THE Unusual Life OF Edna Walling

THE Unusual Life OF Edna Walling

SARA HARDY

A Sue Hines Book
ALLEN & UNWIN

First published in 2005

A Sue Hines Book
Allen & Unwin
83 Alexander Street
Crows Nest NSW 2065
Australia
Phone: (61 2) 8425 0100
Fax: (61 2) 9906 2218
Email: info@allenandunwin.com
Web: www.allenandunwin.com

National Library of Australia
Cataloguing-in-Publication entry:

Hardy, Sara.
The unusual life of Edna Walling.
Bibliography.
Includes index.
ISBN 1 74114 229 6.
1. Walling, Edna, 1895–1973. 2. Landscape architects – Australia – Biography. 3. Landscape gardening – Australia – History. 4. Gardens – Australia – Design. I. Title.
712.60924

Cover, text design and typesetting by Ruth Grüner
Edited by Caroline Williamson
Index by Fay Donlevy
Printed in Australia by Griffin Press

1 3 5 7 9 10 8 6 4 2

This project was supported by the Peter Blazey Fellowship 2004

For Patricia Neighbour;

and for Lois, without whom . . .

PLANTING NEAR STONE STEPS.

Contents

Chronology

1895	Born 4 December; childhood spent in Devon, England.
1911	Travels to New Zealand with parents and sister.
1915	Moves to Melbourne, Victoria, Australia, and settles with family.
1916–17	Attends the Burnley School of Horticulture and Agriculture in Melbourne.
1918	Becomes a 'Girl Gardener' and starts to teach herself about landscape design.
1920	Begins to design gardens professionally.
1921	Starts contributing articles to journals and newspapers. Buys two acre plot at Mooroolbark, an hour's train ride east of Melbourne.
1923	Designs and builds her own cottage at Mooroolbark and calls it Sonning.
1924	Eric Hammond becomes her favourite garden contractor and stone wall builder.
1926	Blanche Scharp becomes her assistant/accountant – and lifelong friend. Trip to Sydney. Becomes regular columnist for *Australian Home Beautiful*.
1928	The building of The Barn marks the first step towards building the village of Bickleigh Vale.
1933	Father dies; mother moves into the village; cousin Edith helps with the workload.

1934	Gwynnyth Crouch becomes an assistant, they work together for seven years. Lorna Fielden moves into the village and a lasting companionship begins. Studies photography.
1935	Sonning burns down, Sonning II built. Ellis Stones becomes second favourite contractor. Develops relationship with Esmé Johnston.
1941	Mother dies. War work includes fund-raising for the Red Cross.
1943	First book published: *Gardens in Australia*.
1947	Listed in *Who's Who*. Second book: *Cottage and Garden in Australia*.
1948	Builds holiday home near Lorne with assistance of Joan Niewand. Third book: *A Gardener's Log*.
1951	Moves into The Barn and sells Sonning. Journalism begins to taper off.
1952	Fourth book: *The Australian Roadside*. Concentrates on conservation.
1965	Donates holiday home to the Bird Observers Club.
1968	Moves to Buderim, southern Queensland; Lorna Fielden follows.
1973	Dies 8 August.

Edna, Brian, and the black cat

Introduction

I was drawn to Edna Walling for several reasons – not least because I *was* her once. I dressed as Edna in jodhpurs, shirt and neck-tie. I walked as Edna with a determined stride, a touch of the masculine. I spoke as Edna, with an uncluttered accent, not exactly English and not exactly Australian (and not achieving Edna's baritone). I sat as Edna – leaning forward, elbows on knees, eyes intent – but this only fleetingly, for most of the time when I was Edna I was lifting heavy loads, wheeling unruly wheelbarrows, building dry stone walls, designing cottages, making gardens and giving firm instructions.

I was performing Edna Walling in a play called *Edna for the Garden*. The play was presented in Melbourne's Fitzroy Gardens in the summer of 1989. People brought their rugs, picnic baskets and fold-up chairs and settled themselves to watch the performance. It was a moveable feast. The play was designed to be enacted in four separate areas of the gardens, each carefully chosen to enhance the telling of the story.

My entrance was made through a long avenue of trees. My three fellow actors played a conglomeration of characters from parents to clients to friends and co-workers, whilst I played Edna from young to old. My final exit saw me disappearing through a leafy bower. I wasn't dead, I was off to Queensland. The audience was left looking at green on green – Edna's favourite colour – the setting sun adding a magical golden tinge to the final image. Apart from the usual distractions that accompany outdoor performances (trams, aircraft, the elements) the play was a gentle success. But the season was soon over. I handed back Edna's jodhpurs, I kissed the cast goodbye and I turned my attention to my next role – which, oddly enough, was to be another 'real-life' gardener: Vita Sackville-West.

I enjoyed being Edna Walling. I liked her strength, her warmth, her vision. I admired her extraordinary achievements: she had 'changed the face of Australian gardens', she had built a village, she had taken beautiful photographs and written informative books and articles and created lovely watercolour garden plans. I especially liked the fact that she came from Devon, for I too was a Devonian, I too had roamed Dartmoor as a child. I was also fascinated by the faint suggestion that Edna was a lesbian. No book or play had made this suggestion directly but the signals were there to be read, if you were so inclined. As an actor I had needed to understand the intricacies of Edna's character, but there were very few clues to help me. Her public persona was blazingly clear (she was a fabulous self-publicist) but little had been written about her private life, and her emotional world could only be guessed at. For a popular personality, Edna had remained remarkably elusive. She was enfolded in a mist. I was intrigued to know more about this extraordinary woman . . . and eventually I did something about it.

By the year 2000 there were three excellent books about Edna's work: Peter Watts's *Edna Walling and her Gardens* (1981) and Trisha Dixon and Jennie Churchill's co-written *Gardens in Time* (1988) and *The Vision of Edna Walling* (1998). Peter Watts's book was the ground-breaking work that brought Edna's name back into the sunlight. All three books give an account of Edna's life as well as an extensive analysis of her achievements and they've been my constant companions throughout my research. However, the main purpose of these books was to explore Edna the garden designer. My purpose here is to explore the woman behind the work – the woman behind 'the mist'.

My purpose is also to explore Edna in context, with more detail than we've seen before. Edna 'the famous woman garden designer' leaps into focus in the mid-1930s – but where did she leap from? And how high did she have to leap? She appears centre stage, 'ready-made', fully talented and without peers or competitors. Was she unique? Wasn't anyone else, male or female, working as she was? Was she really alone in her ideas?

My journey in search of Edna became a long and challenging quest: a tortuous search for clues and fragments and puzzle pieces. Some of the pieces fitted together but there were many gaps.

When I finally plucked up courage and rang the major authority Peter Watts (I was hesitant because my credentials were somewhat peculiar and he might not approve), he instantly offered support and encouragement. He was in Sydney and I was in Melbourne and we talked for nearly two hours. He welcomed me as if he'd been waiting for my call for a very long time. He sent me treasure via registered post – he sent me his 'Edna files'. Two enormous files stuffed with papers browning at the edges. They mapped the journey of his own Edna quest when he pioneered a pathway in the 1970s and brought Edna back from the shadows. As Peter Watts is the first to admit, the files are a chaotic mess full of typed and handwritten notes and correspondence. But in this chaos I found glimmering fragments – little puzzle pieces of information that Peter Watts had not used in his book. A study of Edna the garden designer could not include every snippet that sparkled, and these fragments languished and yellowed until one day they were sent off via registered post to someone that Peter Watts had never met nor heard of. It was a wonderful gesture and the Edna files became an invaluable guide.

My other indispensable guide on this quest was Barbara Barnes, Edna Walling's niece. Barbara Barnes has been endlessly patient and generous in the face of an excess of questioning. Our initial correspondence sparked a friendship and an invitation to stay at her historic property in southern Queensland. The old farmhouse had a room full of boxes containing Edna's papers. The 'Edna room' was useful, but Barbara Barnes was the real treasure. As we sat in the old kitchen, Barbara dug deep for her memories of Aunt. Dotted around the room were items that had belonged to the woman we were talking about – a stool, a pottery vase, a teapot – tangible evidence of the person I sought.

My third major guide was not a person but a library collection. The State Library of Victoria held three boxes neatly filed and numbered plus hundreds of Edna Walling photographs and garden designs. It also held all the back copies of *Australian Home Beautiful* magazine and countless other major sources.

All this material glistened with fragments and clues – all bristling with new questions requiring fresh answers. The quest took me in several directions: to books, to papers and to people. Every so often someone would know someone (who knew someone) who knew Edna. The interviews that ensued were always fascinating, and the people, on the whole, tremendously giving – their memories a charming mix of contradiction. Memory is, after all, a subjective and wholly unreliable process, as is the interpretation of 'truth' and 'facts'.

The point of a quest is that it never turns out how you imagined. The journey, the destination, the Holy Grail, all shift and change as the experience progresses. The fragments that I've gathered and pieced together to form 'Edna' do and do not form the Edna I imagined. She has an extraordinary ability to remain elusive, even when she stands clearly in front of me, shading her eyes from the sun. She does and does not like me delving into her past. She has helped and hindered me on my journey. She is at once difficult and loveable, complicated and clear. She defies categories and definitions, she refuses to be boxed and labelled – and yet she insists that we know her name.

When Edna was in her late sixties she began a memoir about her early years. It is incomplete, and scraps of it have popped up in handwritten and typed drafts in various places. The drafts go over the same memories, each giving a little more or a little less information than others, each revealing and yet concealing the young Edna. They are the writings of an elderly woman looking back fondly and not so fondly on events long past. Inevitably the account bends to Edna's fancy according to how she wishes us to see her, or how she wishes to see herself. Gathered together, the memoir comprises less than twenty pages. It provides few names and no dates but it is the jewel in the crown as far as treasured fragments go.

They say that fools rush in, and I had no idea that this venture would turn into quite such a marathon. But as the fragments and puzzle pieces amassed – to an alarming degree – there was nothing else for it than to try and form a pattern. Here is the result.

Edna's self-built cottage

Chapter 1

Prelude

Wind, fire, water, ashes

One winter morning in 1935 the four elements colluded to defeat Edna.

The day had started in the usual way: breakfast in bed brought by Gwynnyth, and then a speedy dressing into work clothes – jodhpurs, shirt and jumper, thick socks and men's shoes (women's were too feeble). It was a cold morning, and a chilly breeze was dispersing the last of the mist that hung around the nursery where Gwynnyth was already working.

Edna was working on a new plan in her living room-cum-office. She would've liked to have joined Gwynnyth outside, but had to solve a difficult design problem which just wasn't working. False starts lay all over the floor and the new black kitten was playing with them. Brian the dog didn't like the new black kitten, nor did he like the old black cat – and the feelings were mutual.

Brian was an Irish terrier, not a pretty face but he had a loving heart. Brian was Edna's best friend. They'd been together since Edna moved into Sonning, her self-built cottage at Mooroolbark, about an hour from Melbourne. Sonning was a fine little cottage that sat snugly into the landscape, especially now that the garden had developed. Edna had bought a few more acres next to her land and proceeded to build more little cottages with gardens, and the place became known as Bickleigh Vale.

Edna was a few months away from her fortieth birthday in the winter of 1935. She was slim, agile, just under medium height, and surprisingly strong for such a small frame.* She had a puckish whimsical manner topped off by an unruly crop of red hair. Edna had enormous energy and a delightful sense of humour and was one of those people you either took to or really disliked; there was no middle way. It was all or nothing with Edna Walling. As one of her friends wryly commented, you had to be very strong to be a friend of Edna.

Edna was never wealthy but she had done well, even during the cash-strapped years of the Depression. The Who's Who of Melbourne had wanted an Edna Walling garden and she'd worked extremely hard to provide them with one – as had Gwynnyth.

Gwynnyth Crouch was Edna's young assistant; she was impressively tall, had long plaited hair and a gorgeous gap-toothed smile. She proved to be exceptionally strong in all senses, especially during the emergency of the fire. Years later she recalled the events of that day, as did Edna. Their stories differ in the detail but the general picture is

* Edna's driving licence for 1969 states that she was 5ft 3ins (1.60 m) tall but this could be unreliable for it also states that she was born in 1898 rather than the true date of 1895, and that her eyes were hazel whereas others remember them as brown!

the same. I think the fire started something like this . . .

Edna heard Gwynnyth calling from the garden and was only too pleased to leave her task and see what she wanted. Brian and the black cat followed. A gust of wind blew in through the door as Edna went out.

The papers Edna had been working on were pushed towards the open fire, which was barely alight. One of them caught fire and the flame spread from paper to paper across the floor.

The black kitten watched with a startled fascination. The flicker of the flame reflected in her little eyes. First the carpet caught fire, then the wooden furniture, then the wood panelling around the walls, then the ceiling and the rafters.

Gwynnyth and Edna had been talking for only a few minutes when there was a huge and sudden roar. Smoke and flames were bursting from the cottage. Edna ran to get the hose while Gwynnyth ran to rescue the kitten. There was only one tap and one hose and it only *just* stretched to the office window, but Edna managed to poke the end in far enough to get the water onto the flames. There was a moment when it seemed possible that the fire could be put out, that the flames could be doused – but then the water stopped coming. The hose had been torn from the tap and the fitting had broken. The wind rushed in through the open window and the blaze took hold.

How did Gwynnyth manage to find a frightened black kitten in that inferno? She emerged from the cottage scratched and coughing, but with the terrified beast in her hands. She wanted to go back and save the art work, the treasured library – the wonderful Gertrude Jekyll gardening books at the very least. She could see them, she knew she could reach them if Edna helped her stretch through the window. She tried but it was impossible. The heat and noise and thick black smoke were overpowering. They had to move back, a long way back.

The whole house was gone within thirty minutes. They watched; there was nothing more they could do.

At some point Gwynnyth had cut herself quite badly and Edna insisted on taking her into the township for stitches. When they got back, a few of the locals were trying to be helpful – but what could anyone do? Edna's little home was no longer there. Forty years of accumulation – half a lifetime – gone in minutes. No wonder there are gaps in the story.

Apart from the chimney and stone walls, the only thing to survive the fire was a copper nameplate. Edna had made it as a student. She had tapped out the rounded letters of her own name with some reluctance – seeing no point to it. Indeed the nameplate had lain around for seven or eight years until the day Edna saw the perfect place for it. With much hilarity she screwed her name to her very own front door. It must have been a strange moment when she levered the blackened copper sign from the charred remains of that door. A weird symbol of survival: her name.

She had worked hard to find a 'place' for her name. She had built not only a home of her own but a whole environment that suited her needs. She'd made a place where she could be 'herself' – a self that did not generally conform to society's expectations. She had also earned a substantial reputation. By 1935, 'Edna Walling' stood for 'good garden design'. Her gardens were works of art and clients were proud to announce ownership: 'It's an Edna Walling' they'd say and most (though not all) would nod their approval.

As Edna stood amongst the ashes, holding her blackened copper nameplate, she knew that things could have been worse. She knew that she wasn't completely homeless – she had a hideaway. After building Sonning she'd built a tiny one-room stone cottage called The Cabin. This was her hideout, her 'bolt-hole' as she called it. A place where she could work or relax or get away from visitors – actual or potential. Edna's extraordinary success had been a mixed blessing. Her name and achievements had become well known to regular readers of the life-style magazine *Home Beautiful*. Uninvited enthusiasts would roll up to her front door, certain that the famous Miss Walling would be delighted to show them around. The Cabin was secluded. Close friends and co-workers knew about the bolt-hole, and the tiny building was generally respected as being private.

It is through Edna's *Home Beautiful* articles that some of her history can be told. From the 1920s to the 1940s Edna entertained her public with Sonning and Bickleigh Vale updates. These generally concerned building, gardening and furnishing but occasionally there were more personal insights. In the summer of 1936 Edna briefly informed her readers of the fire and how she coped with it: 'With small prospect of sleep that night we decided to occupy our minds with the planning of a new cottage, and by 3 a.m. the plan was complete.' She could have slumped in a corner and wailed (and maybe she did) – but no – enthusiasm and determination were the stuff that Edna was made of. Poor Gwynnyth – she must have been so tired!

Gwynnyth had not lost all in the fire. She shared the kitchen and bathroom at Sonning but always had her own small hut to retire to and keep her things in. It was little more than a tool shed, but at least it was still there. At least she had clean clothes and her familiar knick-knacks around her.

Ironically, Edna had put on her oldest clothes that morning. She'd accumulated several pairs of jodhpurs over the years, all tailor-made to her special design, all now gone. To add insult to injury she had just bought a new tweed suit (jacket and skirt) – the tailor's bill yet to arrive.

The new Sonning, built within three months, was bigger and better and constructed by tradesmen who knew what they were doing. The walls were true, the roof line even, and the chimney did not tilt. For all its faults (and there were many), old Sonning – that rickety, slightly crumpled looking, comforting little cottage – was sadly missed.

It had been the essence of Edna. It had been the house that Edna built – the house that Edna wanted. The dream come true. When Edna screwed the cleaned-up copper nameplate to the front door of the new Sonning she must have had mixed emotions. The new house was lovely, but it was empty. She realised with uncomfortable clarity that she had nothing of her own to put in it.

Earth, water, air

Fire may not have been Edna's friend, but the other three elements could be harnessed to her bidding. She had the magic touch when it came to form and structure. Her gardens were sculptures.

Before we begin this story at the beginning, let us go on a short guided tour of an Edna Walling garden so that we have an idea of what such a creation would have looked like in about 1930. Let us climb into the back of Edna's little Austin and motor down the hill to Melbourne. Let us first wave cheerio to Gwynnyth, dear Gwynnyth, left to carry on with the chores. Dog Brian will jump into the front seat and we will all smile at the black cat and the black kitten, who eye us with disdain as we speed down the driveway towards the dirt road. (Who, we wonder, taught Edna to drive? She appears to have only two speeds – screamingly fast or screaming to a stop.) We are amazed to see so much countryside – we see pasture, scrub, orchard, market garden – and not one string of houses, not one recognisable suburb – not for miles. Mooroolbark really is a hideaway in the country.

How easy it might be to sit amongst the balled-up plants which sway and bob in the back seat of the little Austin. How easy it might be to look quizzically at the back of Edna's copper-red head, which has drifts of cigarette smoke rising from it as she puffs on a very thin roll-your-own. How quickly we might get to know the garden designer if we could ask her a few questions, if we could talk – but of course we cannot – and yet the car speeds on, the roads improve and the houses turn from dots on the landscape to conglomerates in orderly yet spacious lengths of new-built residences. Proud replicas of ye olde English manor house with garden and garage and tennis court to suit. Some even have swimming pools, though the croquet lawn is on its way out. An Edna Walling is definitely 'in' and you can tell who has and who hasn't got one. Houses with a low front fence, a wiggling cement path and a vast front lawn with diamond shaped flowerbeds and roses all in a row have stuck with the old style. Houses hidden within an undulation of foliage allowing but a glimpse of a flagstone path, taking the eye to a pond, to a low stone wall, to a pergola, and far off to a sundial: these are surely the work of Edna Walling.

The car stops, we are not quite sure where, but Edna is already charging towards a front gate, camera in hand, and so we follow.

She stands in the gateway and looks down into her camera, making careful adjustments before taking the photograph. Looking over her shoulder, we see a lily pool set in a well-trimmed lawn. To our left is the house and straight ahead we see a low retaining wall, a post and beam for climbing plants and some steps that invite us forward; trees form a vista which conceals the boundaries so it is difficult to tell how far the garden extends.

Edna strolls past the water towards the steps and takes another photograph. We see a high wooden beam that runs the length of the retaining wall. The beam's supporting posts make frames through which we can see different garden 'pictures' depending on where we stand. The various climbing plants – dark-leafed honeysuckle, golden honeysuckle, decorative vines, wisteria, clematis – are beginning to cover the posts but are yet to travel along the beam. A collection of plants have made their home in the rough masonry of the low stone wall – snapdragons, wallflowers, delicate aster, pink and white daisies, gazania, nasturtiums, cerastium . . .

We go up the steps towards the sundial. Here is a large croquet lawn edged on three sides by a low stone wall covered in plants. The eye is taken by a long border of flowers and shrubs and young and older trees and so up to the blue sky. Edna walks to a corner of the lawn where there is a paved square with chairs and a table and takes another photograph from beneath the shade of the little roof that covers this spot. She then crosses the lawn, goes down some elegant circular steps and proceeds along a stone pathway towards a grass tennis court. She turns to look back to where she came from and takes another photograph. It captures the circular steps, the low retaining wall, the high wooden beam and the table and chairs in shade to the right. We walk back towards the house and head for the front door – which, amazingly, is approached via a substantial pergola – with the sundial at the far end.

There seems to have been some kind of trick; the garden is smaller than we thought it was. The sundial, the high beam, are never far from view. It is the low walls, the trees, the different levels and structures that give the idea of spaciousness, that deceive the eye by suggesting a greater extent than there really is.

But our virtual tour is over. We see our tour guide wander off down a path, teacup in hand, biscuit in saucer, dog at her side. Then she is gone.

Edna photographed this garden for a *Home Beautiful* article that appeared in January 1930. She told her readers that she knew the garden well, but she omitted to say where it was or who owned it. The garden was young, only three years old apart from pre-existing trees. Six years later, in April 1936, Edna treated her readers to an up-dated photograph of the pergola with the sundial. The softening effect of six years' growth is considerable, the pergola posts are hardly visible and one has no sense of the fence line. Just for fun she inserted an extra photograph of a birdbath, saying it had 'refreshed thousands of birds during the past ten years in a garden that I love'. She did not let on that the birdbath belonged in her own garden at Sonning – but by 1936 her readers were so familiar with her column they probably didn't need telling.

Anyone who took an interest in gardens knew who she was and where she lived and what her home looked like – superficially anyway. But few knew how far she'd had to travel to get there.

Edna

Chapter 2

Devon heart

In the beginning was a baby, a red-headed baby born in the city of York in northern England. She was the sister of Doris and daughter of William and Margaret Walling. There were no more children after Edna. For one reason or another, two daughters completed the family picture. Edna was born in the winter of 1895, 4 December to be exact. Queen Victoria (mother of nine) was still alive and well and casting her extraordinarily long shadow over the minds and hearts and morals of her humble and not so humble subjects, while Prince Edward and the twentieth century waited in the wings. Change was afoot – but then, was there ever a time when it wasn't?

A few months after Edna was born, the Walling family was back in William's home town of Plymouth in the county of Devon. Plymouth is the sea port on the south-west coast of England that saw Sir Francis Drake playing bowls as the Spanish Armada was gathering in 1588, and which waved off the *Mayflower* and her pilgrims in 1620. Plymouth had been harbour for all manner of adventurers and warmongers and winners and losers for centuries.

It seems fitting that a woman with a natural gift for building dry stone walls should have the name Walling, but although there are stonemasons amongst Edna's ancestors the association with walls is more to do with being on the outside of them: 'beyond the wall'. The name 'Walling' has its origins in the Anglo-Saxon word 'Wealh' meaning foreigner (the 'ing' indicating 'son of'). Wherever Edna's ancient ancestors came from, the descendants clearly found Devon an attractive place to settle. Edna's family tree has its roots firmly planted in Devon's red soil, and from 1800 the family was based in Plymouth. It seems gently ironic that Edna was born in distant York; their only connection with the place was that Edna's father happened to be working there at the time.

William Walling could have been working anywhere in the mid-1890s, for during that period he was a journeyman salesman working for a furniture dealer. The job took him all over England, which is probably how he came to meet his wife in Buckingham, a village north-east of Oxford, and how their first child Doris was born in Eastbourne, a seaside town in Sussex on the south coast of England.

William worked as a clerk from the age of fourteen and had no intention of becoming a plumber and gas fitter like his father. At least, that was his original plan; but when his father offered him some kind of co-management position in his ironmongery business William took the bait and brought his young family back to the Plymouth fold. Father and son had the same name except that William senior had 'Henry' for a middle name. By 1897 there were two 'Walling' ironmongery establishments in the Plymouth area: 'W. H. Walling' (senior) in the western outskirts, conveniently placed for the road and rail to Cornwall, and 'W. Walling' (junior) situated in the centre of town.

It was the father who had built the business from nothing, but I suspect it was the son who kept things flowing and growing – along with a variety of sideline dealings of his own. William was an expert 'middle-man' or agent. He extended his activities far afield and appears to have enjoyed the travelling, for business trips continued to take him away from Plymouth. His agency work was diverse. Apart from dealing in furniture and hardware, he assisted the monks of Buckfast Abbey to sell their wares, and he handled the import and export of the very latest in meat-slicing machines and scales. Strange to say it was Van Berkel's patented meat slicer and Toledo's 'No Springs Honest Weight' scales that were the root cause of Edna's move to the southern hemisphere.

When baby Edna was brought home to Plymouth, her first address was 67 Mutley Plain. It was a large three-level building with the ironmonger's shop on the ground floor and living accommodation above. Margaret Walling was in charge of home duties and was assisted by a servant. The immediate neighbours comprised a bank manager, butcher, bookseller, dairy keeper and hairdresser. The Wallings were neither rich nor poor; they appeared to live reasonably comfortably yet with an ingrained desire for frugality. William in particular was extremely stubborn when it came to spending money, but Margaret usually saw to it that he paid for the things she deemed necessary.

Margaret Walling née Gough was the daughter of a butcher. Born in 1867, the same year as William, she was working as a milliner by the age of fourteen. She was an excellent needlewoman, and her first-born, Doris, acquired her skills. Her second-born preferred to wield a hammer.

In her memoir Edna tells us that her father had wanted and expected a boy for his second-born. She infers that this idea was so fixed that he ignored the obvious and brought her up as if she were male. On the face of it this sounds extreme.

Edna's mode of dress and manner would attract little attention today, but it drew comment and innuendo in her lifetime. For instance, early in her career a journalist described Edna as having a 'masculine directness' and a 'frankly boyish' personality, whilst other females in the article passed without description. It is true that William treated Edna very differently from her big sister Doris, but then Doris was fond of dolls and Edna preferred a bow and arrow.

I don't know Margaret's medical history so it's impossible to say whether William could be absolutely certain that there would be no more children after Edna – and therefore no further possibility of a boy child. Had Edna taken after her mother and embraced embroidery it's unlikely that William could have *forced* her to put down her needle and take up woodwork.

Very few family photographs have survived, and I found only two of William. The first is a snapshot taken in the mid-1900s when he was in his late forties. He stands behind his trim wife looking relaxed and jovial; he has a sizeable paunch and is smoking a pipe. The second is a studio portrait taken in about 1930. It shows a man with a pleasant rounded face and white wavy hair. His style of dress is distinctive and he wears a noticeably attractive bow tie. He had the reputation for being 'a real gentleman' with a quiet nature, impeccable manners and a fastidiousness that verged on the obsessive.

When Edna was old enough to take herself downstairs to the ironmonger's shop and play with the rows of beautifully organised bolts, nails and hammers – what was William thinking?

Edna's memoir begins:

> My Father thought I would be a boy (he'd had one girl so why not!) and he went right ahead with his preconceived ideas on 'how to bring a boy up hardy' in spite of the turn of events.

Another draft tells us:

> I was sent to the best school in Plymouth. This was not my father's idea – he could think of lots of better ways of spending money than that. He would buy me some tools and set me to work on

> making something. Mother didn't always approve of his ideas. She didn't like his tipping me out of a canoe in order to teach me to swim. Father was determined to make a man of this little girl; always forgetting she wasn't a little boy.

Is it possible that William was more forward-thinking regarding the equality of the sexes than the average Victorian male? Did he thoughtfully encourage the tomboy in Edna, recognising her potential for – what – becoming a carpenter? Or was Edna obsessively pushed so that William could fulfill that desire for a son, which he was too stubborn to relinquish? Or none of the above?

I found only one photograph of Edna when a child, and even this is only a partial view for it was cut down to fit into a small locket. It shows Edna wearing a wide-brimmed hat, a big smile, and long hair not quite holding in ringlets. Few could doubt that it's a picture of a girl, though it's interesting to note that there are no fancy ribbons, no girlish frills – elements that Edna would continue to avoid in adult life.

Edna's memoir is of course a reconstruction of events long gone. Consciously or unconsciously she would have moulded the memories into the shape that suited her best, the one she wished her readers to see. Truth is tricky and we can only speculate on the extent of William's influence on Edna and the accuracy of Edna's description of her rather unusual father.

William's radical method of teaching Edna to swim backfired very badly. She never forgot her sense of panic when he tipped her out of the canoe, and was never able to swim out of her depth without feeling fearful. Margaret was furious about the incident and insisted that William pay for proper swimming lessons. It must have pained him greatly to fork out the extra shillings for what became a series of instructors, each of whom failed to overcome Edna's resistance to swimming beyond the shallow. Her memory of the swimming pool is delightfully evocative, clearly she found its walls particularly comforting:

> [T]hey had just walled in one of the natural rocky pools and lined it with cement and painted it white – how the sea water glistened in the pool, I remember distinctly there were no harsh corners, it was all soft and round and irregular just as though they had been sorry to use any cement at all and would do so as unobtrusively as possible and hurry on the whitewash which helped to make it softer still. How soft whitewash is.

Somewhat ironically, it seems to have been Doris who was in many ways the tougher of the two daughters. Doris was pretty, intelligent and confident. She tended to outshine her younger sister, who was apt to burst into tears quite frequently. These were not necessarily tears caused by distress; sometimes they were due to a sheer depth of feeling. For instance, her parents sang in the local choir, and a beautiful rendition of Handel's *Messiah* or something similar would touch her so deeply that she'd begin to cry. There were times when she sobbed so loudly that a relative would have to escort her from the hall.

The only existing photograph of the young Margaret Walling shows an attractive, energetic face and a complicated hairstyle assisted by curling tongs. Her blouse has intricate stitching, possibly done by herself, but there is no excess of 'show'. She was twenty-six when she married in 1893, by which time her parents were already in their seventies, so it is unlikely that Edna ever knew her maternal grandparents. Margaret was the youngest of four (or more); one brother was a draper and a sister was an accountant.

Edna's many aunts and uncles mostly had a trade behind them. William's eldest brother was an optician who later became a long-serving naval officer, and his eldest sister was a draper. William had eleven siblings, the younger ones benefiting from an improved standard of living – there was money for piano lessons for instance. William's younger sister Lillie was a good pianist and played at various functions. Lillie did what was expected of a young woman – she married and had babies. Less conventionally, she migrated to Western Australia, where some of her babies were born. Her third child, Edith, would one day work for Edna at Sonning.

A photograph of Edna's paternal grandfather, William Walling senior, taken in 1916, shows a stern and wiry man, at ease in his frock coat. One hand is in his coat pocket, the other looks large and strong, still capable of fixing the plumbing. He was seventy-nine at this point, and would live until 1925. His father and grandfather had been master shoemakers, but clearly his chosen trade suited him. His wife, Harriett Walling née Tall, was the daughter of a carpenter, and the Tall family came from Plympton St. Mary, a parish on the edge of Dartmoor. Harriett's photograph shows a Victorian woman possibly dressed in her Sunday best. She wears dark colours with a restrained amount of velvet trimming. Her ample figure looks as if it could burst out of the substantial corset, and her large arms seem unused to the tightness of the sleeves. Her face looks similar to Edna's: neither plain nor beautiful yet determined and strong. When Margaret gave birth to Edna, Harriett was in attendance. I suspect that Harriett had never travelled very far before, certainly not all the way to Yorkshire, so it was a significant gesture.

When Edna grew old enough to observe her relatives she would have seen hard-working, God-loving, clean-living people – and not one of them a gardener.

Edna may have been sent to 'the best school in Plymouth', but the lessons and the teachers made her feel stupid, and she loathed each day. She never responded well to educational structures; the formality didn't suit her. Edna had a practical as well as a creative mind, one that responded to her grandfather's instructions on how to use a saw and build a box but that went blank when asked to explain to the class what happened in 1066. Schooldays were grim, but then a family disaster released her from the torment. One evening the ironmonger's shop at 67 Mutley Plain caught fire. Everything was lost. Fortunately the Wallings no longer lived over the shop; unfortunately the shop was not insured. The family finances were gutted.

The Wallings had a spectacular front-row view of the fire. They were coming home from a fabulous evening, an orchestral concert performed at the Guildhall. They caught the double-decker tram, and the girls raced to the front of the top deck and the parents followed. It was a magical ride with the music still fresh in their minds. The tram trundled around a familiar corner and, far down the road, their attention was caught by the excitement of smoke and fire. How high the flames were, and how pathetically thin the jets of water being pumped by the firemen. It was rotten bad luck for someone . . . And then the awful truth seared into focus. Everything would be different from that moment.

Before the fire the Wallings had prospered. They had moved to a house in Mannamead, a pleasant part of Plymouth. It was probably rented accommodation but it was definitely in the more exclusive end of town. They remained in this house after the fire, so all was not entirely hopeless, though Edna remembers talk of bankruptcy.

Edna was too young to understand the seriousness of what had happened. The event was exciting and it made her feel important – 'that's our shop that's burnt down!' She was especially happy when she discovered that the school fees were no longer affordable. Doris didn't share her feelings; she rather enjoyed 'the best school in Plymouth'.

The rest of the Walling family would have helped as much as they could, but the atmosphere between William and Margaret was probably strained. This may have contributed to Edna contracting pneumonia – the next disaster for the Wallings to deal with. When your child is dangerously ill, fires and bankruptcy pale into insignificance. Margaret and William combined forces and gave all their attention to Edna. Margaret did the day shift, William the night. A doctor administered ghastly treatments involving pipes and lung suction, and tan bark was spread on the road outside to deaden the noise of the horse-drawn traffic. Pneumonia was a killer in the early 1900s.

Margaret was deeply religious and her Anglican faith would have helped to sustain her. William's faith did not run so deep. He sang in the church choir but dozed off during the sermons. During his nightly vigil by Edna's bedside he sang gentle folk songs in the hope of easing her to sleep. Her response was to burst into tears. Acts of loving kindness would always bring Edna to tears. William persevered nevertheless. As he sat through the nights, listening to the rasp of her shallow breathing, he formulated a strength-building plan for her convalescence. His strategy was to exercise her brain as well as her body.

I don't know if William was consciously steering Edna's mind in a particular direction. He was self-taught and, according to Edna, had little respect for formal education – which is perhaps why Edna received so little 'proper' schooling. Whatever William's motivation at the time, his influence was a vital component in her later development.

First he taught her to play a kind of recorder which strengthened her lungs as well as her musical abilities. Then he took her walking. Short walks at first – her legs were like sticks – then longer and still longer. The glittering prize was to walk on Dartmoor, picnic in pocket. Once this prize was achieved it became a regular venture. Father and daughter together.

It is a crisp spring morning and everyone is up very early. Margaret and Doris are not going on the walk, they rarely go. William's strict notch-up-the-mileage regime is too severe for them; besides, Doris has a viola lesson. Margaret makes them a simple picnic: a sandwich and a hard-boiled egg each, beautifully wrapped and slipped into each coat pocket. There is no need to take water, the moors are covered with little streams, fresh and clean (as long as you forget about the sheep droppings).

They could take the tram to Mutley Railway Station but they prefer the walk. The train takes over an hour and a half to get to the moor, so a stretch of the legs first is beneficial. William and Edna are suitably clothed in tweeds and woollens with well-polished boots and the essential waterproof. Each carries an ash walking stick. They look as if they know where they are going, unlike the small gathering of tourists who twitter with excitement on the platform.

Everyone is interested in the weather. Will that famous Dartmoor mist roll in? The moors can be dangerous as well as delightful. A mist can suddenly envelop the moor in an impenetrable shroud; one moment all is clear, and the next you can hardly see your hand. You lose your bearings immediately. There are peat bogs to sink into, bog-grass hummocks to trip you and cavernous gritty holes to fall into. When the mist takes hold, the trick is to keep heading down hill and eventually you'll find a stream which will take you off the moor – unless the pixies get you. The pixies are mischievous little creatures come to torment you. Dressed in green they are difficult to see and impossible to get rid of unless you take off your coat, turn it inside out and put it on again. Then the pixies will have no further power over you. Devonians believe this absolutely.

A sudden shrill hoot calls everyone to attention. A small steam engine puffs and bellows into view. The crowd moves forward but then back as the platform fills with steam and smutty smoke. The engine snorts to a halt, clunking and screeching. Most people climb into the second-class carriage.

It takes only minutes to leave Plymouth. The track keeps parallel with the road that leads to Plympton St. Mary, where Edna's grandmother came from. Edna sits on the right so that she will not miss the point where the road crosses the Plym. She loves the old stone bridge. Its proportions are perfect and it is simply beautiful. The track runs with the river for a while; it's not a wide river but it's a rushing one with great granite boulders making the water swish and swirl. The river slips from view as the train turns towards Bickleigh Vale, making a brief stop at Bickleigh Station. It chugs over a viaduct, through a cutting and enters the enchantment of Bickleigh Woods. The ground is carpeted with bluebells while foxgloves dance towards the sunlight of the track. This vision goes on for several minutes as the train curves around the vale. There are rocky dells and sparkling streams and deep valleys. In a hollow there is a cluster of cottages that look more like over-sized mushrooms than houses. Everyone in the carriage has drifted into a reverie.

The train pulls on, steadily gaining height. The dappled shading of the woodland comes to an end as the lower slopes of Dartmoor roll into view. The colours change as the yellows and greens of grasses mix with the browns and greens of bracken and heather. There is the crisscross of dry stone walls and the occasional groupings of sheep, ponies or cattle. Far off to the right there is a tower, belonging to the little church of Meavy. The tower stays in view as the track comes around the valley of the Mew and bends back on itself.

There is a flutter of excitement as the train reaches the open moor. The extraordinary rock formations known as tors crown most of the hills. There is Mis Tor, King Tor and so on. William and Edna play a kind of game, trying to calculate their height and the distances between them. The game stops when they see the quarry at Foggin

Tor. Huge slabs of granite lie waiting for collection and there's a special little rail track.

The train hoots as the small settlement of Princetown comes into view, along with the imposing edifice of Dartmoor Prison. Everyone begins to stir. This is the end of the line and the beginning of the walk.

The air smells sweetly earthy with a mixture of peat, bracken and heather, and the sky is a cloudy blue. The tourists stand and stare, breathing in the views, but William sets off at a cracking pace and Edna does her best to follow.

For the most part the ground is soft and springy and gentle to walk on. As long as you look where you are going, the tell-tale signs will alert you to dangers. For instance tussocks of rushes grow on the edges of mires, a kind of swamp that should never be walked through. If you get into one by mistake, the tussocks can act as 'stepping stones' to get you out. Another sign to watch for is a circular area covered with a magnificent bright green moss. It looks wonderfully soft and attractive and begs to be lain on like a fluffed-up feather bed – and 'feather bed' is the nickname for these. The circle is actually a deep rocky hole filled with ooze. Animals have a natural instinct to avoid them but humans are less attuned. It has a noticeable wobble when stepped on, so can easily be avoided – unless there's a mist or it's dark . . . But these are minor details. A walking stick and common sense will keep most people out of trouble.

William and Edna have slackened their pace a little. They are heading south towards Sheeps Tor but with no particular destination in mind. They reach Crazy Well Pool, a well-known feature, but do not linger. The pool has been there for centuries but is really the site of an old tin mine. The moor is riddled with signs of early mine excavation, and even earlier settlements. There are ancient hut circles as well as mysterious stone circles and stone avenues. Some are boundary markers but others cannot be explained

William's interest in these formations is practical rather than historical. He uses them to pose questions about distances and gradient. Indeed much of the walk is actually a lesson in scale and measurement and perspective. It's an unusual pastime, but Edna enjoys it. She no longer waits for William to ask a question but makes up her own. She estimates the distance between a boulder and the wizened tree ahead and then counts her steps to see if she's right (three feet equals one yard). When her legs grow longer she will become extraordinarily accurate.

They head for a cluster of boulders for their picnic. The rocks provide a comfortable seat and are perfect for tapping their boiled eggs against. It is only now that they look at the smaller details: the tiny flowers that hide amongst the grasses, the softness and variousness of the different mosses and lichens, the 'pepper and salt' speckle of the granite. When the food is finished they pick out a soft patch of well-nibbled turf and lie on their backs and look for the larks. The hum of insects and the song of the skylarks sends William into a doze, but only a short one. Edna wants to play their game of cricket. A walking stick and some rolled-up brown paper act as bat and ball. The child whose lungs needed strengthening squeals with laughter as she scampers to make a run.

Then it is time to head back to Princetown and catch the train. The journey of return never seems to take as long as the one arriving. They are on the train and trundling down from the moor and around the valley of the Mew and through Bickleigh Vale and past the little stone bridge and into Mutley Station in no time at all.

A roast dinner, a hot bath and so to bed for little Edna.

The enchantment of the Devon landscape would never leave Edna. She would spend much of her life attempting to recreate it.

William's ideas for educating Edna did not stop at country walks. He pressed her into making something for a forthcoming Arts and Crafts exhibition. She resisted because she found his ideas too finicky, and their clash of style led to arguments. He had to finish the thing himself in the end, and Edna was secretly pleased when the adjudicator wrote that the Walling entry was 'pernickety in the extreme'. Vindication did not last. William switched his focus to practical jobs around the house. Making the beds caused tears but she was happy mending Mother's sewing box – and even happier fixing the pothole in the road outside. Margaret praised Edna's efforts, but William always picked at the small detail.

It was the away-from-home excursions that were best. They would go down to the Plymouth docks to see the fishing smacks come in, and sometimes they'd board a cargo ship and talk to the Captain, or hire a row boat and thread their way through the warships and ocean liners anchored in Plymouth Sound. William would also take her to visit the Benedictine monks who lived on the eastern edge of Dartmoor. Edna describes this in her memoir:

> One of the greatest of the many delights I enjoyed with Father was going to Buckfast Abbey with him, he had some business with the Monks, was an agent for their healing salves or some such, and on his periodical visits he would sometimes take me too. The Abbot was extremely tall and quite young, a glorious creature really, he would take us for walks through the woods and I would have to scramble for my life to keep up with his long swinging strides – Father lost a little weight on those days I'm sure. My most vivid picture of this Abbot is of him going down an incline swinging from Birch trunk to Birch trunk with habit and girdle flying out behind. Lunch at the huge refectory table was a most marvellous affair. The fare was good – extremely good, but the setting, the conversation and the laughter was a never to be forgotten experience.

The young Abbot's name was Anscar Vonier, and he became internationally known as a writer, preacher, scholar – and builder. It was through his efforts that the ancient ruin of the Abbey church was restored to glory. Starting in 1907, it took four monks thirty-two years to complete the project (funds and labour being in short supply). Edna was eleven in 1907 and would have seen the beginnings of this inspiring scheme. Discussions about a particular building problem or the qualities of the stone may well have captured her imagination.

The small village of Sonning certainly captured her imagination. She passed through there in 1903 when she was seven. Sonning is on the river Thames halfway between Reading and Henley-on-Thames in Berkshire. Quite how she came to be there I don't know, but she was in a boat and drifted through this village, and was so deeply struck by its beauty that she never forgot its name. It is tantalising to know that there was a particularly splendid house and garden in Sonning that was designed by the famous architect and garden design team: Edwin Lutyens and Gertrude Jekyll. Fifteen years later, the work of Lutyens and Jekyll would have a significant influence on Edna's approach to garden design.

A high wall surrounded The Deanery, the Lutyens/Jekyll creation in Sonning. It was completed in 1901 and owned by Edward Hudson, the proprietor of *Country Life* magazine. Gertrude Jekyll published well over a hundred gardening articles and nine books under the *Country Life* banner, and it was through these publications that her name and ideas became popular. She wrote a particularly delightful book for children and parents: *Children and Gardens* (1908) which would have interested Edna greatly – had she been given a copy. On the first page Jekyll tells her readers that she was 'more like a boy than a girl . . . delighting to go up trees, and to play cricket, and take wasps' nests after dark, and do dreadful deeds with gunpowder and all the boy sort of things'. The book had instructions on how to plan, build and plant, and was illustrated with Jekyll's own photographs and drawings. If ever there was a role model for Edna, Gertrude Jekyll was it. Edna never named Jekyll as an early influence – but then Edna never named *anyone* as an early influence.

Edna was not one of those children who wanted her own patch of garden; planting things didn't interest her. The nearest she came to gardening was to play with the soil, sculpting it into miniature landscapes – a kind of sophisticated form of playing mud pies. It was the countryside and the gaiety of the cottage garden that attracted Edna's young eyes: the hollyhocks in the hedgerows, Nature's own design. There were famous stately homes and gardens in the Devon area – Bicton, Sydenham and Saltram for instance – but I doubt that Edna saw them, and in any case they were rarely open to the public, if at all. The closest most people got to such places was via the pages of *Country Life*.

There came a day when Edna had to go back to school, 'proper' school. She had kept this day at bay for some time by attending morning lessons with a string of retired teachers who lived around the corner or up the road, and who engaged the inattentive Edna not at all. Margaret hunted for something better that would suit her girl – and William's pocket – and found a rather surprising solution: the Convent of Notre Dame.

At the age of about thirteen, Edna was placed with the nuns at Notre Dame Convent. She was there for only eighteen months, but that time was crucial to her later development. The nuns were dedicated to an order founded by St. Julie, a Frenchwoman with a mission to educate the 'whole' girl: heart, hands and head (Catholic or not). It was an approach that suited Edna. She found the lessons inspirational – partly because she found Sister Aimée de Marie adorable, but also because the nuns really did seek to develop the whole Edna – heart, hands and head. To her great anguish, French was her most serious weakness (for she so wanted to speak French with Sister Aimée de Marie), while her two outstanding strengths were drawing and geometry. The nuns worked on the whole Edna but they were especially interested in her drawing and geometry – two of the shining skills that would one day emerge in Edna the landscape designer.

Edna recalled that 'It was a very tearful departure I took of Sister Winifred the Head and my beloved Sister Aimée de Marie before we set sail for New Zealand where life was to begin afresh for the family.' The nuns of the Notre Dame Convent were especially reluctant to see Edna leave their school prematurely and tried to convince Margaret to let her stay on as a boarder. Edna, if not her parents, was tempted by this idea. Who knows what path Edna might have taken if that had happened? – not that Edna could *really* have stood on Plymouth docks and waved and watched and bawled as her mother, father and sister slowly steamed out of the harbour and into the blue yonder . . . Though she had her regrets later on:

> Transportation from one side of the world to another can be a rather cruel affair and we weren't particularly happy for some years – not happy enough to enjoy as we might have the new country. Nothing compensates for the hopeless longing for one's friends – knowing one may never see [them] again – and the exile becomes intolerable at times.

It was all to do with balance. William had weighed up his prospects for the future for himself and his family and had put his faith in scales. In 1911 the Toledo 'No Springs Honest Weight' USA manufacturer was about to launch its best scale yet: the double-pendulum industrial portable. From peanuts to pig-iron, every shop and factory could now be assured of absolute accuracy if a new Toledo was purchased. Good sales managers were required, world-wide. When the Hutchison Scales Company of New Zealand called for the right man, William answered. New Zealand was bursting with good prospects and all kinds of encouraging schemes to attract new settlers. William was forty-four, as was Margaret. Doris and Edna were teenagers. It was not too late for a fresh start. When William weighed up the pros and cons, his head (if not his heart) said *go*. The date of departure was memorable – 11 a.m. on 11 November 1911. At this precise moment William closed his front door for the last time. He gathered up his not particularly happy wife and daughters and took them to the docks. The Wallings boarded their ship, waved their last goodbyes, and left Plymouth forever.

Margaret and William Walling

Chapter 3

Postcard from New Zealand

Edna celebrated her sixteenth birthday on the steamship *Arawa*. It was a five-week voyage to New Zealand, so the ship would have been somewhere south of the equator on 4 December 1911. It was her first birthday in summer rather than winter; indeed she would never have a winter birthday again.

Her emotions must have been as changeable as the elements: a deep sense of longing for all that was 'home' and a rising thrill of excitement for the newness of it all. She had fleeting views of Tenerife in the Canary Islands, Cape Town in South Africa and Hobart in Tasmania. The steamship visited the New Zealand ports of Auckland and Wellington on the North Island before finally reaching Lyttelton on the South Island.

The Wallings disembarked at Lyttelton and took the short rail journey inland to Christchurch, their destination. After the tussle with the harbour and the luggage and the railway, they would have been looking forward to their hotel rooms (even if they were on the cheap side) – but bad news awaited them. Harriett, William's mother, had died. She was seventy-one and had probably been ill when the Wallings left Plymouth, but the news must have come as a terrible shock. The family's grief was surely exacerbated by being so far from what had been home. It was a bad beginning to their 'fresh start'.

It's easier to settle into a place when you have a job. A job gives you an identity, a daily structure, and a ready-made group of potential friends. William had all of this with the Hutchison Scales Company, but Margaret, Doris and Edna had to make their own way and they found it very hard. New Zealand had advertised itself as 'The Scenic Paradise Of The World: the land for the tourist, the health-seeker, the home-maker', but the blurb had not been entirely candid. There were some problems in paradise.

There was a surprising shortage of houses for rent, and it was extremely difficult to find anywhere satisfactory to settle. And although there were numerous government incentives to encourage settlers to develop farm land, the prospects for small business enterprise – William's expertise – were not particularly good. Even the weather was disappointing. Nothing was quite as the Wallings had hoped.

Christchurch, a city with a population of about 60,000, was pleasant enough. New Zealand was of course a colony of the British Empire and though there was a very strong Maori presence – fully exploited in the tourist brochures – the townships had 'Britain' stamped all over them. An extraordinary countryside awaited exploration but, initially at least, it was probably comforting for the Wallings to walk along the banks of the river Avon and see the weeping willows reflected in the water and watch the men practising for the boat race.

What was Edna to do with herself in Christchurch? 'Leave as soon as possible' seemed to be the answer. She had 'a longing for the country' and this was acted upon.

I've no idea how it came about, but a few months after her arrival in Christchurch Edna found some kind of job at Kaituna, a remote cattle station north-east of Wellington. I think her fantasy was that she'd learn to ride a horse and round up cattle and go fence building and, as the sun was setting, boil up the billy, roll out her swag and settle down and watch the stars. She did indeed learn to ride a horse, but the closest she came to working with one was to ride into the one-street town of Masterton to pick up the mail. She was employed, it seems, as a glorified domestic servant. She certainly spent more time in the kitchen than under the stars.

Someone (the housewife?) taught her:

> to make white sauce – dreadful, dreadful white sauce, the kind that all good cooks look on with horror and uplifted hands; nevertheless the kind that goes down with the simple roast dinner that satisfies a working man. I had to be up in time to give Mister and Missus morning tea in bed at seven a.m., on the dot, and was still washing up the dinner dishes at seven p.m.

She did this job, not very happily, for twelve months. I doubt very much that she'd experienced anything like these domestic duties before – they were everything she loathed. Decades later Edna would tell her niece that she had always longed to have a farm of her own. Perhaps working at Kaituna was a step towards this dream. New Zealand was built on pioneering spirit – and government land grants. The possibility of Edna one day owning a farm was not entirely out of the question: all she needed was money.

It's interesting that Edna stuck with her domestic servitude for a whole year. Did she prefer the hardships of station life to the middle-class refinements of Christchurch and the company of her family?

I doubt that the Wallings were so cash-strapped that she *had* to stay put. There must have been something more than washing-up and white sauce that kept her there. Maybe it was to do with those moments of freedom when she could ride off on a horse and dream of a future on the land. At least she could observe how a station was run and what 'man's work' entailed – even if she wasn't allowed to do it. Perhaps it was at Kaituna that she was introduced to that wonderfully liberating garment: jodhpurs.

The experience, whatever it was for or about, must have toughened her up considerably.

By the time Edna returned to Christchurch, William had already left for Melbourne. He had a job as warehouse manager for Toledo Honest Scales. The arrangement was that Margaret and his daughters would follow him to Melbourne in due course, but in the event it was only Margaret and Doris who joined him. Edna had other plans.

Surprisingly, she started to work as a nursing aide in a private hospital in Christchurch. Although it was wildly different from a cattle station, the end result was similar: another form of servitude. Edna was developing an earnest desire to do something *useful* in society. She chose to be a nursing aide to see if she had the potential to make a good nurse. She found much of the experience ghastly, but after six months of bed-pans and disinfectant she wanted to stay on. She wanted to be a nurse. William wanted her to be in Melbourne.

William had been opposed to Edna's nursing idea but had allowed her to proceed because he was certain she would hate it and give up immediately. He must have been most annoyed when she declared her new-found calling – and the desire to stay put.

Was it purely the need to nurse that kept Edna in Christchurch longer than William wanted? Were there particular friends or interests that caused her to be stubborn? Edna gives us no clues. Rather like her leave-taking at Notre Dame Convent, Edna had to choose between her own education/vocation and the will of her father. In other words – there was no choice.

William's somewhat prophetic argument was that Edna would be very much happier having an 'open air' life in Australia. He may or may not have added that her extended stay in Christchurch required his ongoing financial support . . .

Edna complied. In July 1915 she boarded a steamer and slowly slid away from the land of the long white cloud.

Edna boiling the billy

Chapter 4

Australian soil

The World War had begun in August 1914, and Australia had been quick to join in. The people of Australia, and Melbourne in particular, were infected with a frenzy of British patriotism. By the time Edna arrived in Melbourne, thousands of men were being sent to fight in the Middle East. Edna may have seen battleships as she crossed the Tasman Sea and troopships as she entered Melbourne's Port Phillip Bay. If she'd been feeling sorry for herself, dragged away from her new-found vocation, then the sight of so many young men so willing to serve might have put an end to such thoughts. By the time Edna stepped onto Station Pier and into the arms of her father and mother, she was probably ready and willing to put her best foot forward. Here was a second chance to make 'a fresh start' – besides, there was nowhere else to go but forward.

It had been Margaret and Doris's job to find suitable accommodation, but the war made this task even more difficult than usual. There was a housing shortage due to the rising cost of building materials, and a servant shortage due to the steady increase in alternative types of work. Margaret and Doris hit upon a novel solution – a flat. The idea of flats would become commonplace in the 1920s but they were rare pre-war. Arundel Flats was a new building and the Wallings were amongst the first tenants. It was situated on a large site near the corner of Commercial and St. Kilda roads. The flats were fairly small but the location was excellent, right on the boundary between two prestigious areas: South Yarra and the City of Melbourne.

If we were exploring the area for the first time, we'd see that directly beside Arundel Flats (east side) was a large government reserve: the green and gracious Fawkner Park. On the west side we'd see the tree-lined expanse of St. Kilda Road, Melbourne's proud boulevard. We'd hear the clatter of cable trams and the jangle of horse-drawn traffic, with the occasional splutter of an unpredictable motorcar. Cross the boulevard and we'd find the Albert Cricket Ground and the lawn tennis courts, and behind this swathe of green, even more green – Albert Park. Walk north along St. Kilda Road and we'd be heading towards the city. We'd pass empty blocks of land interspersed with very grand Victorian mansions, modest terraces, workshops and factories, and an increasing number of military barracks and police buildings. Cross the road to the east side and we'd find the welcoming undulations of the Royal Botanic Gardens. A little further north we'd find a multitude of boat houses on the banks of the River Yarra, and once across Princes Bridge we'd be engulfed by the bustle of Flinders Street Railway Station. We could pause on the steps beneath the railway clocks and observe the moody grace of St. Paul's Cathedral, or we could watch the more colourful activities around Young and Jackson's Hotel.

If we turned left down Flinders Street and, after a few blocks, right up Market Street, we'd come to a building called Phoenix Chambers. Go to number two on the ground floor and there would be the office of the agent for Toledo and Berkel weighing and slicing machines.

Somewhere in that office would be William Walling, the Warehouse Director.

Phoenix Chambers was a hive of industry. In the basement there were printers and paper bag makers and motorcar furnishing importers; on the ground floor there were insurers and agents and electrical engineers and spirit merchants and the Farmers' & Stockowners' Bureau. On the first floor there were merchants, brokers, the publishers of *Farmer & Grazier* and the Misses Mills and Doolin – typists. On the top floor there was a broker, an agent, a tailor, an embosser and an artist called Miss Low.

Market Street was full of buildings like Phoenix Chambers. William was in his element and his future looked secure. The same could not be said for his youngest daughter.

Edna may have been too earnest to see the irony, but one of the first things she must have noticed about Arundel Flats was that directly opposite was a residence for trained nurses, and diagonally opposite was the Alfred Hospital. How was Edna to relinquish her desire to become a nurse when the object of her desire was but a few steps away?

The answer of course is that she followed her desire and side-stepped William's protests. William ardently believed that Edna should pursue an out-of-door life but he did not seem to have any suggestions as to how she should achieve this. The idealistic Edna wanted to 'serve mankind'. Surely nursing was the perfect profession for a woman who wanted to be *useful* (and earn a living). Besides, there was a war on and nurses were needed. End of argument.

Margaret arranged an interview with Matron Bell so that Edna could enrol for training at the Royal Melbourne Hospital – but there was a problem. Edna recalled the incident in her memoir and she describes it with her usual jocularity but the outcome must have hurt young Edna deeply. It was her lack of formal education that was her undoing:

> 'Has she the leaving certificate?' asked Matron Bell. This winded both of us, and though Mother was clearly planning her graceful departure my crushed expression tempted Matron Bell to suggest I studied and sat for my leaving exam at home and come back again. So off we went in search of the necessary books but it was soon clear that I was not of a studious nature and so I escaped a misguided career and the nursing profession missed a misfit . . . Father was quite right of course, nursing was not a sensible choice of career for his rather odd youngest daughter.

I wonder what Edna meant by 'misfit' and 'odd'. How did she see herself at that time?

A studio photograph taken in about 1914 shows subtle contrasts between the three Walling women. All three wear a similar style of simple white blouse, though Edna's does not look quite as 'crisp' as the other two. The portrait is posed and Doris looks confidently into the camera, while Margaret holds herself a little stiffly and looks into the middle distance. Edna's pose is neither one thing nor the other; she could be daydreaming – or even bored. Her hair is long and not holding entirely firm to its pinned position whilst Doris and Margaret have elaborate hairstyles that are perfectly in place. Edna's skirt is of a plain thick material and her general appearance is less carefully put together than her sister and mother but, all in all, outwardly at least, Edna 'fits'.

As the war progressed and more and more men went to fight, women willingly demonstrated that they were capable of doing 'men's work'. Even so, polite society looked forward to the day when women returned to the home. That was where they belonged. War or no war, it would take a very long time for that attitude to change. The unconventional New Woman with her 'unfeminine' airs was scorned rather than celebrated – she was a threat. Edna was a free spirit, a rather earnest one at this point, but even so she refused to be boxed in – refused to plod her way through the demands of the School Leaving Certificate, for instance. As time went on Edna would reject conventional pathways; this is perhaps why she described herself as 'odd' and a 'misfit'. If Edna's writing style had not been so full of jocular self-deprecation she might have written free spirit instead of misfit. The fact that she wanted a *career* would have seemed odd in this era. Marriage and motherhood is what she was 'supposed' to want (even though there was an increasing shortage of men).

Edna never mentions the possibility of matrimony, and somehow I don't think William or Margaret would have mentioned it either. Doris, however, was a different matter.

Doris had grown into an attractive, intelligent and confident young woman. She was musical, sociable and keen to keep up with the latest trends – especially in clothes. She was also, like her mother, deeply religious. While Edna was trying to find her way forward, Doris was about to meet her future husband – Alfred Oak-Rhind, a company director. She had also become involved in a new religion: Christian Science. Doris's commitment to this religion became total, and Margaret, and to a lesser degree Edna, also took an interest.

The Christian Science movement was founded in 1879 in the USA by Mary Baker Eddy, and attracted an increasing membership in Australia from 1898, peaking in the 1930s. Christian Science attracted a diverse congregation of people, including progressives, artists and the well-to-do. For instance the famous suffragist and pacifist Vida Goldstein was a dedicated early member – as were several of her family, colleagues and friends. Besides the teachings of Mary Baker Eddy, one of the attractions of the religion was that there was a sincere attempt at equality of the sexes. Women played an equal part in services and administration. There was even the possibility that God could be female.

Anyone attending a Christian Science service for the first time would have been entertained at the very least: the teachings were stimulating, the people were interesting and the music was wonderful. It was standard practice to engage professional soloists of the highest quality, and consequently the recitals were superb. The movement grew quickly and the first church was built after the war on prime land in St. Kilda Road.

It must have been a great relief to Margaret that Doris was finding her way in the New Country – and distressing that Edna was not. Poor Margaret: the search for Edna's 'path in life' had gone on and on for months. She escorted Edna to all manner of possibilities. Finally, they tried the Burnley School of Horticulture. Edna's expectations of the school appear to have been minimal, but Margaret was very keen – or desperate.

> Many were the fruitless avenues Mother and I explored before we hit upon the School of Horticulture and I remember so clearly the dampening effect the principal's question 'Is she artistic?' had upon me. That's the last thing I was I felt. Mother's 'oh yes' sounded most emphatic and sincere but I feared 'twas but Mother love. She had said things about my being a landscape gardener to the principal though I never remember the slightest discussion upon the subject before we entered that room – whether she had just thought of it or whether she had it in her mind for some time subconsciously I never knew – at all events the idea did not sink into my consciousness even then or for some time to come.

It was a haphazard beginning to a brilliant career.

The key factor about the Burnley School of Horticulture was that entry requirements were minimal: you needed to have reached Grade VIII in elementary school and you had to be at least fourteen years old. If you attended the course full-time and passed your exams you would earn your Burnley Certificate of Competency within two years. When the school was established in 1891 it was for males exclusively and it was only in the early 1900s that the 'weaker sex' was allowed to partake of lectures plus a modicum of practical work. After much lobbying women were eventually allowed to undertake the full practical course and so gain the full qualifications. It was not until 1916 (the year Edna enrolled) that the first woman gained both the Certificate and the Diploma. This determined student was Miss Olive Holttum (1891-1978). In 1917 Olive Holttum became the first female instructor at the school – and thus one of Edna's teachers.

At last Edna was in the right place at the right time – albeit unwittingly.

Edna enrolled on 24 August 1916, paying her five-pound annual fee in full. She need not have paid the whole sum straight away, most people didn't, so perhaps she was a little more interested in the course than her memoir suggests? Either way, her place was secure, and two weeks after enrolment she began her Course in Horticulture.☼

Burnley (to give the School of Horticulture and Primary Agriculture its shortened name) was situated in the suburb of Burnley by the River Yarra. A twopenny tram fare from Arundel Flats into the city and then another ride east through insalubrious Richmond would have brought Edna to the front gates of the school.

One spring morning in 1916 Edna stood outside those big gates – a new girl on her first day. Dressed in her street clothes (long skirt,

☼ The Enrollment Book for 1916 gives her year of birth as 1896 instead of 1895 thus shaving a year off Edna's age. Was it a clerk's mistake or did Edna have a moment of panic? She hadn't been in a formal school environment since she was fifteen, and now, here she was surrounded by fourteen year old boys, teenage girls and a couple of matronly women.

long coat, large hat), she would have carried a bag which held her work clothes, work books, lunch, and the essential Burnley requisite: a budding knife. As she stepped through the gates she stepped into another world.

It was a rural scene. Cows and bulls grazed in paddocks near the river. Tracks led off to the milking shed and poultry pens, to the silo, dairy and implement sheds, to the gardeners' rooms, the nursery, the orchards. An attractive gravelled path led into the beautiful formal gardens and so to the school building – officially called the Pavilion but generally known as the Elephant House. All students, whether juniors or seniors, headed this way first, for it was the centre of activities.

The Elephant House was a large weatherboard barn of a building that had been converted to contain various offices, two lecture rooms, two common rooms with changing room (girls to the left, boys to the right), and a tiny library. The floor was asphalt and the rafters exposed. Under the same roof, yet immaculately separate, was Miss Knight's fruit bottling department. Her door was always kept tightly closed – her classroom, like her preserved fruit, hermetically sealed from external interference.

A school bell, audible across the grounds to suburbia beyond, rang the changes of the day.

On Monday mornings a list was pinned to the noticeboard assigning different students to different outdoor staff. Each staff member had a specific area to supervise. Mr. Russ was in charge of all nursery work; he was the 'Demonstrator in Horticulture'. It was Mr. Russ who took charge of the new-comers in their first week. An Englishman of few words but with twinkling blue eyes and a friendly manner, he always set the new girls (not the boys) the most horrid weeding task he could find. This, so to speak, sorted the wheat from the chaff. Those still standing and still willing to continue by day five were recognised as 'stayers'. Most students were desperate to please the mischievous, all-knowing, Mr. Russ – he was the revered favourite. Other outdoor staff received friendly nicknames, but George Russ was always 'Mr. Russ'.

Edna was very much a stayer in her first year. She hardly missed an hour except for the afternoon of Monday 4 December. She had a good reason – it was her twenty-first birthday.

For the outside work, males and females, juniors and seniors generally worked together. Women wore breeches with leggings and an over-tunic that covered the legs at least to below the knees. It was suitably modest yet practical. Even so, it was an outfit that would have been forward to the point of shocking a few years earlier.

The atmosphere was jolly. It was strenuous work but there was a lot of fun. Friendships were made, nicknames given, jokes played and there were even sporting activities on the lawn (for those still able to move, that is). Lunch was taken in the common room or picnic style in the gardens.

At 11.30 a.m. each day a senior and two juniors would be excused from work and sent off to the Elephant House to do Room Duty. This was a serious task. The floors had to be swept, the wood chopped for the fire, the milk fetched from the dairy, the fire lit, the big iron kettles filled with water, the heat of the fire so timed that the water was boiling by the time the bell was ringing, so that the tea was brewing when the students started arriving at five past twelve. What a hullabaloo if that tea wasn't ready! A simple lunch was helped along by seasonal benefits. When the fruits and nuts ripened, pockets and mouths were filled – when the supervisor wasn't looking.

Students took pride in their work. There was a competitive zest concerning which team would get the job done best, which individual would get the top marks. Attendance and punctuality was monitored daily, a report card completed weekly. Written and oral exams came at the end of each term. It was a challenge, especially for those well-to-do girls who were doing the course because their parents thought it was a convenient kind of 'finishing school', or because working with flowers might be 'nice'. Of course the study of horticulture could be wonderful, literally seeing the fruits of one's labours grow, but it could also be demanding and tedious. Some students gave up, some opted to go part-time, and some remained steadfast. Edna was steadfast, though she was not particularly fond of the course.

The diploma-winning Olive Holttum was finishing her Burnley studies just as Edna was starting hers. When Olive Holttum became the new and only 'Instructress' she was put in charge of two areas: the Long Border with herbaceous plants and the Australian Border with native plants. Olive was especially interested in native plants which was unusual – the vast majority of gardeners at that time saw little value in them.

Olive Holttum was born near Cambridge, England, and came to Australia on her own in 1909 at the age of eighteen. Her step-mother was an amateur botanist, which influenced all the family. Olive had taught at her step-aunt's boarding school in Birmingham and she probably worked as a governess when she came to Melbourne. She had a practical yet gentle nature. Once at Burnley, her aim was to become a professional 'lady gardener', a job description that included landscape gardening. The study of Landscape Design was an optional extra at Burnley – one that Edna (and presumably Olive) signed up for. Little is known about this class except that student comment indicates that it was unsatisfactory.

Among other things, Olive Holttum taught Edna on the subject of Native Plants. You'd imagine the relationship was a pleasure to both – but not so. Edna didn't think much of Olive, and the feeling seems to have been mutual. Perhaps it was an immediate personality clash, or perhaps their opinion of each other was affected by a professional jealousy that developed later on. In later years Olive became a highly regarded garden designer, writer and adviser, and in the mid-1930s her name began to replace Edna's in the *Home Beautiful* garden column. In other words Olive was one of Edna's ongoing competitors, which may explain why Edna was mischievous when she remembered Olive in her memoir:

> I positively hated working on what was known as the 'Australian border'. The one and only lady instructor (all the rest were men) poor soul, none of us respected her I'm afraid, because she was so sentimental about that blessed border in the school garden that it put me off, perhaps. Little I knew how enthusiastic about native plants I was to become. Mind you, the plants in that border were so extraordinarily depressing that they positively repelled one.

Perhaps Olive was an uninspiring instructor – or perhaps Edna had a blind spot when it came to acknowledging the positive qualities of her competitors! Olive was quiet, modest and practical, and she never blew her trumpet as loudly as Edna did – but then she didn't design gardens as well as Edna did either.

Apparently one of the first things that Edna ever said to Olive was: 'If *you're* working here why cannot I?' The fact that Olive *was* working at Burnley was essential to Edna's concept of a future career. Respect her or not, Olive Holttum was an example of what might be possible.

Olive didn't write a memoir but she did recall her memories of Edna in a single interview. Her comments give us a fascinating glimpse of Edna the student – and a fleeting glimpse of Olive the 'lady instructor'. The interview was conducted by Peter Watts in 1978 when Olive was eighty-seven (she died the same year). The following is compiled from Peter Watts's handwritten notes:

> Olive said that Edna had been a very keen student and a good worker. However Edna found the scope of the course very restricted – and so became discontented. She was among the best of the students, very vigorous, active and interested but yet had

> a nasty streak. She was a disturber of the peace. She wasn't sure, but Olive thought that Edna took drawing classes, maybe at a technical college.
>
> Edna was very strong physically. She volunteered to load sacks of wheat during the great strike [of 1917] . . . Olive doesn't discuss the course at Burnley except to say that the work of renowned garden designers such as Gertrude Jekyll received minimal attention.
>
> Talking about Edna's subsequent career, Olive thought that Edna started working for herself as soon as she left Burnley, that she was shrewd and self opinionated; had an architect friend, made a lot of money . . . Olive said several times that Edna made a lot of money.☼
>
> With regard to her own career, Olive said that she was asked more than once to 'fix up' an Edna Walling garden. That she had thrown away a list of 500 gardens she'd designed herself. Olive does not go into details but she says that she had a breakdown in 1918 and that Miss E. M. Grassick took over her teaching job at Burnley.

Olive's memories, even if tinged with resentment, give us an idea of what the twenty-one-year-old Edna might have been like. She was keen, opinionated and insubordinate. She was also patriotic and willing to support the government against the unions.

The general strike began with the railway workers in Sydney in early August 1917. The subsequent sympathy strikes and union bans seriously delayed domestic and war-front supplies. The government countered with an emergency plan calling for thousands of men – and

☼ Edna's gardens often cost a lot of money to make, but her fees never made her wealthy.

ABOVE: Edna's paternal grandparents came of good Devonian stock. Hariett was the daughter of a carpenter and William was the son of a master shoemaker. They established a plumbing and ironmongery business and had twelve children. LEFT: William Walling junior, Edna's father, became a highly respected Melbourne businessman.

ABOVE: Edna's sister Doris Oak-Rhind with son David and daughter Barbara. Doris liked a touch of style, especially when it came to shoes. LEFT: Barbara grown up and with children of her own – the twins John (aka Mytt) and Jill Barnes, plus Sandy the dog.

ABOVE: Edna at Burnley.

In the public eye

26 The Australian WOMAN'S MIRROR July 21, 1925.

Garden Designing by Women

By EDNA WALLING.

Miss Edna Walling, landscape designer, whose artistic vision is embodied in many beautiful gardens in Victoria. After a two years' course at the Burnley School of Horticulture, she had a further two years of practical jobbing gardening, then, on making known to one or two architects her intention of practising as a landscape designer, she soon got a chance to express some of her ideas.

Edna would 'express some of her ideas' in newspapers and magazines from the 1920s to the 1960s.

Edna shared the story of the building of Sonning and the development of Bickleigh Vale village with her *Home Beautiful* readers. Most of the published photographs were of cottages and gardens but occasionally a more personal image would filter through. LEFT: Edna laying the foundations of Sonning in 1923.

ABOVE: Old Sonning looking well established.
BELOW: New Sonning, a few months after the fire.

A glimpse of the land (18 acres) beyond Sonning on which such Anglo-Australian cottages as this are being built, surrounded by native trees, as a Devonshire village under the direction of Edna Walling, landscape designer.

Cousin Edith sent some of Edna's *Home Beautiful* articles home to Perth so that her family could see where she was living and working. The notes in pencil were made in 1933, those in ink were added many years later. TOP: The very early days of Blanche's 'shed', which eventually became known as The Barn. BOTTOM: Edna at the door of The Cabin which became her temporary home when Sonning burned down.

Sonning's open-air theatre became an ideal venue for raising funds for the Red Cross during the second world war.

not a few women – to volunteer to keep essential supplies moving, and the strike was broken by mid-September. It's not surprising that Edna volunteered. After all, her father was director of a warehouse, and her allegiance would have been with the employers, not the unionists. What is surprising is that she hauled sackloads of wheat – she must have been very strong indeed.

It's possible that Edna did other kinds of volunteer war work, especially before she began her course at Burnley. It was in her nature to 'do good' in this way. Almost every other woman was knitting socks etc. for soldiers, and I'm sure that Doris and Margaret would have clicked away with their knitting-needles, while Edna was off doing something else. Something more robust.☼

It is hard to imagine how intense feelings were around this time. Australian troops were being slaughtered by the thousand, but still the call was to 'send more boys'. There was an urgent, endless need for new recruits and new supplies, and the conscription debate was tearing the nation apart. On a private level almost everyone was dealing with some kind of anxiety or grief. All you could do was carry on as best you could and utter the usual clichés (time heals all, life goes on). And of course it wasn't all bad – business was booming for some people and there were new opportunities for others (every cloud has a silver lining).

Whatever Edna's thoughts might have been on the war, she

☼ Edna could have worked with the Red Cross for instance, or she might have been more adventurous and volunteered for Vida Goldstein's Women's Peace Army which, apart from energetic demonstrations, helped to improve the living and working conditions of women. I don't know how conscious she was of women's politics or any politics at this time.

evidently applied herself to her horticulture course with gusto – and criticism:

> How clearly is remembered the feeling of deep depression with which I listened to one of the first lectures given in the school to which I was sent in search of wisdom. It was on weeds and the lecturer commenced his digression with these words, 'A weed is a plant out of place.' 'Goodness,' I thought, 'I don't think I am going to like horticulture.' It sounded so austere, so dictatorial, so utterly unlike my previous conception of gardens, where foxgloves marched gayly over to the lupin beds and the forget-me-nots romped merrily over the primrose border. And so began a two-years' course of insubordination, fittingly brought to a close with an illuminated certificate which magnificently refrained from telling the world all that I did not know!

Actually the certificate was a plain grey. Edna always enjoyed a spot of elaboration in her writing. She had a seductive way with words. People who knew her say she wrote very much like she spoke, and indeed there is an unmistakable 'voice'. The above quote confirms Olive's memory of a discontented and critical student. And it wasn't just Olive that Edna didn't approve of; she didn't seem to like any of the lecturers. She found 'the few lectures on landscape gardening boring and the lessons on design which were to help us with the drawing of plans extremely tedious'. And she was amazed that: 'the lecturer in "Landscape Design" didn't succeed in putting me off the idea for life'.

But it wasn't all bad. There were some days of perfect bliss, full of 'fun and joyous out of door work under the guiding hand of the head gardener [Mr. Russ]'.

> This old boy seemed to have a soft spot for me; I was strong and perhaps more adapted than some of the more feminine students, and with some pride I began to notice that he gave me work that he would never give the others. He thought that I would plough a reasonably straight furrow so ploughing between the fruit trees was assigned to me. Goodness! What a happy week that was. Then he needed some fresh soil on one of the islands in the artificial lake in the school grounds so I was introduced to a large (a very large one really) wheelbarrow, a mound of soil, a plank and the island. It never occurred to me to put only a little in the wheelbarrow and so with the barrow heaped up I started across the sagging plank to the island and kept steadily at this operation until Mr. Russ came and said 'That will do', and I remember how those intense blue eyes of his twinkled. That I did not displease him was all I ever cared, so deep was my respect.

Ploughing seemed to be the absolute favourite – as long as it was solo.

> I enjoyed enormously ploughing with that dear old draught horse between the rows of fruit trees. He knew that 'cim-'ere' meant turn a bit to the left, and 'gee-'oef' meant a bit to the right. I was terribly anxious to please the old instructor with beautifully straight furrows. However the day came when it was decided that we should work in pairs and the girl they assigned to me had the crookedest eye you could imagine! I was terribly worried that the boss would think those wiggly furrows were mine, and I wasn't as good as he thought I was!

It may be surprising to learn from Olive's interview that the work of Gertrude Jekyll was not given much attention at Burnley, especially as she had published ten gardening books by this time. But then Gertrude Jekyll was part of a new development in garden making – a development that challenged the conventions most loved by Burnley instructors, particularly Mr. Russ. George Russ, revered for his strictly controlled espaliers and his prize-winning dahlias, had trained at London's prestigious Kew Gardens, later becoming gardener at a grand Melbourne mansion known as Rippon Lea. It's interesting that Russ, who promoted the old ways of the Old Country more strictly and proudly than any other staff member, was the one teacher Edna admired. His blue eyes must have twinkled very much indeed.

Edna may not have appreciated Olive Holttum but she certainly took to the other outstanding female figure at Burnley: Millie Grassick (1887–1974). Edna and Millie became friends when they were students together in 1916 – though there was a large gap in their experience. Edna was just beginning while the twenty-nine-year-old Millie was just completing a part-time course begun in 1914. Millie was also the 'Head Girl', which meant she was responsible for the general welfare of the female students. Perhaps it was Edna's particularly bumptious response to the course that initially brought the two together. Millie was also friends with Olive; they had known each other since 1914 and shared an interest in native plants.

Millie had a distinctive oval face and an Irish accent laced with Scots. Emily Matilda Grassick was born in Dublin of Scottish parents, the eldest of nine. The family migrated to Victoria in 1911, two of the Grassick sons having already settled in Australia. Millie's brother Will had established himself as an engineer in Melbourne, and Millie and three of her siblings eventually joined him in 1913. Her father had also been an engineer, and there was a strong tradition of gardening in the family.

Millie gained her Certificate of Competency with a mark of 80.6 per cent (Olive had achieved 90 per cent). Millie's score was above average, but clearly exam results do not indicate potential – or ambition. When Millie left Burnley she was looking for two things: better training in landscape design and a job that utilised her existing skills. She found the perfect combination. How excited she must have been when she told Edna all about it.

With a little help from her engineer brother Will, Millie had gained employment in the office of two of the most innovative architects in town: Walter Burley Griffin and Marion Mahony Griffin. Apart from the fact that the Griffins were creating some of the most interesting and controversial buildings in Australia, they were also remarkable in that they were trained landscape architects. Even the term 'landscape architect' was unfamiliar in Australia at this time – let alone the standard of training. Millie was about to receive the very best on-the-job training that could be found. And that wasn't all: working with her in the office on specific projects would be the well-known decorative artist Bertha Merfield. Miss Bertha Merfield created large-scale murals and panels for private mansions and public buildings, and was a prominent member of the Arts and Crafts Society of Victoria. Millie would learn about plan making from Marion Mahony Griffin and about drafting and design from Bertha Merfield – and to top it all off she was taking classes in painting with the artist and teacher Max Meldrum.

It was all very exciting.

I don't know how much notice Edna took of architects and artists at this point, but Millie's activities must have encouraged Edna to look beyond the simple pleasures of the plough.

The Griffins in particular deserved attention. They had come from their native USA to take on their 'prize' – the design of the new capital city, Canberra. It was Walter Burley Griffin whose name was on the winning design, but his wife Marion Mahony Griffin was a significant contributor; they were a good team. The Griffins took up residence in Australia in 1914 and, apart from many other projects, took an immediate interest in native plants. Their initial interest was aesthetic.

Australian plants were so attractive and so obviously suited to the conditions: why on earth weren't they used in Australian gardens? When they found that there was a dearth of information on native plants, they set about researching and compiling their own list. The resulting index was probably more comprehensive than anyone had managed before.

When Millie Grassick joined the Griffin office in 1917, she was engaged to draft plans. One of the major designs that Griffin was working on at this time was for the new Catholic College at the University of Melbourne – later named Newman College. Here Griffin had the opportunity to create a landscape completely in tune with his architectural concept. The meticulously drawn and labeled landscape plan used native vegetation almost exclusively. Whether Millie worked on these particular plans or not, her daily tasks must have been stimulating – and demanding. All in all, Millie was extending her knowledge in every direction and Edna must have taken notice.

Edna's extra classes in drawing (if Olive's recollection is correct) may have been inspired by Millie's example. The fact that Millie chose to take classes with Max Meldrum – and not just anyone – says something about Millie's desire to learn from particularly interesting and challenging people. Millie knew what she needed to enhance her career. If anyone was going to achieve landscape architect status, then surely she was.

Edna, meanwhile, kept her focus on the task in hand – the study of horticulture and the passing of exams. Her exam results were not exceptional but they were above average. Whatever criticisms she felt about the course, she still knuckled down and studied. She *wanted* that 'illuminated' certificate – even if she wasn't sure what she was going to do with it afterwards.

But what were the exams? What was it that people studied at Burnley to get their Certificate of Competency? A brief overview of the progress of three students – Edna, Katharine and Frank – will give us an idea.

Katharine Crawford was the outstanding student of Edna's year, while Frank Dodgshun found the exams rather difficult. Katharine was five years older than Edna, but most students, including Frank, were about four or five years younger. After the first term exams it was abundantly clear that Katharine was the one to beat – she topped the class with an average of 96.7 per cent to Edna's 80.7 per cent and Frank's 44 per cent.

Surprisingly, Edna's highest mark (beating everyone) was in Fruit Preserving with 99 per cent. It's not easy to associate Edna with the processes of preserving fruit, nor with the making of jams and jellies, but this was what the subject entailed (all behind the tightly sealed door of Miss Knight's classroom).The general quip was that Edna had achieved this lofty mark because she was excellent at soldering down the tops of the tin cans (and Katharine was not). Edna's second-best marks came in Poultry Management (which she professed to dislike) and Chemistry, which I think she did like. Edna's lowest marks were in Flower Gardening (a subject taught by Olive) and Soils & Botany (where clearly the study of plant Morphology, Anatomy and Physiology didn't suit her).

When it came to the comments on the report cards, Edna and Katharine were both described as 'excellent' while Frank was far from discouraged with: 'Takes an intelligent interest in the work; marks do not indicate progress made'.

The mid-year exam saw Edna continue to do well in Chemistry, also in Nuts & Small Fruits and Flori-Culture. Viticulture and Plant Pathology were less impressive, and something went very wrong with Plum Culture where she fell way below average. Again Katharine topped the class with 96.5 per cent to Edna's 76.5 per cent. Edna's report reads 'Alert and hard working student; exam results very good'. Frank was still bringing up the rear, but he had a moment of glory when he beat the other two with his attendance score – and he was appointed a prefect. Katharine was also appointed a prefect. Edna was not.

In the final term ending in December, Edna's attendance record was very poor and Katharine's was even worse, but they still did well in the exams, Edna staying above average and Katharine getting top marks. Frank only just scraped through his exams but his attendance record was 'excellent'. All three are recorded as receiving their Certificates in 1918.

There is scant record of what happened to the twenty-five students in Edna's year. Most took up poultry, orchard or gardening work. Edna is specifically listed as doing 'garden work'. Some few left to join the forces or to be nurses. One went to a florist shop, another to a bank, and some drifted away without a certificate. No one is listed as having taken up garden design.

In 1918 Millie Grassick left Walter Burley Griffin's office and became the second female instructor in horticulture at Burnley. There was a short period when both Olive and Millie were teaching at Burnley, and then Olive left the school to marry Alan Mellor. Olive gave birth to a daughter in August 1920, but in terribly sad circumstances – her husband had died of a heart attack not a month before. Ill health and various difficulties followed, and it would be many years before Olive Mellor managed to return to her profession – though return she certainly did.

Edna, meanwhile, was beginning to find employment as a 'girl gardener'. Her experience at Burnley confirmed her father's belief that an out-of-door life would suit her best. Earth was her element, it suited her 'heart, hands and head' (as the Plymouth nuns would have said).

She enjoyed digging and hoeing and 'just messing about with the soil'. The thought of creating landscapes did not seem to occur to her. Just being with the soil 'was all that mattered for the time being'.

Another thing that mattered was that the World War was over. The men, or what was left of them, were coming home. The women, their war-time duties done, were being asked to move aside. Not all of them obliged.

Edna, Doris and Margaret

Chapter 5

Ladies who lunch

There was a new vigour in the post-war atmosphere, once the flu epidemic was over. New technology was flowing into the country and it was changing the way people worked and lived. Slowly but surely the old social orders were breaking down and new expectations were building up. The impossible dream was becoming possible: to have your own block of land and build your own new house – all within cooee of a railway station efficiently serviced by an electric train. The suburbs were expanding.

A new house was in need of a new garden. Consequently there was a small but increasing demand for gardening advice: general journalistic advice for those creating their own gardens and specific professional advice for those wishing to pay someone to do it all for them. Until this point, almost all professional garden design had been in the hands of architects. It was left to the garden contractor to follow the architect's instructions, and if those instructions were limited – then so was the garden design. Left to themselves, contractors offered a standard arrangement of cement paths, diamond-shaped flowerbeds and orderly straight rows. The 1920s saw a small but growing demand for the professional person who could create a beautiful design as well as manage every element of its construction.

Edna began to see that she could be much more than a jobbing gardener – if she worked extremely hard.

We are watching Edna top-dressing a garden bed with manure. She is somewhere in the prestigious suburb of Toorak. She does not mind the smell of manure, she is not fussed about getting it on her hands or clothes, but she does mind that the lady of the house has been watching her for the last two hours.

It is a hot day. Edna wears a sun hat (which helps to keep her unruly hair in check) and works in her shirt sleeves, having discarded her jacket and tie. She moves freely in her breeches, only a little encumbered by the 'modesty' overskirt. She feels the perspiration trickle as she heaves the shovel-loads of manure out of the barrow and onto the soil. There is a huge mound of manure still to be brought in from the driveway. She wields the long-handled shovel with apparent ease. It is a balanced, rhythmic, circular motion. Almost a dance. Her tools are made for a man's frame, a man's strength, but she was taught from childhood to 'make the tool do the work', and it does, as long as it's made well. There is a nonchalance, a pleasure, as she wheels her wheelbarrow with yet another heavy load, though her arms and back are crying out for a break.

The lady of the house is sipping tea from an elegant china cup. There are biscuits on a tea-tray and thin slices of cake – all carefully prepared and brought by a maid who never looks up. All this Edna can see, for the lady sits at the window which looks out onto the garden. Some of Edna's clients offer her a cool lemonade, or at least a glass of water, but this one does neither. This one sips and watches. Bored yet entertained.

There is something strangely fascinating (thinks the lady) about this girl who looks like a boy. It is pleasing to see that she works so hard (and so cheaply at half the price). It is pleasant to observe that she is well presented and polite. But it is not these things that attract the lady's attention. It is something else, something to do with her manner, her determination, her walk. Something annoying, yet compelling. Is this what the new woman looks like?

Edna is at the hairdresser, a place she rarely visits. It is an exclusive salon in Collins Street, for Edna does not stint when it comes to quality. She has the best shoe leather, the best tailoring (within reason), and her gloves are well made. Swathed and towelled, Edna faces herself in the hairdresser's mirror. A determined hat wearer, she still has a 'peaches-and-cream' complexion but her hand (thinks the manicurist), is not as it ought to be – what lady goes around with short nails and ingrained dirt?

The head-towel is removed and Edna's long auburn locks uncoil down her back. It is strong, thick hair, easier to control now it's damp. The hairdresser is the best in the salon, but she hesitates, looking into Edna's brown eyes for one last check. The eyes say 'yes', and so she cuts. Long, long strands fall to the floor in quick succession. It's not entirely painless, there is a physical sense of disturbance as the cut line reaches the jaw, and then the ear. Edna has to close her eyes when the side parting and fringe are created. As the scissors snip in front of her face, little tufts of hair drift down and make her nose tickle. The general burble and chatter around the salon continues, but everyone knows something extraordinary is going on. Short hair is never seen, hardly ever seen, on a woman (and such beautiful hair too) – it's a sacrilege. And yet there is an easy, acceptable rationale: it is a practical and sensible solution for a woman whose job it is to garden and whose hair never does as it is told.

Edna opens her eyes. She looks at a boyish face, an androgynous face. A face that fits her idea of herself. She feels light-headed, effervescent, a little nervous. The voice in her head says: to hell with what people think.

Edna is at a meeting. A prestigious gathering of some of the 'top drawer' people in horticulture. Edna is not 'top drawer', as yet, but she has achieved a significant step in that direction. She has been elected on to the committee of the Women Horticulturists' Association of Victoria, an organisation formed during the war. It was probably Olive Mellor's idea (before she got married), for it is Olive who is the Honorary Secretary and the guiding force behind many of the activities – not least The Register. The Register is a list of mainly ex-Burnley women who are well trained (and well behaved) and seeking gardening work. Olive keeps The Register at Burnley, which is the Association's home, and places tasteful advertisements in *The Home Gardener* magazine announcing that there are women ready and willing to do 'fruit tree and rose pruning, landscape gardening, and general garden work' – just contact the Hon. Sec.

Edna is one of the youngest and least 'well connected' of the women on the Committee, so it is significant that she was elected on to it. She is surrounded by the wives of some of the 'top men' in the horticulture field. There is Mrs. Cronin, wife of the Curator of the Botanic Gardens; Mrs. Pescott, wife of the government Pomologist (who is also a former Principal of Burnley and the President of the Victorian Horticultural Society); there is the wife of a member of parliament – and so on. There are also of course single women at the Committee table. Although she is not an official Committee member, the gathering is honoured to have in their presence Miss Ina Higgins, the trailblazer who commanded that Burnley open its gates to women. Ina Higgins' pedigree is extraordinary and she needs no man to lend it weight (though her brother is the famous Judge Higgins). Apart from being a pacifist, suffragist and Christian Scientist, Ina is also an occasional garden journalist. She is used to public speaking and doesn't mind who knows it, a fact of which the Committee members are all too aware.

Not all the Committee members are matronly; some of Edna's peers are in attendance. There is Olive of course, and Millie who now teaches at Burnley, and Miss Le Souef, whose uncle runs the Melbourne Zoo, and one or two others.

The meeting is almost over but 'Any Other Business' raises the issue of who to approach for the next round of lectures. Ina Higgins is keen to draw the Committee's attention to the fact that all the lecturers so far have been *male*. Surely the *Women* Horticulturists' Association can do better than that? Mrs. Cronin, whose husband has kindly presented several of these lectures, would be only too pleased to invite a female but asks: who in our community is a recognised expert? (She emphasises 'expert'.) Millie immediately suggests Mrs. Walter Burley Griffin, and Ina suggests the carnation specialist and nursery proprietor Mrs. Denham. There is a stiff silence. Mrs. Cronin, who is, after all, the Chairman of this gathering, knows that Mrs. Griffin is controversial and that Mr. Russ is their carnation expert (she has never heard of Mrs. Denham). Thankfully, someone suggests that the selection topic be held over till next time, almost everyone agrees, and the meeting is closed.

Mrs. Cronin, whose dining room is the venue for this meeting, rings a bell and generous refreshments are brought. Now is the time for tea and chat – this is when the 'real' work is done. This is when the contacts and the favours are exchanged, the women's equivalent of the old school tie. It is here that Edna can enhance her employment opportunities and fish for prestigious clients. And it is here that Edna can learn from Ina Higgins about the radical notion of equal work for equal pay. And it is here, possibly, that Edna can peek into Mr.

Cronin's library and look through his latest *Country Life* magazine, for she is taking an interest in the work of Gertrude Jekyll and Edwin Lutyens. There is a price to pay for all this genteel hobnobbing: Edna must help with the organisation of flower shows and flower-arranging competitions (events which she finds nauseating), but it is a small price when one considers one is mixing with the 'right' sort of people. The people who may one day become clients.

Edna walks to the tram stop with Millie. They don't see much of each other these days. Millie has news. She's planning to go overseas, she needs to learn more about landscape design so she's going to try and get work with a top firm in England. Millie always has ideas, always gives Edna something to think about . . .

Edna is going to a party, a delightful party. All the right people are going – that is, the interesting people, the artists and so on. Edna is invited, or at least her good friend Eileen Wood is invited, and Eileen wants Edna to come. Eileen is three years older than Edna and has a lovely soft face and a winning smile. Everyone likes Eileen, especially Edna.

The party is being given by the Braithwaite sisters who, somewhat surprisingly, live in working-class Preston. Their father made his fortune in Preston through his substantial tannery business, which is why the family home is so far north of the city – though they will one day move to Malvern and Edna will design their garden. The Braithwaite sisters are a lively and intelligent bunch: one is a musician, another an artist and skilled motorcar enthusiast, another is studying to be a doctor and yet another is good at sports. Their only brother died in the war. The grief, in some ways, makes the young women enjoy life even more, and so partying with the Braithwaites is a great deal of fun – teetotal of course.

The Braithwaite house is straightforwardly Victorian, without the over-blown trimmings of a mansion. The house grew as the tannery business and the family grew. There is a pleasant garden with square lawn, orderly roses, and the occasional palm, plus a well-used tennis court. There is an ample driveway and a substantial new garage with two Citroens in residence – one for Mr. Braithwaite and one for the girls.

It is late afternoon on a Sunday and the party is in the garden. Most of the women are dressed in light colours (hem lines are moving above the ankle now), and the men wear cream or charcoal grey. There is a gay array of cordial drinks on a table on the verandah, and plates of sandwiches appear at regular intervals.

Eileen and Edna know some of the people at the party. Millie is there with her artist friend Bertha. The wonderfully creative Alsop sisters are there, and Edna and Eileen go and greet Ruth Alsop who is talking with a tall, slim man with big ears and a red nose. Ruth introduces him as her brother, Rodney Alsop, the architect. Rodney is a gorgeous, gangly, affable man, who has hayfever. He is in his late thirties, and is well known in these circles for his beautifully crafted work with wood and metal, though it is his house and garden designs that are earning him increasing public recognition. Ruth is also an architect (the first woman architect in Victoria) and used to work with Rodney in his Melbourne office. The war, and then the needs of ailing parents, have temporarily halted her career.

Ruth and Rodney used to create superb repoussé metalwork pieces together, but Rodney's design commitments overwhelm him these days. Edna asks if he still has time to do his own garden designs and he's happy to say that he does, with the help of his dear wife. Edna is slightly disappointed with this answer but soon recovers when Rodney launches into a passionate speech about how rarely one sees the architecture of the garden integrated with the architecture of the house. Edna couldn't agree more, but their conversation is interrupted by another of the Alsop sisters.

Edith Alsop, the well known illustrator, playfully nudges her brother aside and steals Edna and Eileen away. She wants them to meet two young journalist friends: Miss Frances Taylor and the newly married Mrs. Katharine Ballantyne. Edna has met Katharine before, when she came to report on a Women Horticulturists' Association function, and is flattered that Katharine remembers her. Frances Taylor overtakes this conversation by asking Edna a number of questions about her gardening work. Frances forcefully explains that she's hoping to set up a new magazine – when she can raise the capital – and is looking for interview stories. The magazine will be called *Woman's World*, and the front page with be illustrated by the wonderful Edith Alsop – and Melba has agreed to be featured in the first edition. Eileen and Edna look impressed, but Katharine has heard all this before and her attention begins to wander across the lawn; she sees her husband talking to Merric Boyd, the potter, and wonders what they are saying.

Edna asks Frances if she is contemplating a gardening column, and if so, who will be writing it? – but there is a loud commotion in the driveway and everyone turns to see an extraordinarily long motorcar driven by a diminutive being whose features are obscured by goggles and a large tweed cap.

The Braithwaites are the first to swarm around this sparkling vehicle and they greet the driver (who you'd expect to be the chauffeur) as if he were a guest. He removes his goggles and cap and appears to be a youth until he – or rather she – steps from the car. She wears silk stockings and sensible shoes and a lovely light blue dress, revealed when she slips off her heavy driving-coat. Her hair is even shorter than Edna's.

It is Alice Anderson, who has just opened her very own garage business. The Alice Anderson Garage offers the usual services plus a driving school, maintenance course, and a unique 'chauffeuresse' service. Alice only employs women, and her staff go through a rigorous Alice Anderson training scheme before they receive their distinctive breeches-and-jacket uniform. The business is beginning to take off, which is just as well, for a large debt rests on those slender Alice Anderson shoulders.

The little group ponders this last thought as they watch the Braithwaites examine the vehicle (cars are 'the next new thing' for the wealthy woman). The tiny Alice Anderson raises both sides of the heavy bonnet with surprising ease. Like Edna, she appears to be very strong, but the appearance is more to do with the strangeness of this unfamiliar sight than a true reflection of exceptional strength.

'Would you care for a game of tennis?' says a young man offering a tennis racquet to Eileen, who blushes and accepts. This annoys Edna – she's not sure why but it's probably because she was about to ask Eileen if she would consider going into a business partnership with her. Edna could do the garden design and Eileen the plant selecting and they could both do the gardening . . . But Eileen has gone off to play tennis. Edna decides to ask Millie instead. But Millie says no. Has Edna forgotten? Millie is going to Europe to learn more about landscape design.

The sun is setting and the party is coming to a close. It has been a delightful success, everyone says so as they wave their cheerios. Edna and Eileen catch the tram and trundle south towards the city. They discuss their plans for a Sunday picnic in the country. Edna suggests they take the train that goes to the foothills of the Dandenongs and explore somewhere there. We might see wild flowers, says Eileen; we might see land for sale, says Edna. She tells Eileen about her fantasy of starting a nursery and garden design business, and how good it would be if she found a friend to be a partner. Eileen imagines the possibilities and is quite taken with the idea, but then her tram stop arrives and she's off and waving goodbye.

It is dark by the time Edna reaches Arundel Flats. William and Margaret are home, and the evening meal is waiting.

It is a Monday morning. Edna is again working in the garden of the Toorak lady who likes to watch. Happily, it is nearing noon, the time when she can stop. Edna has quite a number of clients now, so must keep to a timetable. 'The lady' has had her four hours and Edna has truly earned her four shillings. She must go to the back door, the tradesman's entrance, to receive her pay (one day she will send invoices but she's slow to get that part of the business organised). Fortunately she's very close to Washington Street, where her newly married sister now lives. Edna can pop in and see Doris and have some lunch.

Doris has moved from William and Margaret's small flat to a spacious house on a sizeable block. Doris – Mrs. Alfred Oak-Rhind – has married a widower and father of two. She is not entirely comfortable with her step-children (the feeling is mutual), but everything else is going well. Doris is appreciated by her Christian Science community, which is increasingly attracting some of the very 'best' families in Melbourne. She is financially secure for the first time – though too imbued with frugality to really enjoy it. Doris would be happier if Alfred didn't have a gin and a cigarette each evening – Christian Science teaches that alcohol and smoking are bad for your health – but otherwise, Alfred is a good catch.

Alfred is an affable Yorkshireman in his early forties. He has a soft spot for his sister-in-law, as do his children, Bill and Val. Aunt Edna is always welcome, though preferably not when she's been working with manure. Edna visits Washington Street quite often.

Doris sews and chatters while Edna eats a simple lunch. Doris is an obsessive sewer or knitter; she cannot just sit. Their mother has a similar need to be 'doing'. When Margaret visits Doris they both sit and sew. It's the Protestant work ethic, taken to an extreme in Doris's case. Doris rattles on to Edna about the latest family news, which is that their father has been promoted to Sales Manager and Importer and that his office is now at the top end of Bourke Street. William Walling is becoming known for his astute business sense, gentle good manners and impeccable appearance. This would be splendid if he wasn't so devoted to his tailor. His taste for good suits is verging on an extravagance. William's prospects keep improving but he has no plans to move into a house. He likes Arundel Flats, it's a convenient location and a reasonable rental. Besides, as he says to Margaret, there's more room now that Doris has left.

Margaret, meanwhile, is lunching at home, alone in the flat. She worries about Edna. The poor girl works all day and then studies all night. It's too much. Margaret wishes she could help somehow. But of course she does help, not least by saving up and buying her books; especially the Gertrude Jekyll books, one after another, until Edna has the full set.

One of Edna's most cherished books was Gertrude Jekyll's *Garden Ornament*, published in 1918. This huge tome with its folio pages and golden edging is all about English and Continental garden architecture. It would have cost Margaret a whopping three pounds and three shillings and it would have been worth every penny. It was the perfect style guide for the budding designer.

Edna's memoir omits to mention intensive study after Burnley, but an interview article published in 1922 gives a hint by saying she had 'a knowledge of English and Continental architecture'. It's a tiny clue but a good one. Knowledge of this calibre could not have been obtained at Burnley for it was not on the curriculum. Edna must have taught herself an enormous amount from books and journals.

Jekyll's *Garden Ornament* contains hundreds of photographs showing a glorious range of classic gardens. The photographs are accompanied by Jekyll's engaging and often pithy comments regarding pools, sundials, pergolas, steps, gates and a multitude of other features. The grand historic and the new Edwardian are displayed. One garden in particular must have caught Edna's eye – The Deanery in the village of Sonning. Apart from appreciating the Lutyens and Jekyll design, Edna surely remembered floating through Sonning on the Thames as a little girl. How strange it must have been, to look at the word 'Sonning' and recall another world, another life.

Edna couldn't afford to travel overseas to study, but she could read the appropriate literature, and she could refine her drawing and plan-making skills. She could also view the work of local architects, and experiment with ideas in the gardens of amenable clients.

Edna's first experiment was a disaster. She spent the whole day reconstructing a dull corner, but when the mistress of the house came home Edna was told to put it all back, exactly as it had been.☼

Experimentation was probably the key factor in Edna's development as a designer. It would be her distinctive interpretation of established garden styles that set her apart from her peers, who, after all, studied the same books, the same architects.

Edna's experiments were influenced by two British style 'camps' which had formed themselves into 'the Natural' versus 'the Formal' during the 1880s. The Natural camp was headed by William Robinson, who argued for a wild garden, one that appeared to have been created by Nature herself. Edna particularly enjoyed the natural (carefully constructed) swirl and sweep that she could achieve with this style. The Formal camp was headed by William Morris, champion of the Arts and Crafts movement and promoter of all things related

☼ The client was Mrs. C. Lempriere of Torresdale Rd, Toorak; she was one of Melba's sisters and was otherwise hospitable, plying Edna with drinks, food and funny stories. Edna first met Melba when she was working in the Lempriere garden; the diva asked if she enjoyed her work and Edna answered with a gushing affirmative.

to a vernacular, hand-crafted tradition: beauty through utility and simplicity. Morris called for a return to the dignified seventeenth-century Old English garden – the simple formality that existed *before* 'Capability' Brown created his fantastical landscapes. Both 'camps' were reacting against the popular Victorian Gardenesque, which borrowed from every style imaginable.

Those in the Natural camp tended to have a horticultural background. Those in the Formal camp were architects to a man. The naturalists looked at the Formal style and saw rigid lines and an ignorance of siting, planting and grouping. The formalists looked at the Natural style and saw a mishmash of clumps and no sense of design. Surprisingly, a compromise was found.

By the time Edna began her experiments, many British architects were placing a formal layout close to the house, with a natural layout further away. This combination became known as the Edwardian 'Arts and Crafts' garden – the large country garden style made famous by Lutyens and Jekyll. The Arts and Crafts garden blended three styles: the geometric lines of the Formal, the ornament of the Italianate, and the relaxed undulations of the Natural.

The guiding principle for the architect was that the design of the garden should complement the design of the house. The garden was divided into a series of outdoor 'rooms', each with its own character and each separated by walls, fences or hedges. Signature features of the Arts and Crafts garden included fine flights of steps, well-proportioned pools, circular terraces, extensive pergolas, flagstone paths, retaining walls, and 'wild' natural areas which, in Britain anyway, were meant to reflect the native vegetation of the surrounding countryside. All of these features were to become Edna Walling trade marks.

It is important to note that these trade mark features had appeared in exclusive Melbourne gardens long before Edna started using them. It should also be remembered that Edna had been living within walking distance of William Guilfoyle's Royal Botanic Gardens and that she admired at least some elements of his picturesque style. Edna's touch of genius was to combine these design influences with her knowledge of horticulture – and create a design style remarkably her own.

Melbourne could boast at least three highly regarded architects who were followers of the English Arts and Crafts architectural style: the asthmatic and affable Rodney Alsop (1881–1932), the charming and extremely fashionable Walter Butler (1864–1949), and the engaging Harold Desbrowe Annear (1865–1933). Walter Burley Griffin was in a separate class all of his own. Edna may not have known these fellows personally at this time, but she did have the opportunity to study their work. Plans and photographs of their gardens occasionally appeared in journals, and if all else failed, Edna could always peer over an exclusive garden fence and see for herself.

Walter Butler in particular was inspired by the Arts and Crafts ideal. Born in England, he trained with some of the key figures in the movement and completed his studies with John Sedding, the author of *Garden Craft Old And New* (1891). Sedding's London office was above the Arts and Crafts showrooms of his friend William Morris. Walter Butler worked in this office, and was very much part of the Arts and Crafts 'club'. He came to Australia in 1888 and quickly established a fine reputation. By 1919 he was Vice-President of the Royal Victorian Institute of Architects – with Rodney Alsop a fellow Council member. Butler's amiable yet persistent call for high standards in house *and* garden design did not go unheeded.

Architects like Butler and Alsop would not have wanted Edna to design gardens *for* them; they enjoyed doing their own. But perhaps Edna had the chance to learn from them.

Edna's memoir recalls the eureka moment when she suddenly understood something fundamental about *how* to develop her design style. It was as if she had found the key to a secret garden. It may seem extraordinary that a simple stone wall supporting a semi-circular terrace should have caused Edna to have a near-epiphany experience. Hadn't she seen such a wall before? Surprisingly, the answer is no, or at least not many in Australia. At this time, stone walls, as a design feature, had rarely been used in public or private Australian gardens.

Edna was on holiday when she had her glorious revelation. Exhausted by her gardening work, she spent a few days down the coast, probably with her good friend Eileen Wood:

> . . . one day we were walking around looking over the fences of local gardens, I was terribly bored until we came to one with a stone wall supporting a semi-circular terrace, it was really lovely, I was fascinated and stood rooted to the spot. My friend was giving forth little squeaks of delight at some flower or other . . . 'But that wall, I shall build walls,' I said . . . From then on, gardens for me became a chance to carry out the architectural designs in my head instead of places where one slaved for too many hours of the precious days. I remembered that one of my friends had a brother architect, so I took a day off from that awful gardening and walked into his office, I asked if he would let me design a garden for one of his houses. He had no objections at all – gardening didn't interest him. So one of his clients was persuaded to let me design his garden, as luck would have it the men I got to build my first wall made a splendid job of it, and on we went from garden to garden, building walls, always building walls.

Edna's transformation may not have been as effortless as her memoir suggests – but it was fast. She was designing professionally by 1920, and by 1922 a magazine ran an interview article with the heading: 'Miss Edna Walling – Australia's First Woman Garden Designer'. This statement may have raised the hackles of certain other woman garden designers, but then again, it does seem that Edna was the first to be *making a living* from her work – for no other garden designers (male or female) were attracting anything like the same attention.

The magazine article with the provocative heading appeared in *Woman's World*, the new publication created by Frances Taylor (whom Edna had met at the garden party). Edna's interview reveals a confident woman with definite opinions. These are expressed with an uncharacteristic stiffness, which is probably more to do with the (unnamed) journalist than Edna herself. Stiff or no, Edna is not a shrinking violet when it comes to promoting her profession:

> Australians have not yet fully awakened to the need for a landscape architect to design their gardens. They call in an expert architect to design the interior and exterior of their homes, but the garden is left, with few suggestions, to a contractor. They might just as well ask the cook to design the interiors.

Edna goes on to say that it is the architecture of the house that dictates whether native or exotic trees are used for the garden:

> In a typically Australian home, such as we get in the country, the gum tree is the proper tree setting, and, with broad acres to be laid out in gardens, some beautiful effects can be obtained with them. The average suburban house is not typically Australian, if there be such a thing as Australian architecture, and it is for the garden designer to lay out the garden in keeping with the house. With a typically English house English trees should be employed in the landscape scheme . . . Not that I do not love the gums . . . but in the small suburban garden I find them too hungry . . . I find it easier to grow flowers and shrubs near the deciduous tree, which enables the light to get through in winter.

Edna suggests that stone, with the clever use of cement, can be an excellent construction tool and alludes to 'a sunken garden reminiscent of Italy' that she has recently completed. Edna recommends the Italian style:

> The ideal pergola, to my mind, is that often seen in Italian gardens, heavy concrete pillars supporting a light lath top over which the creepers twine.

Edna had never been in an Italian garden in Italy, but she had seen this style of Italian pergola featured in Gertrude Jekyll's *Garden Ornament.* She would have seen the photograph of the famous pergola of Amalfi with its long curving avenue of bold pillars, and she would have been inspired. It was exactly this 'ideal pergola' style that Edna designed and built for her sister and family in Toorak. Indeed, she used the style to great effect in various places.

Edna enjoyed incorporating Mediterranean features into her designs, when they were appropriate. It was her particular understanding of what was appropriate, and her general sensibility towards architectural styles, that helped her achieve the near impossible task of pleasing both architect and client – and thereby winning the acclaim she deserved. Edna knew how to listen to a client, and how to adapt her ideas to suit. This didn't mean that she *agreed* with the client of course. Deep down, Edna was entirely confident that she knew best. This confidence proved to be the essential ingredient when Edna made her next leap towards success.

It's not clear whether Edna simply fell into journalism, or if it was a calculated push. Either way it was a clever move.

Journalism gave Edna extra pocket money and, very importantly, free publicity. Self promotion was uncommon in the pages of magazines at this time. The artist Margaret Preston was one of the first women to *really* use the medium to promote herself and her work. Both men and women, but particularly women, were shy about using their own names. For instance the *Argus* newspaper began a weekly horticultural column in 1924 with a writer called 'Culturalist'. The column was very popular and fan letters were keen to congratulate this 'Culturalist' chap on his breadth of knowledge. Few people knew that the real name of the writer was Millie Grassick, Edna's friend.

Millie returned from Europe in 1924 having succeeded in her quest to learn more about design. She had worked in the office of Britain's leading landscape firm and was now one of the best trained landscape architects in Australia. Millie Grassick's name would have become very well known (she wrote for the *Argus* and the *Australasian* for twenty years), if she had not followed the norm and chosen the anonymity of a pseudonym. Edna was never so modest. She used a couple of pseudonyms for a short time but otherwise she signed her own name to absolutely everything – text, plans and illustrations – and without the conventional 'Miss'.☼

Edna's robust sentences and black ink plans and sketches shone out as refreshingly different. Garden advice to date had been thoroughly practical and unimaginative. The very few (non-architect) garden plans that had been published thus far had been badly drawn, usually with the aid of a ruler. Everything about them was rigid. Edna's drawings

☼ Edna wrote a monthly article as 'Barberry' for *The Home Gardener* from November 1924 to September 1925 – though she was hardly anonymous for she signed her illustrations with 'EW' or 'Edna Walling'! Edna co-wrote with Katharine Ballantyne as: 'Walltyne' in *The Home Gardener*, October 1924; and as 'EW and KB' in *Woman's World*, September 1924; and under their full names in *The Home* December 1924 and *Woman's World* March 1925. Edna signed a plan as 'Rufus' in *The Garden and the Home*, August 1924 p29; 'Rufus' is Latin for reddish-brown and may have been a nickname, given that Edna was a redhead.

were all swirls and irregular curves and balanced disorder.

Edna's very first article was published in 1921. It appeared in the magazine that would one day be known as *Home Beautiful* but which had the uninspiring name of *Real Property Annual* in 1921. The magazine concerned itself with the serious matter of housing and planning. Side-issue articles were added for light relief, and it was these that eventually turned the annual into a highly successful 'lifestyle' monthly. There were two articles concerning garden design in the 1921 edition: one by Edna Walling and the other by Walter Burley Griffin.

Edna's article offered fresh thoughts regarding paths, borders and lawns: 'Let me plead against the planting of a palm in the centre!' Griffin's article was concerned with ugly housing that was spotting the landscape like a disease. He suggested that houses should be subordinate to the landscape and that flat roofs and roof gardens be used to soften the design. He encouraged simplicity: 'We need but be reminded of the Roman atrium, the Spanish patio, the Italian piazza and the medieval cloisters, to arouse the most poetic fancies of all the past, and make us realise how the habitats even of mere paupers have not been without the simple charm which our most expensive villas lack.'

Edna disliked flat roofs – and I suspect that she disliked much of Griffin's architecture – but she was surely in tune with his philosophy. True to form, she didn't acknowledge his work in her writings, but she must have recognised that she was in extremely good company when she saw that her first-ever article had been published just one page after his.

By 1924 Edna had become a regular columnist for a New South Wales publication, *The Garden and the Home*. Her initial article took aim at the amateur gardener and offered a few hints 'especially directed at the young benedict who is going to eschew football for flowers on Saturday afternoon. Go forth then to your future garden plot armed with a sharp pencil, a sheet of paper and a mind free for the play of the imagination.'

Edna quickly established a recognisable writing style, a provocative combination of artful knowledge and brutish charm. The following extracts demonstrate some of Edna's concerns in 1924, and her particular gift for communicating them:

> Who of you has not observed when wandering the bush or the open country Nature's scheme of planting trees, and then beneath or behind them graceful shrubs, whilst lower down, and hugging the earth so closely, are perhaps tangled wild vines or massed wild growths. Everything is planted so near together that a prim "landscape gardener" asked to contemplate it might raise hands in horror and enquire whether you would ever be foolish enough to want THAT in your garden? Some of the wise people who have the most adorable of gardens would immediately answer 'Yes' to such a question, and they would be right.

> Nobody wishes to have a perpetual view of [their] neighbours' houses and to be able to tell merely by drawing back the dining-room curtains whether Mrs. Brown is washing today or receiving visitors. So the first thing to do is to see about judiciously planting trees on the boundaries.

> The formal flower garden is the only place where one may introduce the geometrical lines in flower beds that are so prone to be ever popular in the majority of suburban gardens. Otherwise than in formal surroundings the unsuitability of these geometrical beds is glaringly apparent and a constant source of irritation to the artistic mind of the man or woman who really has studied the enthralling question of garden design.

> Colour has a very strong influence in making your garden appear small or large. Blues and mauves, to illustrate this a little more plainly, will convey the sense of distance admirably, whereas the warmer colourings . . . will give the sense of concentration. Colour harmony will take care of itself to quite a considerable extent when the reds and magentas are used with a very sparing hand . . . White, used freely in any garden, has a cool and most pleasing effect that is often neglected.

> . . . if you are just building your house, with a good deal of supervision from yourself, have you considered the merits and the appeal of a stone terrace?

By 1925, few could argue that Edna hadn't truly earned the title 'Australia's First Woman Garden Designer'. Indeed, her competitors were so overwhelmed she appeared to be Australia's only garden designer. Everything was going well. She'd found the very best contractor and stone-worker in Eric Hammond; she had a growing client list; and her designs were beginning to equal, if not outshine, those of her architect counterparts.

A person might feel the need for restful weekends and the occasional long lunch after all this effort – but not Edna. All this while she'd pursued a dream. A dream that had taken every spare moment and not-so-spare penny. She had built her own little cottage in the country: Sonning.

Edna was nearing thirty. She had lived with her parents in Arundel Flats for over ten years. It was time to leave home.

Edna and Brian at Sonning

Chapter 6

Love

Decades after the event, Edna recalled a particular night and a persistent woman: Olwyn Connor.

> Always remembered her turning up at Sonning one night well late in the evening to realise she intended to stay the night! Sonning was only half built and there was nowhere for her to sleep but with me! in my quite narrow single bed! I can't remember who slept on the outside but I know that who didn't had to hang on to the one who did!

The night in question was in 1923. Edna remembered Olwyn as 'a charming and amusing person' who adored everything to do with horses. She also had a keen sense of humour: 'She'd laugh at people – kindly of course, but even now I can see her screwing up her eyes and hear that low chuckle.' Clearly Olwyn wasn't overawed by Edna's forceful personality, nor hesitant about inviting herself to stay the night.

Edna must have been surprised to receive such a nocturnal visit – she was, after all, miles from anywhere in the middle of a cow paddock in a half-built shell of a house.

Edna would willingly share whatever she had, but whatever she had was severely limited at this stage. Food, bedding – there was only enough for one, and Olwyn surely knew this. Who can say why Olwyn arrived so late (or how – by horse?). Let us hope she came with suitable provisions. A midnight feast perhaps: sandwiches, cake, a thermos of tea – or maybe a drop of something alcoholic? The nights can get chilly when the mists float down from the Dandenong hills. A drop of heart-warming brandy might have been what Olwyn brought. But then again, 'nice young girls' didn't generally travel with a hip-flask, it wasn't 'proper'.

However, two young women clinging to each other in a too-narrow bed wouldn't have raised an eyebrow of innuendo in the early 1920s. There was nothing improper about it – how could there be?

Edna was no puritan. From her early twenties she enjoyed a drink and a smoke (pleasures some called vices), but it's unclear how 'forward' she was when it came to intimate or sexual relationships. To many people, to religious people like Doris for instance, partaking of alcohol was sinful, awfully sinful, and so was sex outside marriage. Edna was not like Doris. Edna made her own religion, her own rules. She was an independent spirit who had discarded much of her Protestant conditioning – but not all. It's clear that Edna had a preference for women when it came to intimate relationships, but it's not clear how she approached, or indeed understood, her preference.

Whether Edna consciously invited it or not, her distinctive individuality was especially attractive to young women seeking something 'individual' for themselves. Edna exuded the something they wanted: an independence of spirit, a strength of purpose, a playfulness, a kindness, and for some an intriguing 'otherness'. As we have seen, Edna named her otherness as 'misfit' or 'odd' – her half-joking way of saying she didn't fit the standard female mould. She may have recognised her otherness as an aspect of her sexuality, or she may not. There are subtleties rather than clear-cut certainties. Even Edna's understanding of the term 'sexuality' would have been a world away from the informed and liberated use of the word today.

For all Edna's independence of mind, spirit and body, she was a woman of her time. It was not the age of enlightenment as far as sex education and sexuality was concerned. When Edna's sister Doris went to her wedding night in 1918, she had no idea what was to occur in the marital bed. Her mother certainly hadn't told her. Some three decades later, Doris's own daughter Barbara was not much the wiser when she approached her wedding night.

In Edna's early days, the general populace knew little or nothing about homosexuality; it was still 'the Love that dare not speak its name'. The majority believed that any deviation from the heterosexual norm was perversion. Homosexuality was, at best, a subject for mirthful scorn; at worst, a vile and criminal obscenity. The word 'lesbian' was hardly in the vocabulary at all. The idea of sexual desire between women was too extraordinary for words; it remained as silent, as invisible, as lesbians themselves. Indeed, many women who would now be called lesbians didn't recognise their intensity as sexual desire; they simply loved their very best friend – who loved them in return. They would have been horrified by the suggestion that their love was anything but pure. And if they did have an inkling, if they did share their bodies as well as their hearts, why then – they kept quiet about it, and who could blame them? There were no positive role models for women who loved women. Novels and films of the period, if they alluded to lesbians at all, portrayed them as pathetic victims, or bitter, sadistic, mannish, grotesques. No woman in her right mind would wish to be associated with that. Silence was all.

If Olwyn desired Edna, and/or Edna desired Olwyn, they may not have known what to do about it.

When the famous English author and garden-maker Vita Sackville-West wrote about her sexual 'duality' in a secret journal, she was attempting to understand her feelings for women. As she wrote, she recalled her first real love: Rosamund. In 1913 she was in love with Rosamund at the same time as being engaged to Harold Nicolson. Vita would stay at Rosamund's house, and secretly creep into Rosamund's bed, creeping away again early in the morning. Both of them knew that their feelings for each other should be kept secret, that their love was somehow 'wrong', but neither knew why. They did not recognise their feelings as sexual: 'It was passion that used to make my head swim sometimes, even in the daytime, but we never made love', said Vita to herself in her journal. Vita overcame her uncertainties and married Harold, and so began a loving, lasting and unusual marriage. By 1917 they had two sons and all seemed blissful – until Harold was forced to tell Vita about his own 'duality'. He'd caught a venereal infection and had to explain that he'd caught it from a man. It was only through Harold's explanation of his homosexuality that Vita began to comprehend her own same-sex desires. Until this point she had not understood what homosexuality was: 'I didn't even know that such a thing existed between men or between women.'

Edna's world was less sophisticated than Vita's. It seems likely that, in her twenties at least, Edna was naive about homosexuality. If the nature of Edna's 'oddness' included feelings of what we now call lesbian desire, then she probably repressed them.

Repression of one's feelings inevitably results in some kind of limiting effect, emotionally and/or physically. There may be no connection, but Edna was not a warm person physically. She did not give hugs or kisses. Some people found her very stern, but her friends knew she had a soft, romantic heart. If Edna was fond of you she would not express it with a cuddle, but she would give you love. Love in the form of boundless enthusiasm – especially if you were helping with one of her 'schemes'. It was her work, her ideas, her projects that took most of her attention, most of her passion. She could sweep people up with her enthusiasms, buoy them along with her encouragement, overcome difficulties with her keen sense of fun – and send herself up in the process. That was her attraction. On the flip side, she could be argumentative, moody and selfish – especially if she didn't have a 'bolt-hole', a room of her own, to escape to. For all her enthusiasms, it was imperative that Edna spent time on her own.

A single woman, Edna always had a single bed, its narrowness an indication that she wished to be alone when she tucked herself in at night. But then again, a narrow bed was never an impediment to passion, if passion there was.

As the sun rose and the birds screeched, on the morning after Olwyn had slept with Edna, there was no time to lay abed. There was work to be done – walls to be built, wood to be sawn, materials to be collected – and there were people expected. Bill Oak-Rhind, Doris's stepson, was catching the morning train from Melbourne, and Katharine Ballantyne, Edna's journalist friend, was popping down the hill to see how things were going. Edna was up and dressed and out to inspect the property while Olwyn was still in a daze, blinking at the brightness of the morning – for it shone most forcefully through the gap in the unfinished roof.

How sweet the air, how blue the sky, over Edna's little patch of country earth; how peaceful the cattle, as they grazed on their *own* side of her self-built fence. How satisfying the views of undulating hills, drifting far into the distance to the north, west and south. How graceful the peaks of the Dandenong ranges, their misty dark presence behind the hill that Edna now called home.

There must have been moments when Edna just stood and breathed deep, enjoying with all her senses the view, the breeze through the trees, the cattle, the mixed aromas, the swish of a horse's tail, the warble of a magpie. This was living. This was the dream . . . half the dream anyway. Edna was halfway there – with more than a little help from her friends – old friends and new friends, not to mention relatives, who had all been wonderfully helpful.

Katharine Ballantyne and her husband were Edna's near neighbours; they had a house and eight acres further up the hill. The hill had once been part of the Arnwood Estate, a 112-acre homestead consisting of orchards, grazing land and an area of bush. Edna's two-acre plot was grazing land dotted with spindly trees, she-oaks mainly. Her plot was halfway up the hill, a fact breathlessly commented on by visitors who arrived by rail. It was a three-mile, cross-country, uphill walk from Mooroolbark station to Edna's place. Hardly anyone owned a car, and in any case, there were few roads and none of them sealed.

The railway station was a convenient stop-off point between the larger townships of Croydon and Lilydale, and the train journey from the city took barely an hour. Mooroolbark farmers and fruit-growers were the main users of the railway, but in earlier decades the timber merchants had dominated activities. The hills had long been denuded of their forest, though there were still some beautiful bushwalking areas to the east, behind Edna's hill.

Edna bought the land in 1921, having discovered it with her friend Eileen Wood. The original plan may have been to buy land together. They had at least discussed the idea of forming a landscaping/gardening partnership. Both Burnley graduates, they had compatible skills and could have made a go of it. Dream or reality, the idea fell through, perhaps because Eileen became engaged to be married. The story goes that the pair were out bushwalking and happened to come across a 'For Sale' sign. The subdivisions of the Arnwood Estate had not sold as quickly as Taylor and Sharp had hoped.

Taylor and Sharp were a contractor and timber merchant partnership with offices in the city. They had bought up large areas before the war, and from 1918 were advertising the subdivided blocks as suitable for small farms or weekend homes. Buyers 'only' needed to pay a five-pound deposit, and a pound a month thereafter: 'Interest 5 per cent per annum, payable quarterly. Residue, if any, at the end of 8 years.'

Edna emptied her savings book and paid her five-pound deposit in a characteristic rush of enthusiasm. She had found what she was looking for. It was only after she'd signed the papers and started the payments that reality kicked in. She suddenly realised how expensive it was going to be to have a house built in the country, even a very small one. It would take her years to save the money. The original day-dream had not included a scene where she built the house herself. That was just too extraordinary a scheme, even for Edna.

The idea of a single working woman wanting her own country cottage wasn't unusual. Single professional women were heading for the hills and establishing weekend houses or hobby farms in increasing numbers. *Woman's World* magazine reported on the new trend in 1921:

> In the foothills of the dividing range there are scores of mountain cottages of quaint artistic design owned by bachelor women. Overlooking the Dandenong ranges, at a spot within twenty miles of Melbourne, five such cottages have been erected, and the row has become for all time 'Spinster Crescent'.

Woman's World was aware of the difficulty of finances and offered some helpful suggestions:

> The next problem – building – is not one to be solved alone by £ s. d. Bush carpenters are gradually becoming extinct, and the estimate for building a one-roomed hut in Melbourne stretches to breaking point when the proposition is taken to the country. Roughly speaking, a nicely finished room 10 ft. by 10 ft. should

> be built for £70. One of the best solutions of the problem . . . is buying the ready-made house in sections. One of the leading timber mills has a two-roomed hardwood cottage nicely finished inside and out, with chimney complete, which can be erected by them practically anywhere for a sum not exceeding £200.

The 'ready-made' was the solution for the woman with savings, or with a nice little inheritance. But all was not lost, *Woman's World* had an answer for the woman with hardly anything:

> Another scheme which has proved satisfactory is the aeroplane-case cottage. Aeroplanes arrive in this country in huge wooden cases lined with three-ply and roofed with malthoid. These cases could be purchased at an average price of £10 and are easily converted into two and three room cottages.

Ideal – except for the cost of transportation. The train was one thing; transporting such a large item halfway up a hill, was another. Edna couldn't afford it. For a while, she gave up on the dream.

At this point Edna did something that seems uncharacteristic – though it may have been the way she dealt with overwhelming problems. She pretended the problem wasn't there. She focussed on her extremely hard-working life in the city and ignored the 'fact' of Mooroolbark for months and months.

Margaret Walling observed Edna's neglect of Mooroolbark with a mother's dismay. She was a practical woman, and in her mind ignoring Mooroolbark was a terrible waste. Margaret was an organised as well as a supportive mother. When Edna arose each morning she found clean clothes in the drawer and was assured of a cooked breakfast; when she staggered back to the flat at night there was an evening meal waiting. Edna could never have achieved so much in her work if she hadn't been looked after in this way. Similarly, Edna may never have achieved so many of her dreams if her mother hadn't given her the occasional little 'push' when needed.

Margaret and William had been supportive of Edna's desire to own land, and interested in her idea to have a cottage. They had faith, and neither had asked the obvious: *how*? But as the months rolled by, Margaret began to wonder: *when*? Margaret knew her daughter. It wasn't just money Edna was short of. She had somehow mislaid her enthusiasm – the key to motivation. Edna needed a little push of inspiration, so Margaret developed a plan. Unbeknownst to her daughter, she went on a trip to Mooroolbark with a friend. She climbed the hill, found the plot, and had a good look around. When Edna sat down to dinner that evening, Margaret made her move.

It was just a short conversation, retelling the story of her day: how easy the train ride, how pleasant the walk up the hill (when taken slowly), how splendid the views, and how beautiful some of the trees. Edna could only remember spindly trees on her land, but Margaret assured her there were some beauties – yes, on *her* land, not the plot next door. The local stone looked very attractive too – a lovely texture of pale ochre yellows to dark reddish browns – and so *much* of it was just lying around . . .

And that was it. The flame had been lit and Edna was afire with ideas. There were saplings in the bush that could be cut for rafters, sand by the roadsides that could be mixed with cement. The roof would be a difficulty – but then William chipped in. He offered to send up a load of packing cases from the Toledo Scales warehouse; when covered with malthoid they'd be perfect for roofing. Simple calculations suggested that Edna's only substantial cash outlay would be on cement – and a horse. A horse to literally share the load. Suddenly all the answers were there. She had the brain and the brawn, she could put it all together. And if enthusiasm ever flagged, or doubts niggled, there was Margaret to offer support:

> When I began building Mother would come and spend the day and sit on a box talking to me whilst I did the stonework. I soon found I relied on her quite a lot and would delay certain parts of the work until she was there and we would talk over the placing of the windows and the fireplace – their proportions and other details – I always felt safe if she approved for I liked her ideas.

William contributed his wisdom from the soft comfort of his fireside chair. He did not want to sit on a box in the middle of nowhere; country walks were not his style any more. But he helped by suggesting solutions to practical problems, and by donating the occasional eight shillings, so desperately needed for the next bag of cement.

Mooroolbark local residents took a good humoured if quizzical interest in developments. It did not take long for everyone to know who Edna was and what she was attempting. The young woman in jodhpurs was endearingly dubbed 'Trousers' by one of the council members, which is why her private road later became known as 'Trousers Lane'.

The locals looked forward to Trousers' next visit. It was like waiting for the next installment of a good yarn – what would the girl do next? She was wonderfully stubborn about doing the hard labour herself. The blokes were itching to lend advice, if not labour, but she liked to do as much as she could herself – her way – however unorthodox.

It was an especially interesting day for the Mooroolbark community when William's packing cases arrived at the railway station. How would that young woman get them up the hill? With a sledge, of course:

> Having a horse, I felt that nothing was impossible, more especially as 'Adam' was amenable to any work that had been invented for him to date!

> A sledge was soon made, and proudly we drove into the station and loaded up. It was a strange and eventful trip with the first load, but we arrived intact, and made many more trips before completing the transportation.

Edna gathered her stones in the same way, having to go further and further afield to collect them, as more and yet more were needed. Eventually she had to compromise and use less stone and more wood. She would spend weekends or more camping on site, working away, with visits from local friends like Katharine Ballantyne, or city friends like Olwyn, or relatives like her step-nephew Bill Oak-Rhind.

Bill was a gem. Just a teenage schoolboy, he mucked in with Edna, spending every weekend he could, working with Aunt on the cottage. His younger sister Val sometimes joined them, but Doris didn't visit. Her energies were focused on her own domestic haven; she was now the proud mother of three-year-old David, with a new baby on the way.

One of Edna's new friends was Alice Houghton. The Houghton family owned the farm next door, while Alice's sisters ran a boarding house nearby, so between them the Houghtons saw to it that Edna and Bill were well fed – at 1s 6d a head. Edna either went to the Houghtons for meals, or food was sent over in a basket. There was an interesting unpredictability about the basket meals; Edna was never entirely sure which was the white sauce and which the custard. Bill, a thoroughly amenable chap, didn't really mind what it was, it all went down the same way after all.

Miss Alice Houghton was not your typical 'country lass'. Her permanent address was a pleasant street in St. Kilda in a house shared with a sister. She gave her occupation as 'Home Duties' in the Rates Record, but then so did Edna, so it's not a reliable indication of how she spent her days. Alice Houghton must have shown a keen interest in Edna's activities, for she later became Edna's assistant, probably the first regular assistant Edna employed.

There was much laughter, and not a few tears, as the cottage slowly emerged, stone by stone, rafter by rafter, packing case by packing case.

When Edna returned to her 'real' work and city life, she'd entertain her father with the latest stories of achievement and disaster. There was the day when the whole frame began to lean at a ridiculous angle, and would have fallen over but for their emergency props. They eventually worked out what was wrong; they'd forgotten to put in the absolutely essential tie beams. They fixed it, after a fashion, though the structure never returned to its original plumbness. William was especially tickled by the stories about the horse and sledge, but perhaps seeing that 'enough was enough', he gave his daughter the cash to buy a new spring cart.

> And so one day 'Adam' and I went forth to the market, and for a few pounds secured a dear little cart and some second-hand harness. I was a little crestfallen at learning that harness had to be bought, too, but was not at all deterred when the dealer asked, 'Has he ever been in harness before?' You see, I did not know that horses that are really hacks quite commonly kick a conveyance to pieces on first acquaintance with it – and I had hitched him up to a sledge!! My complete fearlessness, entirely bred by ignorance, was evidently contagious, for although I replied in the negative nothing more was said, the harness was adjusted, a surprised-looking horse was backed into the shafts, a few pound notes handed over the side, and off we went. I was so glad that some of my neighbours were working in their field as we neared home, so that I could proudly wave to them.

By the end of 1923 it was official: a cottage was born, and Edna's rates almost trebled to prove it. The dwelling wasn't truly finished of course, as every owner–builder knows; there were still things to be done and errors to live with. There was a tiny ongoing problem concerning borer in the rafters, and a certain irritation when the wind changed direction and the fireplace guffawed a chimney-full of smoke; and then there was the little matter of the bedroom window that gave a wonderful view when Edna lay in bed but no view at all when she stood up – but such things were minor. Edna had a roof of her own. She was home.

A couple of years after she'd settled in, she gave her *Home Beautiful* readers a candid description of her house-building adventures. She alluded to her need for economy, her indispensable 'Chief Mate' Bill, her 'four-legged friend Adam', the obsessive fascination of stone gathering and placing, and the rotten fact of borers being in the saplings she'd cut for rafters. She included photographs, humorous cartoons, and a brief description of the finished interior:

> [T]he furniture consists chiefly of ancestral cast offs and bush products eked out with the ever-useful packing case. But for a splendiferous bath heater and a porcelain bath, supplied by a generous parent, everything is of the very simplest nature, only those things that are essential being admitted.
>
> A room 18ft. x 10ft. with double glass doors leading on to a piazza overlooking a little flower patch and nursery garden is the main room. Off this is the kitchen, bathroom and bedroom. You go up two steps into the bedroom, because it is built on the side of a hill.
>
> There is a stone chimney in the kitchen, bedroom and main room. Domesticated relations regret the absence of a range in the kitchen. I, however, prefer the open fire, not being domesticated.

'Not being domesticated' meant that Edna was cooking the bare necessities over an open fire whilst receiving her main meals from the Houghtons; it also surely meant that she was paying for domestic assistance. With Edna's increasing workload, she had little time and no inclination for washing and ironing (assuming she possessed a wash tub and a flat iron). Edna knew that her approach to home building and home living would not suit many people and readily acknowledged this to her *Home Beautiful* followers:

> [T]here are certain drawbacks which make me hesitate to honestly recommend to my fellow-readers the building of their own cottages in stone. I mean, of course, the readers of my own sex . . . my circumstances were peculiar. My training in outdoor work as a garden designer had taught me how to overcome certain inevitable difficulties and had rendered me indifferent to an unusual amount of 'dirty work' and the knocking about of the hands . . .

The 'fair sex' was not generally acquainted with stone-work, carpentry, and the trench digging required to build one's own outdoor lavatory (the latter detail not alluded to in Edna's article). There was no electricity, no piped water, no sewage system, no 'mod cons' beyond the heavenly porcelain bath with its wood-fired water heater. There were some softening features: feather cushions provided by her mother and fitted curtains sewn by her sister, a wind-up gramophone with a modest collection of classical recordings, a wide selection of books, and a put-me-up for guests. What more did she really need?

Edna's desire to have a home and lifestyle 'of the simplest nature' was influenced by three factors: her very real need to be frugal, her rejection of the stereotypically feminine, and her aspiration to achieve 'beauty through utility and simplicity' – as influenced by the philosophy of William Morris. She cared deeply about the design of her cottage, how it functioned in terms of sunlight and shade, how it opened onto the outside 'room' of the piazza, how the whole sat easily on the landscape, a snug fit rather than a raw blemish, the local stone an echo of the local stone. She'd made mistakes of course, but such idiosyncrasies simply added to the general character. The cottage had heart, or whatever it is that certain dwellings have when they immediately say to you: welcome, be at peace here. Perhaps it was that sense of peace that reminded Edna of her childhood vision of the dreamy village of Sonning on the river Thames. 'Sonning' – it was a pleasant name to give a country cottage.

For the first time in her life, Edna was in command of how she wished to live. Not even her mother could compel her to have a cooking range if she didn't want to have one.

There was no single day when Edna moved into her cottage, no significant date when she called the place Sonning. She gradually spent less time living at the flat and more time living at the cottage. She stayed with her parents when it was convenient for city activities, but otherwise she went home. By 1925 the transition was complete. She listed her name under the Country Exchanges section of the telephone directory as: 'Walling E. Miss, Landscape Designer, Mooroolbark' – and her number was 3. It was the magic of the telephone and the efficiency of the post office that gave Edna the ultimate freedom to live, and work, as she wished.

It must have been marvellous to come home, knowing it was truly her home, with everything arranged as she wanted it, and no one but herself to accommodate in terms of taste or habit. To wind up her gramophone and play her most rousing piece of Beethoven, 'conducting' the finale with gusto if she felt like it. To light her fire in her very own handmade fireplace, to pour herself a drink and settle into her cosy armchair and read a book, or simply gaze at the flames. To fill her beautiful porcelain bath with water from her efficient little wood-heater; to cast off her old clothes, and the old day, and sink her body into the enveloping warmth, relaxing, easy breathing, the steam rising and clouding, the single candle-flame flickering, the packing-case walls whispering, and her body slowly releasing the muscle-aches of the day . . . To climb the two steps to her bedroom, to tuck herself into her narrow bed, to gaze at the moon and the stars and the darkness from her pillow-level window, and to drift very gently to sleep . . .

I wonder if Edna felt lonely at first, living on her own after twenty-eight years of co-habitation. She may have felt the need for some companionship and protection, for she soon acquired the perfect friend for the purpose: a dog. One of her friends bred Irish terriers so perhaps that is how she came to bring home a little bundle of a puppy with wiry hair, floppy ears, and a big Irish terrier nose. It was his dark brown eyes that were especially captivating. When he stopped wriggling he could look quite intelligent, even noble, so Edna called him Brian Boru, after a legendary Irish king. It was an odd sort of name for a dog, but then Brian was no ordinary sort of dog. Brian, and of course Adam the horse, were well-loved companions in the early days, and it was not long before they were joined by a black cat or two – much to Brian's annoyance. Edna found great comfort in these companions, and owned a dog or at least a cat for the rest of her life.

Edna's four-legged friends were not her only companions. There was a diverse range of interesting people all around the neighbourhood and she enjoyed spending time with them.

Closest of these was Katharine Ballantyne, Edna's journalist friend. Katharine had a home in Melbourne under her husband's name and a home in Mooroolbark under her own name, and appears to have been of an independent nature. Just a couple of years older than Edna, she was born Katharine Bryndwyr Griffith, on her parents' farming property west of Melbourne. As a young adult, she lived in South Yarra. She married William Ballantyne in 1919. She developed strong links with Melbourne's Royal Show as a journalist and administrator, and, given her interest in agriculture and horticulture, it's possible that she and Edna knew each other before becoming neighbours in Mooroolbark. Either way, the two put their heads together and created a handful of magazine articles during 1924 and 1925.

Most of the articles consisted of gardening advice, but their major success (from Edna's point of view) was a feature devoted to Edna's design work. It appeared in the up-market Sydney magazine *The Home*, and was surely a crucial boost to Edna's career. The article included eight photographs detailing two of Edna's gardens, plus a segment from one of her plans, and a photograph of the newly built Sonning. The text was minimal but all was in praise of Edna's city and country designs. It was probably Katharine's contacts, rather than Edna's, that had gained them such a highlight in a 'top drawer' magazine.

Katharine appears to have adopted a supportive role in the collaboration. The influence of her more 'literary' writing style is evident within the articles, but the overall effect is dominated by Edna's ideas, Edna's work, and certainly Edna's drawings. The collaboration didn't last, perhaps because Edna didn't actually need a co-writer; she was doing very well by herself. The two remained close, geographically at least. Apart from being long-term neighbours in Mooroolbark, they became city neighbours for a time. Katharine's Melbourne address was Arundel Flats during 1926, just a corridor away from the Wallings.

There were other interesting interconnections between city and country people. Eric Hammond, Edna's brilliant stone-worker and garden contractor, was a fruit grower near Mooroolbark in the early 1920s. The two didn't officially work together until 1924, by which time Eric Hammond had moved to the city, but he clearly had links with Edna's part of the countryside. He may well have heard about the woman known as 'Trousers'. Edna was a couple of years older than him. They were chalk and cheese in temperament but of like mind in their understanding of beauty and quality. It was an important and long-lasting relationship based on mutual respect. Eric Hammond advised Edna on how to fix some of Sonning's faults, and was destined to work on many of the cottages that became Edna's village of Bickleigh Vale. They may not have socialised, but they certainly spent a great deal of time together.

There were new and old friendships for Edna to cultivate in the wider surrounds of the Mooroolbark area. For instance Blamire Young and his family became residents from 1923 and were soon part of Edna's social network. Blamire Young was one of the leading artists in watercolour in Australia, his wife Mabel was a wood-carver, and their daughter Ida a poet. Apart from being a watercolourist of extraordinary ability, Blamire Young was also a wine buff, art lecturer, art critic, after-dinner speaker, designer for 'high class' theatrical evenings in Melbourne and Sydney, a prominent member of the National Rose Society of Victoria – and much more. Unusually for the time, he favoured modernist rather than traditional art and particularly welcomed Margaret Preston's work. Time spent with the Blamire Youngs must have been especially pleasant – a generous flow of good wine and even better conversation.

Edna seemed to have the best of both worlds: friends in city and country, increasing work opportunities, an assistant in the form of Alice Houghton, and her own little house plus four-legged companions. What more could she need? A new acquaintance saw an obvious and rather urgent requirement.

Blanche Scharp was a determined young woman with a capacity for adventure, independence, and meticulous efficiency. A pharmacist by profession, she was looking for something 'else' to engage her mind when a mutual friend introduced her to Edna.

One Saturday afternoon in the winter of 1926, Blanche visited Edna at Sonning. Blanche had an interest in Edna's work, but it appears to have been a social rather than business call – though it was the business end of Edna's life that caught Blanche's eye that day. Blanche happened to glance into the corner where Edna had her office. She admired the drawing board with its near-completed plan, half garden design and half delicate watercolour, but she was *appalled* by the chaos that appeared to be Edna's attempt at invoicing and accounting (it was tax return time and the mess was laid bare). Blanche insisted on coming back the following Saturday to sort it all out. It was the beginning of a long, fruitful and sometimes bumpy relationship.

Blanche Scharp was born in the pleasant Melbourne suburb of Kew, and was twenty-four when she met Edna, who was thirty. Blanche's father was an accountant, a respectable one – though he had been friend and bookkeeper to the wealthy, powerful and notorious John Wren. The association ceased when Mr. Scharp realised that shady deals were going on. Presumably Blanche acquired her aptitude for accounting from her father. She was the sort of person who kept lists and tallies in tiny neat handwriting, and was canny when it came to money. Her fiancé of several years, Louis B. Marshall, was not good with money, which is why Blanche took command of the purse, and perhaps why the house they eventually bought was in Blanche's name only. Blanche 'wore the pants' in the relationship, metaphorically – but sometimes literally. She adored horses and spent as much time as she could riding through the countryside. When a teenager she rode on her own to Beaufort to visit country relatives. The trek took three days, and at night she simply camped under the stars. Blanche was a gal who liked to go her own way. She gained her driving licence when she was eighteen, and had her own motorcar by the time she met Edna.

Small of frame, large of bosom and sharp of nose, Blanche was just the sort of bright spark that Edna enjoyed.

For the next few months, Blanche worked as a pharmacist during the week and spent almost every Saturday, and some weekends, at Sonning. Louis, her patient fiancé, was rather put out by this turn of events, but he adapted. This was fortunate, for Blanche would devote much of her time to Edna over the next few years. Louis was an easy-going chap. He went fishing when Blanche was busy with Edna, though sometimes he went to Sonning and lent a hand with practical jobs.

One of the myths about Edna is that she didn't like men. This is untrue: it was fools she couldn't stand. Edna and Louis liked each other. Understandably, there were jealousies, on all sides, at different times. For instance, Louis can't have been too pleased when Blanche announced at the end of 1926 that she would be spending her summer holiday driving to Sydney with Edna – in Edna's new car.

A motorcar, a motorcar, how had Edna ever managed without a motorcar? Like everyone else, she had walked, or used public transport, or relied on her friends, or driven her horse and cart, but that was hardly feasible for the long-distance country jobs she was now being asked to undertake. A motorcar was vital to her career.

One day Edna drove home, somewhat gingerly, in her brand-new, two-door, four-seat, soft-top Fiat 509. It was the model with plenty of 'Power, Pep and Personality' and cost £345 (the price of a small house). It was absolutely perfect – especially as William Walling was paying.

It was a long drive to Sydney and the roads were poor, so two drivers were essential. Edna and Blanche planned their route carefully, giving themselves six days to get there, five days to get back. There would be time to stop and explore a little; time to take notes about interesting plants and collect a few specimens; time to find a good camping spot, or a reasonable hotel if they preferred. They would have to pack their camping gear and luggage and food and petrol and water very carefully, for there had to be room for the third member of the party: Margaret Walling.

Margaret was far more adventurous than William when it came to leaving the comforts of Melbourne, but I doubt that bedding down in a dusty swag by a dry creek was her idea of fun. Blanche kept a sketchy account of the journey in her tiny appointments diary, and it appears from this that Margaret was found a hotel each night, while the drivers camped out on alternate nights.

Blanche's diaries are a treasure of tiny clues. She scarcely wrote anything in them, yet kept them year after year as the decades passed. It is from Blanche's all too brief notation that we know that the first day's journey began from Melbourne at 8.30 a.m. and ended at 10 p.m., at Lakes Entrance. It must have been a relief to all to find a hotel so late in the evening. Undaunted, they set off early the next morning, and were less tardy on subsequent days. They'd buy provisions along the way, and stop at some picturesque place and have lunch or a short tea break. On the morning of the third day they crossed the New South Wales border and headed for Merimbula. The road wound through hilly countryside, sometimes wooded, sometimes pasture, and then turned towards the vast blue magnificence of the Pacific Ocean. When they crested the hill that led into Merimbula they saw a lagoon and lakes and brilliant white beaches and the swell and fall of thundering waves. It was irresistible. When they reached the shoreline, Edna and Blanche slipped into their bathers and ran into the sea.

It's unlikely that any of the three had seen such a wondrous coastline before, or undertaken quite such a journey.

There are photographs that show the threesome at various stopping points. There's one of Edna sitting on the running board, rolling a cigarette, knees wide apart, hair short, expression determined. Or there's another snap of her half disappearing under the bonnet of the Fiat, doing an oil, spark plugs and water check. Photographs of Blanche show her wearing similar garb to Edna – shirt, tie and jodhpurs, plus a cheery smile – though she looks particularly petite behind the driving wheel. Margaret, meanwhile, wears the standard protective clothing that most women wore in a motorcar: a hat with plentiful gauze to cover the face, and an all-enveloping overcoat. She sits with a statuesque pose, very much the Englishwoman abroad.

The Fiat earned the nickname Psyche on the journey. It's an interesting choice, given that it comes from Greek mythology, a topic one does not immediately associate with Edna. The name can mean butterfly or soul, but in this instance it probably reflects the trials that the Fiat had to overcome before reaching a safe haven. The original, very beautiful Psyche had to perform a number of almost impossible tasks before she could be reunited with the one she loved – Eros. She succeeded in the end, with much help from Eros.

Psyche, the beautiful Fiat, had a mighty thirst for oil. There were a couple of mishaps with tyres and a few minor repairs. Eventually however she too succeeded, and roared into Sydney on the sixth day, rolling to a stop outside a hotel. Edna ordered the doorman to cart the luggage and *all* the camping gear to their rooms – clanking blackened pots and all – for the Fiat was a soft top and she didn't want anything stolen!

They had a fascinating few days investigating Sydney. They explored the bays, the architecture, the gardens, the vegetation; they sent postcards, they met people. Edna took notes and made contacts and marvelled at the natural rock landscapes, the cliffs, the beaches, the beauty of it all. And then they packed their things into Psyche, and began the long journey home.

There's nothing like a long trip to really get to know someone, and a close bond was established during the Sydney adventure. Blanche was adopted into the Walling family circle. They exchanged birthday and Christmas presents, they socialised, and Blanche stayed overnight with Margaret and William if she worked a late shift in the pharmacy at the Alfred Hospital opposite Arundel Flats.

Blanche was doing relief rather than full-time work as a pharmacist at this stage, which meant that she had free periods when she could work with Edna. She'd accompany Edna on design jobs in city and country, sharing the driving and various practical tasks. Importantly, Blanche also shared Edna's dream for Sonning; a dream that saw the transformation of a cow paddock into an idyllic scene, a place where there was a garden with an abundance of trees, where the architecture of even the simplest out-house was sympathetic to the land, and where there'd be a nursery for shrubs and trees of many varieties. Blanche cared about what Edna was trying to do. She wanted to help where she could.

Edna's plans for her land were developing splendidly. She'd completed her payments for it by late 1927, and she'd even managed to increase her holding to three acres, the extra acre for the development of the nursery. She had planted mostly deciduous trees around Sonning: 'Liquidambers; Golden, Silver and Italian Poplars; Lime Elm; English Ash, and lots of others, with a sprinkling of evergreens'. Her vision was progressing well, but the view beyond her fence was threatening to turn ugly.

The acreage around her property was beginning to change hands. Katharine Ballantyne had wisely bought nine more acres around her land further up the hill, thus securing it from prospective pig or poultry farmers or insensitive weekenders. Through this good fortune, the land above Sonning was reasonably safe from 'invaders', but the land below might be sold off at any time, to *anybody*.

The primary owner of the land below was Mrs. Whisson, proprietor of the Victoria Coffee Palace in nearby Lilydale. She'd purchased the plots as an investment, and it was doubtful that arguments concerning aesthetics and rural beauty would have discouraged her from selling to a prospective pig farmer if she was offered a good price. The obvious solution was for Edna to buy the land (about seventeen acres), but it was far from obvious how she could stretch her finances to achieve this.

It's impossible to say what Blanche felt for Edna personally, but clearly Blanche had invested much of her heart, as well as head, in Edna's work and vision. Blanche now proposed to deepen that investment by making a financial commitment. She wanted to buy the couple of acres directly below Sonning – a purchase that would require a complicated subdivision. Rather than approach Mrs. Whisson with a proposal, Blanche offered to pay Edna £100 in advance in anticipation of eventually owning that plot. For her part, Edna would design a building and garden to suit the plot, and oversee the construction. It was a deal. Edna now had the wherewithal to bargain terms with Mrs. Whisson.

In March 1928, Edna and Blanche sat down with Mrs. Whisson and made her an offer she did not refuse.

A few months later, Edna was officially the owner of Mrs. Whisson's acres, but it was a nerve-racking period financially. Although Edna's income was steadily increasing, so were her expenses – wage payments, loan repayments, running costs, rates. Her profit margin was very narrow. Even so, thanks to Blanche, Edna could now expand her dream. She could sleep soundly, knowing that when she looked through her pillow-level bedroom window in the morning, twenty acres of the view was safely under her protection.

Blanche, meanwhile, was on the verge of becoming indispensable. She had not only helped to build The Cabin – Edna's one-room, stone-walled, many-windowed, steeply-roofed, hideaway cum bolt-hole

– she had also agreed to work for Edna *full-time*. It was a surprisingly lateral move for someone determined to run her own pharmacy one day – and of course to marry the ever-patient Louis.

Blanche must have loved working with Edna very much. She was about to earn less, work more, and put her own plans on hold. Blanche gives us no clues in her diary as to why she chose this direction; however she did keep the letter that Edna sent her confirming the full-time arrangement. As it is one of the very rare pre-1930 letters that has not been burnt, lost or thrown away, it is worth quoting in full.

To set the scene: it is April 1928, and Blanche has taken five weeks' work as a locum pharmacist in Finley, New South Wales. She is earning £6 a week and staying in a not-too-pleasant boarding house. She has written to Edna about her starting date, and has asked her about borrowing a book by A. A. Milne. Edna is on holiday with an unidentified friend at Airey's Inlet, a settlement on rugged coastline about three hours' drive along challenging roads west of Melbourne. Edna must have told Blanche the story about her father tipping her out of a canoe when a child, for she refers to her fear of swimming out of her depth. Edna's nickname for Blanche was 'Buve', short for 'Buvelot' which was Louis' middle name – which tickled Edna no end. Edna's handwriting is difficult to decipher; words in square brackets are estimations.

> Airey's Inlet,
> Victoria. 22.4.28
>
> What a rotten shame! I can't for the life of me remember you asking me to send you a book & haven't got your first letter with me here dear. You mentioned – I remember – that you had "Now We Are Six" so I am wondering if it was "When We Were Very Young" that you asked me for?? I did not skip through your letter – on the contrary I enjoyed it so thoroughly I read & reread

it again, which is all the stranger that I overlooked the request. P'raps you didn't put it in dear?!

How very rotten about Louis' accident. I wish I had known, I could have taken him up something to read or at least found out what he was in need of.

The pub here gives one a jolly good meal which we partake of every other day – it's 3 bob a head so [it's] got to last two days!

I'm getting rather a good swimmer, yesterday I swam quite 3 yards – nothing I know – but when I add 'out of my depth' you may feel moved to admiration. I feel confident I could swim miles and miles but somehow I just don't! The Inlet is a topping place to swim in, it is always so beautiful calm, you can come out of the breakers & then go for a swim and then 'bask in the sun until you are saved'. It will be, perhaps, of interest to you to learn that swimming is a most excellent 'reducer' so I must bring you down here & put you through your paces my girl!!! But I am thinking you may have been reduced more unpleasantly at the place you are boarding at.

I take it that you are [working] an extra week that will be May 7th or thereabouts that you will be returning to Melbourne. Well now [Buve] if you hurry up to Sonning & not stay fooling around town you should be in time to see some of the chrysanthemums. I shall want your help in listing what varieties we have, & in a hundred & one other ways & don't forget we start on a strictly kept salary basis for you dearie – the rotten part about it is you won't get quite as much as you do as a chemist – but we will say £4 per week, which seems damn little for all you do old chap.

I shall expect you to start on May 10th (ahem!) & the hours will be 8.30 to 5.30 (ahem! again)

Yours Edna

> We will have our own holiday – a deliciously happy holiday one day dear.

The signature, and touching afterthought, was squeezed into space in the margins.

Edna's comment about Blanche 'reducing' or losing weight seems strange, for Blanche was not large – except for her bosom. Edna was quite obsessive about body weight; she appreciated a slim female figure when she saw one, and strove to keep her own proportions lean. She never wearied of saying that the physical demands of gardening were good for the waistline as well as the plants. Even so, I doubt that Edna would have raised the 'reducing' topic if Blanche hadn't declared some unhappiness about her shape – women's fashions of the period called for narrow hips and a flat chest.

At the time of writing the letter, Edna had just completed a *Home Beautiful* article in which she'd quoted from A. A. Milne's *Now We Are Six* – so Christopher Robin was 'in the air' at this time. She called her article 'How We Put Up Our Little Stone Cabin' and gave Blanche an appreciative mention as her 'offsider':

> My fellow 'mason' had never done stonewalling before, but very quickly developed the stone sense, and would have a number of stones in position whilst I was mixing the mortar.

The 'fellow mason' also appeared in one of the photographs – her small frame seated in a large wheelbarrow.

After some minor delays in the city, Blanche packed a suitcase, waved a cheerio to her family and fiancé, and drove the twenty miles to Mooroolbark. Her small neat handwriting, in blue ink fountain pen, marks the occasion in her diary for 6 June 'Started at Sonning'. Underneath this statement, added in pencil, is a rare expression of emotion: 'V. very happy'.

Edna and the Fiat

CHAPTER 7

Billy Vale

Edna was entering the busiest and most demanding phase of her career so she was fortunate, and doubtless 'very very happy', to have Blanche come and work with her at Sonning.

Blanche's responsible influence had already eradicated some of Edna's chaotic excesses. Gone were the days when she neglected to send the necessary invoices, and gone the days when a client blatantly omitted to pay what was owed. Sometimes a client resented the fee for a visit, or disputed the cost of her travel expenses, or simply never paid. Edna didn't care to pursue her non-payers with the necessary paperwork, though there had been occasions when she argued the point with a client, or simply never finished the job. But incidents like these were rare now that Blanche had overtaken the management of the accounting. There was one client however, who would always sweep past the formalities of 'administration' – Dame Nellie Melba.

One day in 1927, Melba rolled up to Sonning in her chauffeur-driven motorcar and hallooed Edna's name in the general direction of the front door. There being nobody home but Brian the Irish terrier

– who excelled himself with the happiest of greetings – Melba left a note on the kitchen table requesting that Edna attend her at Coombe Cottage, her country estate just across the valley. The upshot of the audience was that Edna undertook to employ three 'girl gardeners' to maintain Melba's country grounds. As Melba was away from this residence quite often, Edna was to take responsibility for overseeing the work and for paying the wages, for which of course she submitted regular invoices for reimbursement.

The arrangement worked well unless Melba was without a secretary. Edna had not made this connection until one evening Melba telephoned and asked her to come over and keep her company. Melba loathed being on her own and if there were no guests in the house she'd seek alternatives. Busy though Edna was, she did not refuse the invitation. Who could say no to Melba? Besides, there was always half a chance that Melba would remember to settle their account.

When Edna arrived she was shown into Melba's boudoir, an ornate room packed with impressive mementos. Melba was sitting by a cosy log fire, opening her mail and, after the initial delighted welcome, she resumed this task. As they chatted, Edna noticed that Melba was sorting her mail into two piles, a letter pile and a bill pile, and when the last of the envelopes had been opened she watched Melba slowly but steadily feed the papers from the bill pile into the flames of the fire – chatting all the while. Edna recalled that 'It was one of those periods when she was without a secretary, and I couldn't help hoping – for all concerned – that one would be forthcoming again soon.' Edna was too polite to press for payment, but as Blanche kept reminding her, 'carrying' the Coombe Cottage wage bill was costing an extra £9 5s a week.

Edna chose to remain patient; a cheque would come eventually. Edna knew that the benefits of Melba's patronage and friendship far outweighed the difficulties. Melba liked Edna, she approved of her endeavours and appreciated her talents and did not hesitate to say so.

A highlight of Edna's career was when Melba ceremoniously launched Edna's exhibit of a full-scale garden for an Arts and Crafts Exhibition at the Melbourne Town Hall: 'She said all sorts of nice things about me and I shall never forget my mother's expression of pride.'

It wouldn't have been difficult for Edna to tap into the 'old girl' network of Burnley and secure three suitable gardeners for Melba, though their temperaments, as well as their efficiency, would have been an important selection factor. Melba had fired her male gardeners for accidentally mowing down her pansies with the new motorised mower. She had a temper, did Nellie Melba. Fortunately, Edna had an extraordinary intuitive ability to see qualities in people they didn't know they had. This uncanny gift guided her when she selected Joan Anderson to be Head Gardener.

Joan was the younger sister of Alice Anderson, the woman who had set up her own garage service employing an all-female staff of mechanics and chauffeurs. Alice Anderson had attracted the same kind of media attention that Edna had experienced. They had both been noted for their 'frankly boyish' appearance as well as their success in unconventional occupations. Joan Anderson had followed in her elder sister's footsteps. She too had a boyish appearance and unconventional occupation – though 'girl gardener' was not nearly as extreme as 'girl mechanic'. Joan Anderson graduated from Burnley in 1924 and like many of her Burnley peers she was eager to learn more about landscape design.

Joan quickly proved that she had all the skills required. She was excellent at her job and, most importantly, Melba enjoyed her company. The three girl gardeners lived in a cottage on the estate and Joan was often invited to the 'big house' for a chat, and even to dinner if Melba needed the company. The two underling gardeners were virtually ignored, probably much to their relief.

Joan made fairly frequent visits to Sonning (possibly to pick up the wages) and Edna always greeted her with a very warm welcome

– so warm that Joan often stayed on to the wee hours. Blanche was usually there, and of course Brian, and with the extra good cheer of a drop or two of gin, everyone had a jolly good time. It was not *all* work at Sonning.

Edna was surely delighted when Melba asked her to design a garden to replace the tennis court at Coombe Cottage – though Blanche may have been less happy, given Melba's 'bill burning'. Edna drew up two contrasting plans: a relatively modest Garden Of Old Fashioned Flowers and a rather expensive Water Lily Garden. Melba was immediately attracted to the formal elegance of the water lily garden but was aghast when she saw the estimated cost – outlined in detail by the ever efficient Blanche. It required extensive stonework and thus labour and Melba took fright. Her coffers were not what they had been, and she decided to drop the whole idea. It was disappointing; a garden created by Edna for Melba would have been a fine tribute to their friendship. Edna's efforts were not wasted however, she took the opportunity to 'recycle' the two plans for an article on 'new garden designs for old tennis courts' a few years later after Melba's death.

The friendship between the diva and the landscape gardener was tenuous, Melba was, after all, Edna's boss. Even so, when Melba gave Edna a copy of her published memoir, she inscribed it with a fond: 'To Edna with love from Nellie Melba'. It was a cherished gift. Interestingly, Joan Anderson was not honoured with a similar gesture, perhaps because she left Melba's employ after 'only' a year. Joan was keen to go overseas and learn more about her profession. Like so many of Edna's employee trainees, Joan was eager to establish a career of her own, and in time she succeeded.

When Edna acquired the land below Sonning she gave her 'new estate' the temporary name of Pig and Whistle. Friends and relatives were cordially invited to come and explore Pig and Whistle – and come they did. They picked their way through the unpromising terrain, they squinted into the middle distance, and they tried to imagine the picturesque setting that Edna was describing. Some said it was terrific and some said it was overly ambitious. They generally enthused about the *idea* of transforming a dull hill into a rural oasis, but they invariably worried over *who would buy*? Who would want to buy a plot of land that could *only* be developed in line with Edna's ideas? Edna optimistically reminded them that Blanche had very happily bought under that agreement; but in truth she was well aware that the scheme was a nerve-racking gamble.

Edna had purchased Mrs. Whisson's seventeen acres at a cost of £50 an acre, which meant that she carried a debt of £850, plus interest. Blanche's £100 had provided Edna with the initial cash to secure the Whisson land; however the same £100 had also served to buy Blanche the two-acre plot she wanted. This meant that Edna had sold those two acres for the same price that she had paid for them. Edna had not started her village scheme to make a profit, but she couldn't possibly make it work if she didn't at least cover her costs.

Putting the financial worries aside, the first exciting venture for the Pig and Whistle experiment was to build a dwelling for Blanche. The construction work began in September 1928, about three months after Blanche had started full-time employment at Sonning. Surprisingly, the dwelling that was erected was more of a utility outbuilding than a charming little cottage – in fact Blanche called it her 'shed'. Her choice of building appears to have been guided by her limited budget and practical needs. Blanche didn't require a roof over her head at this point; she already had that at Sonning. What she really needed was a stable for her horse, garage for her motorcar, a workshop and storage area, and some sort of 'man's room' where (presumably) Louis might stay. If all this added up to a 'shed' rather than a cottage – then at least it kept the rate bill down.

Edna incorporated all the elements that Blanche wanted under a broad A-frame roof which rested on low walls. The roof had the height to provide good loft space, yet the low walls made the overall shape appear to sit snug into the landscape. Blanche added the final touch. Instead of double doors, she wanted an open archway to run through the centre of the building and end in a courtyard beyond – and that's what she got.

Edna managed to press a local labourer into 'discovering' his latent skills as a builder, and she economised on materials where possible – but without repeating the mistakes she'd made with Sonning. Purchases included five motor packing-cases for the walls, six loads of stone for the base, timber for the frame, galvanised iron and green paint for the roof, and a tar and sand application to protect the outside walls. Amazingly, the costs were kept to under £45.

Ever on the lookout for topics for articles, Edna used the project as the basis for an item on 'Beauty in Outbuildings'. She alluded to Blanche as her 'neighbour' with a 'farm', which gave her the freedom to discuss farm outbuildings in general as well as Blanche's project in particular. The 'neighbour' was acknowledged for her idea of a central archway and the cleverness of placement:

> The building has been so placed as to be right on the south boundary of the property, and in such a position that the archway comes in the centre of the lane by which the farm is approached. The lane is on the east of some beautiful gums and blackwoods, and is, therefore, cool and shady in the afternoon. Through the archway one may glimpse the fine old gum-tree that is 30 ft or so from the north side of the building. It is between this tree and the building that the stone-paved courtyard will be.

The simple frame, with its pleasing placement, was a heartening indication that the village ideal had potential. The seventeen acres, plus the three acres of Sonning, were far from a unified picturesque scene, but it was now possible for Edna's friends and relations to imagine what 'could be', given time.

Perhaps it was the completion of the shed that stimulated Edna and Blanche to think about a name, not only for the new building but also for the whole village. Pig and Whistle was all right as a private joke, but something better was needed as a 'proper' name. Edna's thoughts returned to her childhood home: glorious Devon and the sweet country lanes, the dear little cottages, the steam train from Plymouth that chuffed along beside the river Dart, then past the beautiful stone bridge and on through Bickleigh Vale, then around the little church of Meavy and up towards the moors and the big stone tors . . . It was the romance of Devon that Edna wanted to re-capture in her naming, and it was the essence of that romance that she wanted to capture in the whole village. The eventual choosing of the name was important enough for Blanche to record in her diary – albeit without ceremony: October 11th 1928 'Called the place Bickleigh Vale'.

Blanche didn't record when her own property was named. Good-a-Meavy was the official title but people generally called it by its nickname: The Barn. Edna had a penchant for nicknames or shortened names and it wasn't long before Bickleigh Vale became Billy Vale – but that was just between friends. From now on, visitors and potential buyers would know the place as Bickleigh Vale, Mooroolbark, Victoria.

All this while, numerous other activities had been engaging Edna and Blanche – with the help of the Irish terrier Brian – in diverse and sometimes very challenging ways. For instance, there had been the particularly unusual job that they had done in the Melbourne zoological gardens. The design was straightforward enough – but the situation was peculiar in the extreme. The experience went something like this.

It was a dark and moonless night, and the lions were roaring loudly. Brian kept very close to Edna, but it was debatable who was guarding whom. Brian, Edna and Blanche were in the middle of the zoo, planting out the new garden that had been constructed next to the bear enclosure. The zoo officials had asked for the work to be done at night to avoid inconvenience to the public, so powerful lights had been erected. The brightness of the lamps, and the occasional noise of the workers, had disturbed the sleeping bears, who in turn disturbed the lions, who in turn disturbed the whole zoo – thus waking the entire neighbourhood! The lions, tigers and monkeys were the loudest in the their complaints, but there were other noises, shrieks and cackles, and a weird mournful lilt, all coming from the darkness beyond the halo of the work site. Edna and Blanche were stoic. They'd had a fit of the giggles when the growling first started, but cold and fatigue had dulled their senses to all but the loudest roar. Brian gallantly held his ground, ready to fend off beasts of all kinds, but his face was a picture of misery. When Edna paused for a moment to ease her aching back, Brian took the opportunity to sit on her foot. She gave him a cuddle and a kiss on the head – 'What a comforting doggie you are, and what a fuss those big pussycats are making!' Brian wagged his tail – the word 'pussycats' always made him smile . . .

And then there were challenges of a more 'human' nature, where the importance of a commission or the influential status of a client could bring an extra excitement – and indeed *tension* – to the day. The commission for Cruden Farm, for instance, falls well within this category.

Edna's client for the Cruden Farm job was Mr Keith Murdoch, Managing Director of the *Herald and Weekly Times*. His newspaper empire included most of the publications to which Edna contributed her articles – not least *Home Beautiful* – so it was particularly important that she do a good job. Keith Murdoch had an impressive reputation. He was generally known to be charming and clever; those closer to him knew that he aimed for, and expected, excellence. A long-term bachelor, he had recently taken a very young bride – Elisabeth.

When Keith Murdoch gave Edna the commission to work on Cruden Farm, he was still extremely angry about what had 'happened' to the farmhouse – with good reason, for it was quite a story.

Cruden Farm was a country property near the coastal town of Frankston, south of Melbourne. Keith Murdoch had bought it as a wedding present for Elisabeth in 1928. The farmhouse was old, in need of some renovation, and alterations were undertaken when the newlyweds were overseas.

The architect who undertook the work was the highly regarded Harold Desbrowe Annear. His task was to renovate the farmhouse in keeping with its character, but for reasons never really explained, he ignored his instructions and gave the Murdochs what he thought they should have – at four times the expense. His design also included plans for an elaborately formal Italian garden, but fortunately the Murdochs returned before this was started. They were too late to save the farmhouse however.

With such an influential and infuriated client, Edna's Cruden Farm commission was going to be an especially tricky assignment! The added tension appears to have brought out the worst in Edna – or as Blanche so succinctly put it in a brief but revealing diary entry: 'Edna ghastly'!

Imagine how things might have been for Blanche on the morning that Edna went off to make her first visit to Cruden Farm: Blanche standing red-faced and alone beside the potting shed, as the Fiat roared off down the driveway, Brian looking out of the passenger window, Edna not even waving goodbye . . .

Perhaps the day went something like this.

Blanche's temper was still boiling as she potted up the last of the seedlings. She banged the flower pots onto the shelf and decided to make a cup of tea. She felt she'd earned it after such a beastly morning. As she washed her hands under the outdoor tap, she thought again about how *grumpy* Edna had been over breakfast. Edna could be so moody, so bossy, so Spartan! Even making a pot of tea could take an eternity because Edna wouldn't have a cooking range. Edna didn't see the *need* for a cooking range – but then Edna rarely did any of the cooking!

Blanche was feeling sorry for herself. She poked the fire and ate a biscuit. She had thought of going back to Melbourne a day early but she knew that was silly. It was only a tiff. She looked at her small gathering of belongings, neat and orderly in 'her corner' of Sonning. She picked up her little diary, her tiny green book of lists. She regularly used the book to keep track of savings and expenses, the amount she'd paid for cheese and eggs, the ten shillings she'd loaned Edna, the date the shillings were paid back – why was she always having to lend Edna money? It was comforting, to keep account. She rarely used the diary to record events or emotions, but that morning she'd written just three words: 'Edna deserted me'.

As she made her pot of tea, she remembered that she'd done her own form of 'deserting'. When she'd first met Edna and regularly skipped off to Sonning, she had written two words for a weekend away: 'Deserted Louis'. She thought about Louis; she was losing count of the number of years they'd been engaged. Perhaps it was time to start her own pharmacy – that's what she really wanted to do.

Perhaps. She ate another biscuit while the tea was brewing. It was a lovely teapot, made by some potter that Edna knew. Rotten horrid Edna!

Meanwhile . . . It was a two-hour drive from Mooroolbark to Cruden Farm, ample time for reflection.

Edna turned the Fiat into the driveway of Cruden Farm and was delighted by the possibilities of the landscape; it was a lovely pastoral setting. But her delight turned to dismay when the farmhouse came into view. It looked absurdly grandiose. It had been given an elaborate façade in the manner of an American colonial mansion – the kind you'd see on a Louisiana plantation. A gap-toothed portico with eight white columns announced a self-important two-storey frontage, yet tucked behind was a typical Australian country house.

Edna frowned; she could see that her design would require much 'deception of the eye' to overcome the clash of styles. It was going to be even tougher than she'd thought. She could feel a tension in the back of her neck, the preamble to a headache. She knew why. She turned to Brian, who was enjoying the rare pleasure of sitting in the passenger seat, and told him to stay in the Fiat – she wouldn't be long.

Edna grabbed her notebook, and walked around the outskirts of the house, observing the lay of the land, assessing what might be salvaged from the remains of the nondescript garden – it was amazing the amount of damage a few builders could do to a garden . . . She wished that she had brought Blanche. Such a silly blow-up they'd had about *who* was supposed to have done *what*, and *when*. She knew that Blanche wasn't as happy as she had been. It was probably the workload; given that Blanche lacked the necessary training, she tended to end up with the more laborious tasks. It couldn't be helped! Even so, Edna regretted being grumpy. She'd had a bad night and came to breakfast in a bad mood, mainly because she was anxious about this job.

Edna completed her circuit of the grounds and returned to the Fiat to get Brian and the tape measure. Brian was a good helper, he'd sit on the end of the measuring tape and stop it from sliding. She didn't really need to use a measure, she could simply step out a distance with extraordinary accuracy, but she thought she'd better double-check for this job; besides, Brian enjoyed it.

After about an hour or so, Edna pencilled the last of her notes and wound up the measure – which was difficult because Brian was reluctant to relinquish 'his end'. Edna laughed, she felt better, calmer, now that she had started the Cruden Farm job. There were plenty of possibilities – rather splendid ones actually; the ideas were already spinning. 'Come on Brian, let's buy Blanche a present on the way home. What would she like, do you think?'

And so life went on . . .

Mr. Keith Murdoch must have been pleased with Edna's ideas, for she was commissioned to do further work on Cruden Farm. Her 1929 plans included a formal Rose Garden for the south-west of the house, and various informal borders and plantings to the north-east where the tennis court was situated. Her 1930 plan focussed on the grounds in front of the house, an area that included the driveway and turning circle. Edna's copy of the 1930 plan shows that the driveway was to be planted with an avenue of lemon-scented gums. Low stone walls were to line the latter part of the driveway and continue on around the outskirts of the turning circle, then connect with the taller walls of the new Walled Garden and existing Rose Garden. The walled gardens were to have wrought-iron gates at the various entrance/exit points; the grassed turning circle was to have five trees (in groupings of two, two and one) and an invisible gutter. Drawings in elevation featured two of the wrought-iron gates designed for the walled garden, plus a sketch of two standard bay trees in large tubs situated either side of the front door.

The garden that resulted from this design was a masterly demonstration of elegance and grace. The proportions, the curves, the balance of informal to formal – they all produced a wonderful harmony of space.

Once it had matured, the most breathtaking feature of the design was the avenue of lemon-scented gums (*Eucalyptus citriodora*). The pale smooth muscular trunks, in their decidedly irregular and close-planted formation, perfectly complemented the gentle curve of the sandy-gravel driveway. The sway of the branches, the rustle of the leaves, the scent of lemon, the glimpse of fields between the pale grey tree-trunks – all combined to create an extraordinary and sensual experience.

There has been some doubt as to who suggested lemon-scented gums for the driveway. Edna's 1930 plan clearly names this species with a caption saying 'Lemon Scented Gums replacing planting of broom', but it's possible that the suggestion came from elsewhere. Edna favoured exotic rather than native trees at this time, so it was an unusual choice for her to make – unusual, but not out of the question. After all, Edna's plan follows the requirements of the classic Arts and Crafts Garden: the formal design around the house leads to the informal garden further on which then blends with the 'wild' or 'natural' pasture beyond. The choice of lemon-scented gums fits perfectly with this scheme.

Visitors arriving to spend a weekend in the country with the Murdochs would have spent an hour or so driving through the Victorian countryside. They would have turned their motorcar into the driveway, they would have been greeted by the slender pale-grey trunks of the lemon-scented gums, then they would have noticed the beginnings of a low stone wall, elegant, curved, formal. They would have caught sight of the eight slender white columns of an impressively styled portico, and perhaps noticed a high stone wall with an inviting gate as they got out of the motor, as the front door opened, as the weekend began . . .

The slender pale-grey tree trunks had prepared the eye for the straight white columns of the façade. The difficult transition from Australian/Victorian countryside to Louisiana-style plantation mansion had been achieved.

Of course, not every design decision of Edna's was inspirational and not every client was happy with her work. For instance, Elisabeth Murdoch, for whom the Cruden Farm garden was being made, found Edna's manner to be overly brusque, giving her little or no opportunity to discuss ideas. In later decades, Elisabeth Murdoch was to make the Cruden Farm garden famously her own; she preserved and enhanced most of the architecture of Edna's original design and extended and developed a much larger area to her own design. When a fire savaged the lemon-scented gums in 1944, Elisabeth nursed the famous avenue back to life, and when she found that the walled gardens created too much heat for some of the plants, she rearranged the planting. In 1930 however, Elisabeth was the particularly young and inexperienced 'Mrs. Keith Murdoch', and it was regrettable but perhaps understandable that the brusque and breezy Edna took more notice of the husband than the wife.

Since the mid-1920s Edna had had a dream run. She had created gardens great and small, for town and country, for Victoria and interstate. She had worked for the 'big names' in the community: Ballieu, Darling, Fink, Grimwade, Moran, Ritchie. She had worked on a diverse range of projects – from a garden for the Peninsula Golf Club, to a design for a fountain inside the aviary at the zoo, to a private open-air theatre in Kew. She'd also done 'love jobs' such as the family garden for her sister and brother-in-law, and 'mates jobs' such as the Box Hill garden for her contractor Eric Hammond. At the other end of the scale she had influenced an ever-increasing number of garden enthusiasts via her journalism. Apart from her regular articles, she'd started a 'reader request' series where a lucky *Home Beautiful* subscriber would be chosen for 'The Garden Plan of the Month'. Readers were invited to describe their block and their needs for their garden and Edna would select the one that seemed useful to both owner and general reader and present a plan, plus plant list and guidelines in a following issue of the magazine. The requests came by the sack-load. Edna was swamped with snapshots and descriptions and drawings – often inadequate ones, judging by Edna's rather desperate plea for clearer instructions and at least *some* measurements!

Edna's star was shining bright. She was *the* garden designer, the chosen one. Everyone wanted 'an Edna Walling', and Edna did her best to ensure that they had one – whether she designed it for them or advised them on how to do it themselves. Everything was going splendidly, Bickleigh Vale was taking shape, life at Sonning was good, and all manner of schemes seemed possible.

Then came the shock-waves that marked the beginning of the Great Depression. Stocks and shares began to fail and the value of everything changed. Many wealthy people were financially ruined, and a great many more people were thrown out of work.

It was *not* a good time for Edna to be trying to sell her plots at Bickleigh Vale. However, it was not necessarily a bad time to be a landscape designer: there were still wealthy people in the community and they could still be tempted to spend, especially when the cost of labour became so cheap. It was the clever strategists who survived the Depression the best. For instance, Keith Murdoch immediately negotiated a 13 per cent pay cut for his employees at the *Herald and Weekly Times* – a cut that would have affected Edna's payments. Keith Murdoch's domestic staff also accepted wage cuts, and doubtless Edna reduced her fee for working on the Cruden Farm design for 1930; but at least the project went ahead and the garden was built. Local stonemasons and labourers would have been grateful to get the work, albeit at a reduced rate of pay.

The first three years of the Depression were the worst, and this is reflected in the marked reduction in the number of plans Edna completed. However, during the rest of the decade she received some of her largest and most significant commissions; this didn't mean that she became wealthy – far from it – but at least her business survived.

Edna's father managed to survive the financial crisis, initially. William Walling had become Managing Director of Toledo Berkel Pty Ltd. – a promotion that was celebrated in the society magazine *The Home* in 1930. William Walling was one of five businessmen to be highlighted under the title 'Melbourne men of mark'. His photograph shows an attractive-looking gentleman with silver hair and dapper bow tie, and the caption describes him as 'a prominent figure in Australian business circles'. According to John Renwick, a business partner, William was one of the best-dressed men in Melbourne, and his turn-out could be appreciated by all as he drove around in an open-top Buick. John Renwick also suggests that William had a mistress, a professional woman who worked in Collins Street. If this is true, it may explain why there appears to have been a growing distance between William and Margaret; why it was Margaret, and not both parents, who visited Edna at Sonning for instance; and why Margaret turned increasingly to her religion for comfort.

Life in the household of Edna's sister and brother-in-law was not as it had been either. Although Doris's husband was reasonably secure financially, he and the four children were increasingly harassed by Doris' well-meaning but severe devotion to Christian Science. It was not such a happy family.

Whatever was going on *beneath* the surface, Edna and her family appeared to be better placed than most to face the difficulties brought by the Depression. Even so, the 1930s were a particularly challenging decade for Edna.

The first of Edna's challenges was to find a full-time offsider to replace Blanche – who had at last married the ever-patient Louis. Blanche would continue to do Edna's bookkeeping and would occasionally assist on jobs, but her attention was now fixed on setting up a pharmacy and saving to buy a house. This was all very fine, but where on earth was Edna to find a replacement with anything like Blanche's efficiency and sensitivity? The stalwart Alice Houghton, daughter of the neighbouring landowner, continued to share some of the load, but a full-time live-in and at least partially trained offsider was what Edna needed: a young woman willing to learn and work hard and receive pocket-money pay, and whose personality was compatible with Edna's. Interestingly, it was quite a while before such a person was found!

Another of Edna's ongoing challenges was to find the 'right' sort of buyers for Bickleigh Vale. Now that the task was even more difficult than originally anticipated, Edna was inspired to attempt a spot of grandstanding salesmanship. In late 1930 she wrote an article for *Home Beautiful* that was, in essence, a double-page advertisement saying: land for sale at Bickleigh Vale! She must have been on good terms with her editor, W. A. Shum, for no other contributor to the magazine was ever given quite such a personalised platform to air their wares. The article was called 'Adventure in Landscape Gardening':

> [T]hose rolling acres that I coveted so long came into my possession, and are now safe from despoilers of the landscape, and available to those who long to build themselves a quaint little English cottage surrounded by sturdy young trees and shrubs of their own planting.
>
> The land has been split up into five pieces as a commencement, but permits the making of one or two smaller pieces without harm

to the plan that is eventually to present a series of delightful landscape pictures. It is desired that all the cottages will be screened and sheltered with trees and shrubs, so that each will appear to be the only one on the landscape to those living within, except perhaps for a tiny peep of some distant stone chimney or a thread of blue smoke curling up from another. There will be thickets of Birches and Poplars, and groups of Lilacs and Spireas. There will be blossom trees in plenty and masses and masses of Iris. There will be the red of the Liquidambers and the gold of the Silver Birches, and Barberries and Crabapples, and Oaks and Elms and Willows. All will flaunt their beauty in the mellow season of autumn.

In one corner a nursery has been formed, roughly an acre in extent. Here the trees and shrubs are being raised for making the landscape pictures. Here plants selected from other nurseries as being suitable for this adventure are brought to be grown into larger specimens . . . Amongst those already present in the nursery there are Purple Leaf Birches, Yellow Birches, Silver Birches, Swamp, Red and Scarlet Oaks; Elms of many varieties (not the English, which is the worst offender of all for suckering); many varieties of the Ash; American, English and Mexican Hawthorns; Hackberries, Golden Willows and a little low-growing pussy willow of most charming habit; Pear trees with beautiful autumn foliage; Golden and Lombardy Poplars. There are old-fashioned Weigelias, Japonicas, Viburnums and Spireas, Lilacs and Hydrangeas. There are climbing roses, red vines and honeysuckles for the walls, and Lavender and Rosemary for around the doors. There are specimens of clipped Box and Privet for the trimness that is often right in the most informal schemes.

Water – the most important of all factors in a country habitation, is available from the O'Shannassy water scheme, so no loss of young trees need be feared in the event of a drought during their first tender years.

> As much of the land as it was possible to plough has been cultivated and sown down with oats to open up the ground . . .
>
> The remaining land has grey and woolly tea-tree and white swamp gums scattered about in picturesque groups. It is already 'landscaped' for someone.
>
> It should be emphasised that these blocks are only for those interested in English cottage design, the planting of trees and shrubs and the preservation of the existing landscape.

But no one was tempted to buy.

Apart from the lack of funds, it was probably the *idea* that was too challenging for most people. Edna's scheme was a particularly unconventional adventure. While the wonderfully diverse yet non-native choice of plants may concern some of us today, it was Edna's concept of 'the preservation of the existing landscape', the unusual method of subdivision, and the thought of not having complete control over one's own block of land, that surely worried people in 1930. The only other scheme to equal and possibly surpass Edna's adventurousness was by Marion Mahony and Walter Burley Griffin, who placed modern domestic architecture in a bushland setting at Castlecrag, a rocky harbour promontory north of Sydney. The Griffins proposed to build a suburb of low-lying houses made with local stone in pre-existing bushland. There were to be no fences or boundaries, and native trees and shrubs were to be planted right up to the walls of each house. The scheme was begun in the 1920s but, like Bickleigh Vale, the unusual nature of the project, and then the dire economic climate, interrupted its progress.

Two years passed and there were still no purchasers for the Bickleigh Vale land. Feeling increasingly desperate about the burden of her loan, Edna made a bold and risky move. She decided to go ahead and build the first cottage. If a cottage was visible, with its own pretty garden already landscaped, then – surely – a buyer or renter would be found. She approached a local labourer, Alf Pollard, and told him that she didn't have any money but if she could just get one place built very cheaply she would be able to carry on – would he do the building? Alf Pollard found himself saying that he would!

The place that Alf and Edna built was a simple little cottage with white wooden walls, a stone chimney and steep sloping roof. As with most of Edna's cottages, the exterior walls were low, just above door height, and the ceilings were 'coved' or arched. It was not your usual style of country cottage. Edna told her readers in her next 'village news' installment that the cottage was quaint and unconventional – yet far from grotesquely 'original'. She also just happened to mention that it was built at a very low cost.

Wonder of wonders, by mid-1933 a Miss Emily Hansen, news-agent of East Melbourne, had bought the little white cottage for her weekend hideaway. Even better, Grace Hughston, a widow of Caulfield, was moving into a second little cottage – and there were more buyers in the offing.

The gamble had paid off. Edna's financial drought was breaking and 'Billy Vale' was at last taking shape. The village was even becoming 'official', for certain legalities were now having to be faced. In March 1933, Edna had the land surveyed and sensitively subdivided into eighteen allotments of differing sizes; although the Shire of Lillydale approved the subdivision, it also insisted that a road be put through the middle of it. It was a terrible blow to Edna's vision but there was no way around it; all blocks had to have proper access. The legal requirement was that a straight passage of land, 50 feet wide, be portioned off for the throughway – it was small compensation that the name of this travesty would be Bickleigh Vale Road.

It was an abomination, a complication and an extremely unwelcome expense. However, there was a loophole and Edna exploited it to perfection. The regulations allowed for roadside planting, and Edna took advantage of this. Working within the spatial limitation, she planned to give the roadway gentle curves, and then accentuate each curve with massed plantings of trees and shrubs so that one never saw straight ahead; there would always be a bend and then another bend. The overall effect would be of a winding country lane.

Edna immediately began her preparations. Once the road had been built it would be vital to get the trees and shrubs planted as soon as possible, otherwise the lane would look terribly raw and be a poor advertisement for potential buyers. But it was an enormous amount of work – in the nursery, let alone the planting – and she needed help, she needed a team, she needed to organise. But then something really awful happened and it stopped her in her tracks. Her father died.

On 22 March 1933 William Walling's heart faltered and then stopped. He died in the Alfred Hospital, just across the road from Arundel Flats, his home of twenty years. He was buried the next day in St. Kilda Cemetery in the Church of England section and was duly given a simple gravestone: a large sandstone slab with a small metal plaque saying: William Walling 1867–1933. And that was that.

But of course something like that affects all the family and friends in different ways. Edna was a crier, the tears would have fallen, she loved her father very much. But then there was Margaret, a widow suddenly, numb and dressed in black; and there were William's various business colleagues, solemn, and worried perhaps – for William had recently left the security of Toledo Burkel and set up his own partnership. Doris would have been buoyed up by the teachings of Mary Baker Eddy: there is no illness, there is no death; but there is, surely, great sadness . . . Who knows what the undercurrents were? Funerals, and their aftermath, are never easy.

There was, however, a surprising silver lining to the whole affair – the arrival in Edna's life of the wonderful Edith Cole.

Lorna Fielden's woodshed

Chapter 8

Burning the candle

Edith Cole was a determined sort of person with a strong character and optimistic outlook. In fact, she was very like her cousin Edna. The family connection goes back to Plymouth. Edith Cole's mother was William Walling's younger sister Lillie. It was Lillie who'd been the accomplished piano player and Lillie who'd married Ernest Cole, a farmer's younger son who had no hope of inheriting the farm. This lack of prospects probably motivated the Cole family to steam off to West Australia in 1912, with the one-year-old Edith in Lillie's arms.

It's strange that the Cole family made no attempt to live anywhere near the Walling family, for they both travelled to the southern hemisphere within months of each other. Perhaps they didn't get on, or perhaps they didn't realise how very *far* everything was from everything else. Whatever the rationale, it seems likely that the antipodean Wallings and Coles maintained occasional contact via postcard and letter. However infrequent these missives may have been, they must have increased in number around the time of William Walling's death, for it was not long after William's demise that someone had the bright idea of suggesting that Edith Cole should go to Melbourne. Cousin Edna was in serious need of a helper, someone who could dig and answer the phone and clean and type and keep all sorts of 'things' in reasonable order. And if this helper could also bake a potato and fry an egg it would be even better. For her part, cousin Edna could offer free board in The Cabin, excellent tuition in horticulture and design, tons of work experience, and a small amount of cash at the end of each week. It was a deal. In mid-1933, Edith Cole arrived in Melbourne, ready and willing to begin.

There was a definite family resemblance between the cousins, especially when the twenty-two-year-old Edith was wearing the work-a-day jodhpurs and shirt. Each of them had an open face and a wide smile, and each had a slight yet strong body. Edith turned out to be a wonderful addition to the Sonning camp. She was hard-working and enthusiastic as well as gentle and kind. The happy bonus was that Edith and Edna shared many interests, not least classical music. This was a lovely change, for it had taken Edna much effort to persuade the bookkeeping Blanche to appreciate even a short piece of Beethoven. Blanche firmly believed she had no ear for music and was determined she wouldn't like it, until she finally gave in and really listened. Now here was cousin Edith who could even play classical music on the piano – which is perhaps why an old piano found its way into Blanche's barn.

Edith Cole was not the only family member to be living at Bickleigh Vale, for Margaret Walling was also taking up residence. Now that Margaret was a widow, it was decided that she should move out of Arundel Flats and split her time between her two daughters. She would spend short periods in Toorak with Doris and family, and much longer periods at Downderry, the new cottage that Edna was building for her. Margaret was sixty-six and in fairly good health, but she had become anxious since William's death and there were times when her anxieties caused extra tension between herself and her offspring. But on the whole the arrangement worked well, and Edna in particular put much effort into ensuring that her mother was as comfortable as possible. Even the name 'Downderry' was significant, for it had been one of the family's holiday haunts on the southern coast of Cornwall. There were doubtless many practical difficulties that had to be overcome before Margaret moved in, but what a proud and happy moment it must have been for her when she turned that key and opened her front door and stepped into her new home.

Edna's daily working life was made considerably easier with cousin Edith as a helper, yet the business was expanding at such a pace that it was clear that a fully trained assistant was also needed. Her ideal would have been to find a person who was both trained and experienced, but, as Blanche probably told her, she couldn't afford the wage for such a person. The next best option was to look for a suitable Burnley student who was about to graduate. Edna wrote to Burnley and asked if a 'suitable girl' could be recommended. She explained that she was looking for someone who would be interested in nursery work as well as ordinary gardening, and that her tentative proposal was that 'she should receive half the profits of the nursery' and be agreeable to bachelor conditions: i.e. 'a large room over a garage on the boundary of the nursery'. The response to her letter was an invitation to meet some of 'the girls' for herself, and Edna proceeded to do this in a variety of ways over the next twelve months. She went to the school and gave talks at student association meetings, she gave a guided tour of Sonning, and she even took a couple of groups around some of her city gardens. Yet she did not approach any of the students with a tentative job offer. It was not that she was being excessively careful about finding the 'right girl', it was more that she had changed her mind about employing an inexperienced person. She was becoming so busy that she didn't have the time to train anyone properly. She might have shelved the whole idea if the Burnley students hadn't tempted her with a splendid offer.

The Burnley students got together and offered a sort of 'thank you' for all her generous efforts regarding lectures and tours. They suggested that they come to Sonning and plant out the newly made and horribly bare Bickleigh Vale Road. Edna was delighted. One Saturday morning in July 1934, a chattering band of cheery young women boarded the train to Mooroolbark and volunteered their services for the weekend. When the work was done and a high-tea given, Edna made a bee line for Gwynnyth Crouch, a very tall young woman with long plaits and an engaging gap-toothed smile. She took Gwynnyth aside and asked if she'd consider coming to work at Sonning. Gwynnyth blushed and smiled and looked into Edna's eyes and said: 'Gosh. I mean *yes*!' – or words to that effect. She had just turned nineteen, and was about to graduate from Burnley, so the timing was ideal. Everything about Bickleigh Vale and Sonning and Edna appealed to Gwynnyth. It was a lifestyle, a philosophy, that she hadn't realised she was looking for – until she'd found it.

Apart from being tall, Gwynnyth had generally 'risen above' her fellow students in achievements, especially as she was the only one of her peers to have a garden plan published in *Home Beautiful*. It's unclear how this came about, but in May 1933 'Miss Crouch, of the Burnley School of Horticulture' supplied the layout plan and plant list for a subscriber in want of some fruit trees and a lawn. Gwynnyth displayed no talent for drawing, but her plant list was meticulous and the advice was clear and practical. Perhaps Gwynnyth's name had been suggested to Edna as a possible candidate for the nursery job, or perhaps Edna simply saw the glowing potential of this outstanding young woman during the working-bee weekend. Either way, it was the beginning of a remarkable working partnership that lasted for seven years.

Gwynnyth Crouch had received a good education but her childhood had not been easy. Her father had drowned when she was small and her mother had been left with six daughters to care for. There had been emotional as well as financial turmoil, and it had fallen to

Gwynnyth to hold the family together. Edna's job offer represented far more than employment; it was an opportunity to experience a different way of life. Apart from Edna's influence as a teacher, there'd be a whole new world of cultural pleasures: art, music, craft and literature were part of the texture of life at Bickleigh Vale. There was even live performances, for Edna had built her own outdoor theatre in a suitably sloping part of the garden and periodically invited all manner of artists and friends to give and enjoy performances.

It was all very stimulating, but as Edith Cole had soon discovered, it wasn't all roses. There were barbs and black spots. Edna could be selfish and demanding and argumentative as well as utterly charming and delightful. There were 'pros and cons' to the Sonning experience, but Gwynnyth would not have missed it for quids.

Edith Cole must have been delighted when Gwynnyth arrived to share some of the load, for 'the load' included looking after Edna and Sonning and the animals as well as working in the nursery and the office and going out on jobs. 'Girl Friday' is an inadequate term for what these women undertook. Work started at daybreak when not only breakfast but also lunch and dinner was prepared. Edna appears to have had a paid cleaner who probably 'saw to' the laundry and other regular domestic chores, but there was always an extra bit of mending, ordering or general caring – what some might call 'mothering' – to be done in the process of seeing that Edna had what she needed to get on with the job. Part of the week was devoted to ongoing tasks connected to administration, design, and nursery business, while the other part usually involved two or three days further afield maintaining gardens or creating new ones. If a new garden was to be made then the preparation was extensive. Many of the plants came from the Sonning nursery so these had to be lifted and balled the day before, a process that could go on late into the night, leaving little time for sleep before the whole lot was shifted to the work site next morning. A very long day of planting would follow, perhaps several days if it was a big job.

Of course Edna shared all these tasks – and more – for it was she who visited new clients, prepared new designs and oversaw all aspects of the business, as well as writing garden columns and managing Bickleigh Vale. Edna was phenomenally busy, and the only way she could have managed all that she did was to have excellent support – and she had that with Gwynnyth and Edith.

If Edna behaved badly, if she was moody or over-demanding, then her co-workers were generally forgiving. Working with Edna was too interesting and stimulating to carry a grudge for long. In later years there would be a number of assistants who came and then quickly went. The set-up was too demanding or perhaps too unconventional. It took a certain kind of young woman to happily camp in a stone cabin or a bachelor-pad better known as the 'man's room next to the potting shed'. There was no electricity, no mod cons, no easy access to hot water, and the lavatory was a dunny. The outside of the dunny was made to look attractive with climbing roses and so on, but one of the regular tasks was to remove the 'night soil' so that it could be used as compost for the nursery. Edna often spoke about the joys of collecting and spreading cow manure but even she kept silent about the secret ingredient that made her young plants grow so well. Some of her clients would have fainted had they known.[*]

Edith Cole stayed with Edna for fifteen months and then she went back home to Perth. She might have stayed longer but an illness – or was it exhaustion – depleted her reserves and she needed some home comforts. Her time with Edna may have been arduous but it was also educational, for by the end of 1934 she was not only writing gardening articles for *The West Australian Gardener*; she was also advertising her services as a garden designer in the same magazine.

[*] It was Blanche who spilt the beans about the night soil; the sanitary arrangements steadily improved over the decades, as did the other amenities.

Edna was sorry to see Edith go. She dearly valued her cousin's companionship as well as her assistance, for they shared a similar sensibility. The beauty of a petal, the delight of a poem, the clowning of a cat – these were part of the daily friendship. Edna wrote to Edith about a month after she'd returned to Perth, and most of the letter is reproduced below, for it gives us a rare and personal picture of life at Sonning in the spring of 1934:

> Sonning
> 25.10.34
>
> Darling old girl
> Where shall I begin with so much to tell you? One thing I shall have to do & that is get something to catch the drip on my desk! It has rained terrifically ever since yesterday . . .
>
> . . . The double pink Hawthorns are just coming out & one or two foxgloves are quite out. Oh! how I shall miss you this year. You were so appreciative of all the beauty.
>
> I have been looking forward to writing to you so very much & here I am sitting down in the morning when I should be doing Youngman's plan, but if I wait until the evening I will never write for I'm always too sleepy.
>
> I came home with three new jumpers the other day! You'd love them. One is a blue & white aertex . . . another is brown & white stripes . . . I look like a sailor boy in it, & the other [is] silk & 'wiv' ties to tie the floppy collar, the whole lot came to 30/-.
>
> What fun we used to have when I came home with parcels & how patiently you always listened to all my ramblings . . .
>
> I went up to Hamilton which is beyond Camperdown with Hammond to Betty Youngman's cousin's station, the garden of

which I am designing – going to unravel the measurements this afternoon – the first since you left.

Got some beautiful enlargements from garden photographs of the Village Scheme which are up at the Emily McPherson School of Domestic Economy on exhibition. I will send you some small prints when I get them.

Later . . . The Youngman's plan is going horribly slowly. I think you would have liked the Manifold's which went to them last week.

I'm trying to get Blanche interested in a garden shop. It would be wonderful in conjunction with Sonning & a headquarters for me in the city.

Oh! did I tell you about Pinkies family of four (now one, called Simon which I fear may be Simonette) he is just beginning to lap milk which is good because Pinkie must go. Gwynnyth & Blanche have been putting their heads together about it!

It would be so pleasant to go on writing to you dear but Youngman's plan is biting me badly! Oh! we heard Masefield reading his Reynard the Fox & other poems over the air – it was divine.

I'm looking forward tremendously to your next letter dear, so write to me as often as you can.

With very much love
Yours affectionately Edna

Edna was almost thirty-nine when she wrote this letter, and just about at the peak of her career. She was moving along at a staggering pace, though it is pleasing to see that she still gave herself time to smell the flowers, listen to the radio and buy herself some new jumpers. But the *work* was the main thing with Edna, and a new commission would have been particularly exciting.

The 'Youngman's plan' that was causing Edna difficulty was a big commission for a property at Grassdale near Hamilton in the Western District of Victoria. It would have been a long drive from Melbourne, so it's likely that Edna, Eric Hammond and Betty Youngman stayed with the Youngmans for a couple of nights or more, depending on how much measuring up there was to be done. Accommodation for the country trips was unpredictable. The 'lady designer' might be treated as a valued guest or be sent to the maid's quarters – which is partly why Edna tended to travel with camping equipment – she could always camp by the car if necessary. Presumably Eric Hammond did the same, though he might have had the extra option of dossing down with the workmen who were constructing the garden. Doubtless the Youngman family displayed good hospitality on this occasion, though this too could have its problems in terms of social demands and etiquette, for this was still the era when people 'dressed for dinner'. Despite her preference for more casual attire, Edna probably packed skirts and frocks along with her jodhpurs and shirts when she spent weeks at a time working on a country property.

We can easily imagine Edna in her work clothes, for there are enough photographs to give us the image. But as no photographs have emerged that show Edna in any other types of clothing it is more difficult to imagine her, say, appearing from the guest room of a large country property wearing a 1930s evening gown. According to some people, she scrubbed up very nicely, according to others she looked rather odd when she wore a dress. Perhaps she was most comfortable in the smart casual category, looking like 'a sailor boy' in her nice new jumper.

Edna seems to have been much more relaxed about the other job she refers to in her letter: the Manifold plan. The 'Manifolds' were probably Mr and Mrs A. Manifold, who owned 'Boortkoi' in Hexham, another substantial country property in the Western District. Edna appears to have worked on different aspects of this large and gracious garden over a period of five or so years, and it is here that she built one of her very best Amalfi-inspired pergolas. Apart from the actual work involved, the journey to these country properties must have been challenging. Although cars and roads had improved by this time, it was still an achievement just to arrive at these places, and it's little wonder that Edna preferred to travel with a friend or assistant. She knew how to change a tyre but it was always nice to have someone to chat to while she was doing it.

It's interesting to learn from the letter that Edna was having a photographic exhibition at the Emily McPherson School of Domestic Economy (a new school in the city), though she does not clarify *who* took the photographs. The answer may be that they were taken by various photographers, including Edna. The photographs of Bickleigh Vale that appeared in *Home Beautiful* during the 1930s were taken by named and unnamed photographers including Clifford Bottomley, Duncan Wade and Edward Cranstone. Each of these men helped Edna to develop her skills with a camera but it's unclear when she first started to learn. From the sound of the letter, she was yet to experiment with developing her own film. Whoever took the photographs, their exhibition presented another terrific opportunity for people to become aware of Edna's work and the Bickleigh Vale scheme. It was 'creative publicity'. It's a shame that her plan for a shop and H.Q. didn't come about, for it was a clever idea to have a foothold in the city. Blanche must have rejected the idea; after all, she wanted a pharmacy not a gardening shop.

Edna's desire for a city H.Q. was probably in answer to the increasing competition that was nipping at her heels. To date it had been the architects and garden contractors who had been her main competitors, but now there was a growing number of female Burnley graduates offering their services as designers and nursery owners (male graduates tended to become employees, and few, if any, seemed to take up design). Ten or so of these 'Girl Graduates' got together and published a leaflet advertising their wares. Each was developing a little business of her own in a suburb of Melbourne, which meant that each had the potential to capture some of Edna's suburban clientele. Most of these graduates had been working professionally for at least a couple of years and one, Joan Anderson, had had further training overseas. Joan Anderson was the young woman that Edna had employed as head gardener for Melba, the one who used to ride over from Melba's Coombe Cottage to visit Edna and Blanche at Sonning. She'd spent three years in Britain and Europe gaining further training, and had returned to put her new expertise into practice. Graduates like Joan Anderson were an important development in terms of new competition, but they had a long way to go before they'd be *real* contenders for Edna's 'king of the castle' crown. Even so, Edna kept her eye on them.

There was a handful of top architects who were recognised for their garden design, such as Marcus Martin, but otherwise it was Edna's name that reigned supreme. Yet it was a small kingdom. Gardening was not the popular mainstream interest that it is today and Edna's celebrity was modest compared to the *really* famous. She was a tall poppy in a small field and thus became the main target for criticism from up-and-coming competitors. For instance, when Edna was giving a talk to a gathering at the Royal Melbourne Show, it was Joan Anderson who felt compelled to jump to her feet and contradict her. It was a minor disagreement about the uses of native plants in the suburban garden, but it was a significant moment for both of them: the new hand was criticising the old hand, in public.

Joan Anderson continued to be critical of Edna's methods in subsequent years. She said Edna over-planted, didn't understand different soil conditions, and didn't make enough use of native plants. There is an element of truth, but also a hint of resentment in her criticisms. Joan Anderson didn't make much headway as a garden designer and eventually left Melbourne and took over The Hermitage, an historically significant house in country Victoria. Ironically, the few gardening assignments that she worked on thereafter were usually on existing gardens designed by Edna. She married quite late in life and became Joan Jones, the wife of a grazier.

Joan's career seems typical of a number of Burnley women who made good progress in the early stages but who discontinued the work due to marriage or an inability to forge ahead. The 1930s was a tough time to be trying to start up a garden design business, and it wasn't necessarily easier to work for an established garden contractor. Working for someone else meant that you followed orders and had little scope to develop your own design style. It was tough to get ahead, whether you were new to it or not.

Apart from the architects, there were only two experienced garden designers who could equal Edna in terms of reputation and popularity, and both of them made their names through garden journalism rather than garden design. They were her old mate Millie Grassick, and her old adversary Olive Mellor.

Millie Grassick was a well-loved columnist, but her use of a pseudonym and then her marriage to Ernest Gibson camouflaged her identity. Though her work was significant and appreciated, 'Millie Gibson' did not become a well-known name. Olive Mellor (née Holttum) stopped teaching when she married, but then she was widowed and it was years before she found her way back to her chosen profession. Her initial step towards this aim was to have her gardening articles published in *Home Beautiful*, and the first of these appeared in April 1934. Her second step was to place an advertisement for her new garden design business in the July issue. The ad was not a modest three-liner but a quarter column block. Her name and her 'New Service' was writ large. Olive Mellor was back!

It's unclear how popular or competitive Olive's New Service

became, for most of her gardens and plans have disappeared. However, Olive's journalism remains to tell us at least part of the story. Between 1934 and 1936, it was Olive who maintained a regular presence in *Home Beautiful* and Edna who slipped to intermittent contributor. Edna regained her regular status in 1937, and sustained it for the next ten years, but then Olive took over again and held the ground. As far as I can tell, the two kept their distance. They were not friends and there was no comradely cross-referencing of ideas from one columnist to the other – or if there was, it was in the form of criticism. Olive went on to produce about five gardening books during the next two decades and she became well known through her broadcasts on local radio, but it was Edna who held the competitive edge. When Olive started winning ground within the pages of *Home Beautiful*, Edna was having her articles published further afield. She was writing regular columns for the *Adelaide Advertiser*, and one-off items for the *Sydney Morning Herald*. Olive achieved a great deal, but Edna was always a few steps ahead.

Everything was rolling along well for Edna. She'd found the perfect assistant in Gwynnyth, she'd weathered the worst of the Depression and prospects were good.

And then – disaster. The elements colluded to destroy the object that was dearest to her heart

One Thursday morning in the winter of 1935, Edna was at work indoors at Sonning when she answered Gwynnyth's call from the garden, left her paperwork and went outside. As the door closed behind her it let in a gust of wind which blew onto the dying fire, which spat out a vagrant spark, that fell upon a discarded piece of paper that was on the floor with other pieces of paper, and each caught alight, one after the other, taking the flame across the floor and over the rug and under the furniture and up the wall and into the roof. So started the blaze that brought dear old Sonning, cracking, howling and twisting, down to the ground. All that could be salvaged was a frightened kitten that was rescued by a very brave Gwynnyth, and a blackened copper nameplate that had somehow clung on to the remains of the front door. Everything else – papers and books, jumpers and socks, tables and chairs – everything else was gone. Just like that. Edna was left standing in her oldest jodhpurs and most worn-out boots, pale, trembling, and with an aching heart.

Losing Sonning was like losing a friend. Sonning had a character, a spirit, even a sense of humour, and of course many faults, many endearing idiosyncrasies, many memories – all interwoven into Edna's life. If Edna had made Sonning, then in many ways Sonning had made Edna. Their strengths and weaknesses were one; day by day, they'd held each other up. How soul-destroying then, when Sonning was destroyed. Edna knew she could rebuild, and she knew she could do a better job, especially with the help of a cheque from the fire insurance. But that wasn't the point. Sonning was gone, and it was an awful aching loss.

Of course the other heartbreaking element was the destruction of all that had been inside Sonning when it burned down: half a lifetime's accumulation. We can imagine the sentimental value of at least some of the things that were destroyed by considering a particular book that survived the fire because it wasn't in the cottage on that day. This book was Edna's copy of the oratorio to Handel's *Messiah*. The inside page reveals the copperplate handwriting of a nine-year-old Edna who'd written her name, Plymouth address, the date of March 1905 and the inscription: 'From Mother & Father'. The existence of this slim volume gives us an unusual view of Edna – a young Edna singing Handel's *Messiah* in a choir. We could picture her somewhere in the back row of the chorus, her red hair and bright face just discernible amidst the orderly flock of fellow choristers, the pages of their scores being turned at the same time, almost the same time, as the rows of faces concentrate on one fixed point, as they all breathe in with one accord, as they all sing out with one great voice: 'Hallelujah'. There must have been so many treasured mementos of this nature: the inscribed book from Melba, the letters from dear ones, old and new photographs, gramophone records, notebooks, paintings, rugs, good old shoes, a fine pewter collection, a new tweed suit, a filing cabinet, a brooch, a gold-nibbed fountain pen, an oak chest . . . All gone.

As Edna told her *Home Beautiful* readers a few months after the fire: 'The experience of suddenly being bereft of everything . . . is a marvellous revelation of the kindness and sympathy there is in the world . . . I wonder if those who were so very kind realise just how much they really did at the time.' Edna wore a brave face in public, but her friends knew that she was devastated. And yet there was something in Edna that almost thrived on difficulty: here was a chance to re-plan, to improve, to build again. She soothed her aching heart by embracing the challenge with enormous energy, and by January 1936 she was able to tell her readers that good progress had been made. Sonning number two had risen from the ashes:

> Sonning 2 is complete, and it is much the same in its outward appearance except for an added respectability, which I secretly regret. However, as the years advance, one is apt to drop the romantic for the comfortable, perhaps, and so there stands now a cottage with sufficient 'mod. cons.' to satisfy the most fastidious housewife, and soon a Fortunes Yellow will once again be clambering over the stone chimney, and shrubs to soften the walls are already in place.

The addition of 'mod cons' included the kitchen sink:

> The absence of a sink in the previous cottage was undeniably a great inconvenience, but the objection to them was still as strong as ever until we hit upon the idea of a wooden one. Amongst the

> marvellous collection of cast-off family possessions that find their way from time to time to the more commodious outbuildings of Sonning there were some wash tubs, and, although old, the kauri was still good, and from this has been made the dearest little sink you ever saw. I was so pleased with it that I bought it a beautiful long, broad piece of kauri to sit in, and now my visitors queue up waiting their turn to wash up!

There were all manner of ingenious features. She eliminated dust-catching ridges from window fittings and skirting boards, she designed fitted cupboards that were the right height and shape for the purpose required (a very new idea at the time), she made little contraptions to keep small things tidy and out of sight, and she made a kitchen table that was fixed to the wall so that it didn't need legs, which made it easier to wash down the stone floor with a simple swish of the hose. She even reversed the fibrous plaster sheeting in some instances so that the rough side faced out – the smooth seemed too conventional for a robust little country cottage. The suppliers of the sheeting were horrified until they saw the result, and then they adopted the method as a selling point.

All in all, the whole place showed a quirky, efficient and pleasing use of materials and space. And of course descriptions of Sonning 2 became another useful advertisement for the ongoing developments of the Bickleigh Vale scheme.

One of the people who read about those developments was Lorna Fielden, a teacher at the Junior School of the Methodist Ladies' College (MLC) in Kew. Lorna made an appointment to visit Edna and she liked what she saw. She purchased a plot in 1934 and, according to Blanche's diary, a tiny stone cottage was built for her at the beginning of 1936. It was called Lynton Lee. Lorna was so pleased with Lynton Lee that she bought an adjoining plot and requested that Edna transform her little cottage into a larger residence.

Edna was delighted to oblige. A little *too* delighted, for Edna's ideas were ambitious, and building proceeded whether Lorna was there to approve 'new directions' or not. There were occasions when Edna saw opportunities to improve on her original design and Lorna had a few surprises when she made her visits of inspection. The owner/architect relationship is always a tricky one and, reading between the lines of Edna's recollections, the friendship between Lorna and Edna was forged and truly tested during the building of the extension:

> [T]he chief request made by the owner of Lynton Lee at the time of discussing the plans ran something like this: 'I simply *must* have some lavender bushes on which to dry my handkerchiefs!' It was a comparatively simple wish to gratify; the disposition of the rooms, the fenestration, the pitch of the roof, the design and proportions of the stairway, etc., were to follow . . .
>
> Someone once said that 'to know a person you must build a house for them,' and it is true. Arguments there will be and tolerance there must be on both sides . . . Atmosphere is not always easy to achieve and one cannot afford to throw away any chance that will help to provide it . . . In the original plan of Lynton Lee the back door was to be sheltered by a small porch; just in time it was realised that an extra room could be provided under the roof by the addition of another gable.

The process of argument and compromise doubtless held its own special 'atmosphere' but the end result was splendid. In fact Lorna was so enchanted with her country haven that she decided to give herself a twelve-month break from MLC and even considered total retirement. Lorna was a reserved and gentle woman in her late forties; she had a round face, plumpish body and wore her long dark hair pinned fairly tidily to her head. Her dedication to teaching had always put her health at risk. She needed a long rest, so she spent the year of 1938 settling into Lynton Lee and Mooroolbark. She gradually got to know Edna and Gwynnyth and Margaret Walling and Blanche Marshall. She read and she listened to music and wrote poetry and got a cat and wove rugs from her own spun wool and made patchwork quilts and tended her garden and dried her handkerchiefs on the lavender bushes that grew by the new back door. She loved to cook and was very happy to share the occasional meal with Edna, or bake her a cake or take her a tasty dessert, and on some days she'd pick a bunch of flowers and place a vase of them in her own cottage and another vase of them in Edna's cottage and generally help the days along with touches of kindness. It gave her pleasure to help Edna in the ways that she could – typing was another thing that she helped with – and Edna reciprocated by doing all sorts of practical jobs that Lorna found difficult: repair jobs around the house and the heavier work in the garden and errands that needed running or lifts given in the car, for Lorna did not drive. The two women were marvellously compatible and mutually helpful. They had similar interests and tastes and, very importantly, they respected each other's need to spend time alone. Lorna's move to Bickleigh Vale was very good for both of them.

Lorna recovered her good health so successfully that she resumed her post at the Junior School of MLC and taught for about three more years. Then she retired for good and made Lynton Lee her permanent home. Lorna enjoyed her privacy but she obviously had no objection to Edna referring to her presence in the village in magazine articles. Though Lorna's actual name was never mentioned, Edna's followers became quite used to reading about her helpful 'friend', or more specifically 'the Mistress of Lynton Lee':

> The Mistress of Lynton Lee said, 'Smell that!', handing me a jar containing some dull red berries. 'Glorious, how do you describe that?' 'Ambrosia', she said dreamily! She had gathered them from her Russian cranberry (which is *Eugenia ugni*, a little evergreen

> shrub from Brazil). In the evening when she came over to share my fireside she brought me a small pot of jam. It was certainly food for the gods; I can only describe the flavour, and the fragrance, as a cross between pineapple and sweet peas. Grasping secateurs the next morning I toured the garden, taking clippings from every specimen of the little eugenia I could find, and now hundreds of them are rowed out ready for the onslaught we expect when others get to know about this luxurious fare.

Lorna Fielden became such a consistent part of Edna's daily life that it must have been hard to remember how she'd managed without her. The garden path between Sonning and Lynton Lee was well trodden. Not a day went by, hardly a day, without the two seeing each other. It was a splendid arrangement that became part of the tapestry of village life: Edna and Lorna, friends and neighbours, independent and close.

By most accounts, Lorna was a kind, generous and devout person. Her devotion was to Christian Science and the teachings of Mary Baker Eddy, which meant that she rarely sought conventional medical assistance for her ailments, and she certainly did not drink alcohol or smoke. She lived to a ripe old age so her methods obviously succeeded. Most people remember Lorna as 'a very nice person', though some recall that she could be an intellectual snob, especially when it came to English literature. She had the power to make the less well educated feel intellectually inferior, and Edna was afflicted with this feeling on occasion. Lorna tended to be a 'know-all'. This could be very helpful when Edna was searching for a suitable quotation for an article but it could be very annoying when it came to discussing Lorna's garden. Lorna had a fantastic garden but she sometimes 'forgot' that it was Edna who had originally put it there! All in all, however, Lorna really *was* a very nice person and Edna must have been especially pleased when she made Lynton Lee her permanent home.

Another thing that must have pleased Edna was that she had managed to pay off her debt to Mrs. Whisson (or the bank) for the Bickleigh Vale land. By late 1935 she was the title-holder of fourteen lots plus the new access road – plus Sonning. She still had an overdraft, but her financial situation had improved. Although Edna may have begun the village scheme in a dreamy romantic haze, by the mid-1930s she was protecting that dream with legal realities. Those wishing to buy plots were required to agree to a covenant. The wording of the covenant differed slightly for each buyer but the meaning was the same. This is the wording of the covenant that Lorna put her signature to:

> [T]hat not more than one dwellinghouse with the necessary and proper appurtenances may be erected or stand upon the above-described land and that no dwelling house may be built thereon except in accordance with a design to be prepared or in writing approved of by Edna Margaret Walling her executors or administrators (such approval not to be unreasonably withheld) and that the said land may not be used for the purpose of poultry or pig farming or for the agistment of live stock other than live stock reasonably required for the domestic use of the registered proprietor or proprietors for the time being of the said land.

The covenant, along with the like-minded enthusiasm of the original purchasers, ensured that the subsequent development of this cluster of subdivisions kept faith with Edna's scheme. It was an extraordinary and unique achievement.

Edna had a celebratory Sonning The Second house-warming cum fortieth birthday party at the end of 1935 and then she took Gwynnyth to Tasmania for a working holiday. The two stayed in Hobart with Edna's old friend Eileen Bamford and family, and they all had a marvellous time. Relaxation and exploration was combined with preliminary work on at least two major commissions. One garden in particular, Greenacres in Hobart's Sandy Bay, was a huge undertaking, and Edna returned to Tasmania a number of times to complete this and other work. She had now designed at least a few gardens in all the south-eastern states of Australia, and her journalism had covered a similar if not wider geographical area. Well-to-do people seeking to renovate or build a new home would engage a 'name' architect for the house – and Edna for the garden. It was now fashionable to have 'an Edna Walling'.

My candle burns at both ends;
It will not last the night;
But, ah, my foes, and oh, my friends –
It gives a lovely light.

Edna St Vincent Millay

We have observed Edna at work and at rest, with friends and alone. We have read some of her letters and articles and we have come to recognise her particular writing style or 'voice'. We have a picture, a sense, of who she was. And yet the light and shade of Edna's character can still hold surprises.

The 1930s was a roller-coaster decade for Edna. Her father died, her house burned down, her village was born. Somewhere in the middle of it all she had an intense, and apparently secret, relationship. This most elusive story drifts, like an invisible thread, through the fabric of the decade.

At some point during the 1930s Edna went through some difficult and at times underhand manoeuvres so that she could be with a particular person in private. The person in question was Esmé Johnston. It was known that the two were friends, but the extent of their intimacy seems to have been a well-kept secret. So well-kept that only one letter remains to give us the clue to what appears to have been a period of extreme emotional intensity.

Esmé Johnston was a sparkling personality with a successful career in radio and journalism. She was a year older than Edna, well educated and the daughter of a high-ranking public servant. She began her career on the stage in Melbourne and then started writing and editing for various newspapers. By the early 1930s she was also acting, announcing and writing for radio, first for 3AW, then for 3XY, two well-known radio stations in the city. She wrote a popular Children's Hour series which was broadcast daily by 3XY, and she became a regular writer for *Home Beautiful*, specialising in reviewing the latest in interior design. Her very first article for *Home Beautiful* was about her experience of building her own cottage near the beach in the Melbourne suburb of Brighton in 1930. One of Esmé's interests was architecture and she was able to design her house to suit her needs. She was also involved with the building, though she was not as hands-on as Edna had been.

Perhaps Esmé and Edna met at a *Home Beautiful* staff gathering, or at the house of one of Edna's clients, for Esmé sometimes wrote about the interiors of homes that had an Edna Walling garden.

Esmé was full of enthusiasm and fun. She had an open, rounded face, wore fashionable clothes, and was generally well liked. Her pleasures ranged from swimming and riding to theatre and books. She enjoyed a drink and a joke and had a remarkable ability to mimic all kinds of voices and accents. She was ambitious as well as talented and her career made good progress. Even her pet cockatoo had made a name for himself, for he had been pictured on her shoulder in publicity shots, and was a character in one of her 3XY radio programs. By the mid-1930s, magazines like *Radiogram* were running small promotional items on her various talents. One such item related that Esmé was known by three nicknames – Pony, Johnny, and Dimples; and Pony was the name that Edna adopted.

The early years of Edna and Esmé's relationship appear to have been troubled as well as intense. The cause of the turmoil is not clear, though the key was probably the nature of their *feelings* for each other. These feelings were surely complicated by the fact that Esmé married in July 1936.[*] Esmé was thirty-nine when she married Alex Good, a fellow journalist in his early twenties. The circumstances are unknown, but the marriage didn't work and divorce proceedings began three years later. The relationship must have failed very badly to force the couple into divorce, which meant a lengthy legal process and the real possibility of tarnished reputations.

Complications between Edna and Esmé appear to have come to a head in about January 1937, which is probably when the following letter was written. Edna had been away, working on various country jobs, and had just arrived back in Melbourne. However, instead of returning home to Sonning, she set up camp in an empty house in inner-city St. Kilda. Edna had somehow secured the role of 'caretaker', looking after the place until the new owners moved in. There was the slight possibility that Edna might do some design work on the garden but otherwise it was an *extremely* unusual job for Edna to be doing.

[*] Esmé Johnston was born on 27/11/1896, so it's interesting to note that she gave her age as 32 instead of 39 on her marriage certificate of July 1936; her husband gave his age as 24. Esmé died in 1978.

She wasn't being paid, but at least she had somewhere private to live in Melbourne. And that was the point. The house was near the beach and just down the road from where Esmé was living in Brighton, i.e. conveniently placed for Esmé to visit on her way home from work at 3XY. Secrecy as well as privacy seem to have been very important.

Edna was desperate to see Esmé and to make her aware that they would be alone in the house. She also seemed particularly eager to discuss aspects of their relationship. She refers to her own suitably 'bottled' emotions, and the need to sort out certain 'feelings' that Esmé did, or perhaps didn't, want to feel. The underlying and repeated plea in Edna's letter is: *please* come and see me at this address as *soon* as you can. She seems to have gone to great lengths to set things up. There are no other examples of Edna taking on a 'caretaker' role anywhere else in her career.

This printed transcription cannot convey the intensity of the handwriting, the hurried scrawl in pencil, the largeness of the capitals, the firmness of the underlining, the lack of paragraphs. Nor can it show how every bit of space, every bit of margin, was filled till the words disappeared off the edges of the paper.

Edna scrawled her letter on a long narrow cut-off from a large sheet of drafting paper. This wasn't unusual; Edna often used scrap paper. However, her use of little crosses or 'kisses' (xxx) in place of some of the full-stops and ellipses is unique.* Edna posted it to 3XY,

* No other letters sighted by me have this distinction. Lucky chance brought this treasure into my hands long after I'd given up hope of finding anything remotely like it. The letter had been in an old plastic bag with other papers and photos that a great-niece had rescued when Esmé died (one of the photos was used for the cover of this book). It was a heart-thumping moment to open the fragile, tightly folded piece of paper and read the highly charged sentences written upon it. Here were signs of intimacy and vulnerability, signs of the Edna I'd imagined but not found – till this moment.

not Esmé's home, which suggests that it was not to be seen by Esmé's husband – or anyone else for that matter. It was painfully private. Desperately urgent. Entirely different from Edna's usual tone.

The full stops, ellipses and brackets are Edna's, the paragraph separations are mine, and the letter is presented in full. Words or dashes within square brackets indicate words that are uncertain or indecipherable. The letter is undated, but December 1936 or January 1937 seems the most likely time of writing.

7 MARYVILLE-STREET
ST. KILDA

My dearest Pony,

I wish my mind were readable by you by telepathy. The 'phone is always somehow inadequate; and letters are only letters. But I <u>did</u> love to hear your voice over the 'phone x x x Matters <u>begin</u> to be settled-down, although there have been so many preliminary doings, and the digging-in here has meant a good deal of moving-about, arrangements & general unavoidable what-nots . . . I WANT so much to see you & talk about yourself & myself x Heaven knows, though the 'phone is speech-with-you Pony dear, I am diffident in more ways than one when talking that way – about keeping you too long, & about possible undesired listening-in. And to myself I never seem over the 'phone as the just-as-myself person, though <u>you</u> do to me x x x

(Please regard with lenience the appearance of this stationery. It is the last I have, and I shall [renew] a clean envelope or so tomorrow, Monday x) <u>If</u> this letter fails to reach you on Monday morning, it will mean my failure to get the stamp shortly (this being Sunday) which I should have got yesterday x But I do hope for the best, now, so that [this will await] you when you reach

3XY. Otherwise it will be in the afternoon, & I so much hope that it will be welcomed whenever it comes . . . Darling, I want to know that you are well in mind & body – not pipped by any part of life, and that you are still looking forward to seeing & talking with me, about all manner of things. I hope it ~~may~~ be soon, Pony, if you can find the [appointable] occasion. Life has me as impatient as I have ever been, to sit beside you and have you talk to me, and me to you x x x

I now begin to write [of] the position, about myself, as exactly as I can see it x Please always do take for granted that your work with 3XY is continually thought of by me, – that I should so much love to have a long, uninterrupted exchange of minds. And here is the position:- This is a pleasant kind of house; Maryville-street runs east off Brighton-road, with a sign up 'To Ripponlea station,' which is a stone's-throw from here; the garden here is pleasant, back and front; there is no furniture in the house, which is quite a new one (or newish) & as clean as a new pin; I get no pay; but I'm sure to be OKEY, with one thing & another x x x Let me tell you now that my long & quite laborious tramps have made me thank goodness to be under a roof in Melbourne with the ability to see daylight about the meetings with you which I so much miss, & which I so much missed while on the move . . . I said 'I get no pay' but that doesn't mean that I'm going to starve. I put various items in the larder; and you have been responsible for seeing me through a somewhat depressing (or perhaps 'desperate' wd. be a better word) itinerary. You HAVE, Pony, and I HAVE been so anxious to get settled somehow so that we might be able to meet with my chin off my chest, & you not feeling that – well, feeling things you didn't want to feel x x x My own 'bottling' should keep me all right, now.

I have a comfortable stretcher & spring mattress & a quite

deep & restful kapok (I suppose) mattress – a good rest for the old feet, which have felt it! Tell you everything when I see you, beloved x x x I don't know, yet, after all, just how I stand. It's called a caretaking job; but it really means keeping the garden & house as they should [be], with cooking-gas for me, and the [truck] sent down for me without my asking x

NOW, I shall be here every evening & night. Even though the agent, & the new owner, have duplicate keys, I feel that you might not be averse to sitting on the stoop with me on your way home; or to calling on your way home & taking me up the road with you for a talk. I DO want so much to see you, somehow; and of course my 'bushings' have made me for the time not of a suitable appearance to ask for your company in the city x Do understand that my larder will be all right, and everything else probably so pretty soon . . .

Even now, I am not quite clear about what is expected of my movements; but I have been going like smoke here to improve the job, and am quite hopeful x But, it does tantalise me to feel that, when I say how much I want to see you, I am still so much up in the air. WILL you call for me, WHEN you can, and either sit with me, or walk with me, AND talk with [me]

Please understand that there WILL be daylight x THIS is my postal address; [hope] you are [-] . – ALL my love, and much hope, for you (& for me). I want [you] x [-]

This, my darling Pony, is a mixed-up position, even now, with the roof over my head x I want to improve it; want to get a move on, into your company. I am full of hope. But I AM missing you terribly x

The letter never really ends, but goes round and around the outer margins till the words fall off the edge.

What was it all about? Edna appears to have gone to extraordinary lengths to find a private, if not particularly comfortable, place that was conveniently situated for Esmé to visit. And what was the rush? She hadn't even gone home to Sonning to pick up a change of clothes. She was at pains to assure Esmé that she had food and gas and a bed. Edna's sister was living in a large house in Toorak, so she could have stayed there, or with other friends, but she didn't. Why was this top-class designer being a 'caretaker'? It's all very strange.

Perhaps Edna and Esmé were having an affair. Or perhaps they'd had a passionate friendship before the marriage but then jealousies intervened. Or perhaps Edna had been too intense for Esmé's comfort and there was a need to talk it through . . . Who can say?

Esmé married for a second time in later years, yet the subtleties of attraction are so complex, so changeable, that anything is possible. Unlike Lorna Fielden, Esmé was unhampered by restrictive religious convictions, unfettered by the ultra-conservatism that was prevalent in middle-class Melbourne at the time. Yet there were boundaries, even for free spirits. A whiff of scandal would have damaged both Edna and Esmé's careers.

The pair remained close for the rest of their lives, so presumably the intensity calmed to a manageable equilibrium.

It's extraordinary that the St. Kilda letter has survived, for almost all the other correspondence between the pair has disappeared. Esmé Johnston could have read Edna's letter and then destroyed it, yet she didn't. In fact she did the opposite. As the years went by she placed it with other Edna-related papers. She kept it with her unpublished manuscript of her biography on Edna, written after Edna's death: a biography that is warm and jaunty but free of specific dates and scant on facts. A biography that makes no mention of the early days of their friendship, though happily celebrates their later years.

Esmé remained a constant and perhaps elusive presence all through Edna's life. It was a presence that was subtle, and yet always there, somewhere in the background. Somewhere between the lines.

Edna appears to have bottled up her emotions, but she might have confided in Blanche Marshall. Blanche and Louis Marshall moved into their new house around this time (for which Edna designed the garden), and a few months later Blanche became pregnant. It was probably because of this pregnancy that she decided to spend a few weeks resting at Sonning in mid-1937. If Edna had wanted to do some 'unbottling', those few weeks would have been a good time.

It's interesting that Blanche chose to go to Edna's home for her extended rest, for Sonning was on the Spartan side when it came to home comforts. Edna's friendship was clearly important but a secondary consideration may have been that Margaret Walling was close by. Blanche got on well with Margaret. They'd go on shopping expeditions, and doubtless there was much talk about the coming baby. Margaret was motherly, which was comforting for both Blanche and Edna. Yet it's worth considering whether Margaret's presence, as a close neighbour to Edna, may have felt restrictive at times. It may even have inhibited some of Edna's movements in relation to Esmé. Is it possible that Sonning was never completely private for Edna, with her mother and other neighbours just across the way?

Neither Edna or Esmé offer any further clues.

Edna's answer to emotional difficulties was to throw her energies into her work. Apart from her usual jobs, she started building another new cottage called Winty, and was soon telling her *Home Beautiful* readers what a lovesome little cot it was and how lots of delightful things would be planted just as soon as she'd found someone to take it on – which was Edna's way of saying 'Cottage for sale'.

One of the things that would have taken Edna's attention at this time was her discovery of an impressive workman called Ellis Stones. Ellis Stones was a beginner when it came to garden construction, but he was a magician when it came to placing boulders and rocks in 'natural' positions. He could make them look as if they'd been there forever. If Eric Hammond was too busy to take on a garden job, then Ellis Stones became Edna's second choice.

Ellis Stones was the same age as Edna, so he was forty in 1935 when they first met. Edna was working on a suburban garden where Ellis Stones happened to be doing some odd-job carpentry on the garden owner's house. He overheard Edna saying that she needed someone to build a curved stone wall and he offered to have a go. Edna was skeptical. After all, he was a carpenter who knew little about stone, but she gave him a chance and the result was very good. Ellis Stones (soon to be called 'Rocky') had a feeling for stone. Edna knew at once that he was a natural. She told him he should throw away his carpentry tools and come and work for her. And she meant it. She was soon offering him contractual work on garden jobs and building work on Bickleigh Vale cottages. It was a turning point in his life.

He was a likeable man, with a strong physique, though he had a noticeable limp due to a war wound gained at Gallipoli. He'd been through tough times, and was determined and strong-willed, which is probably why he and Edna argued with great gusto when they disagreed – which was often. Edna could give Eric Hammond the briefest instructions and he'd know what she wanted and produce it to perfection. Stones was unpredictable. He had an inventive and creative mind which was useful in some circumstances but entirely misplaced in others. Hence the arguments. However, his rock gardens were marvellous creations and Edna knew it. She knew it so well that she even told her *Home Beautiful* readers about him. This was an extraordinary show of support, for she almost never recommended the work of her peers.

They had a strange kind of relationship. Respectful from Stones's side (he called her Miss Walling), appreciative from Edna's side (she chose to call him Andy, his middle name), yet always volatile, always horns clashing. Arguments or no, Edna and Ellis continued to work together for many years until Ellis earned a reputation of his own. In fact it was Ellis Stones who eventually inherited Edna's 'king of the castle' crown.

It was just as well that Edna had found another good contractor because her workload was increasing in all directions. Things were also developing in the village: Gwynnyth Crouch's mother had decided to take on the new cottage called Winty, and would be moving in with at least two of her daughters just as soon as Ellis Stones had built the extension. This was especially good for Gwynnyth for she would have a 'proper' bedroom at last, instead of a bed in a shed. And there was more good news: two more subdivisions had been sold, which meant that Edna was designing two new cottages. This was a landmark development, because it meant that Edna was at last in a position to settle her debts. One of these debts was the £100 she owed Blanche for the 'repurchase' of The Barn. Edna had always owned The Barn on paper, but Blanche had been the unofficial owner since their gentlewoman's agreement back in 1928. It's a sign of Blanche's commitment to the ideal of the village, and to Edna, that the sum had not increased with interest over time. It was also a sign that Blanche was relinquishing her hold on that plot. After all, she had many other things to think about, for the other good news was that Blanche had given birth to a baby daughter – of whom Edna was godmother – and it would not be long before there was another baby on the way.

Midst all this energy and activity we pause briefly to mourn the passing of an old friend. One spring afternoon, when the blossom petals were falling and the bees humming, the Irish terrier known as Brian tottered to his basket and laid his body down. He was very old, and it was only to be expected, but it was awfully sad when it actually happened. He'd had a jolly good life and been a very good friend: a brave fellow when needed, and a gentle one when required. He'd seen Edna through the best of times and the worst. He'd been her mate and her little shadow since the early days when they'd camped together in the cow paddock when Sonning was just a dream. He was just a puppy then, with the rather grand name of Brian Boru, after the Irish king. He had served that name well, for he had welcomed guests, worried strangers and been most cordial with dignitaries. He had put up with the black cat and other lesser cats because his mistress asked him to, and he had rarely lost his sense of humour. The bundle that was his body was gently lowered into the ground in his favourite part of the garden. And then a few months later the old black cat was buried at a tasteful distance from him. She had died not so much from old age but from boredom. Her adversary had gone, and the great game was over. There was nothing more to do but rest in peace.

People were quick to give Edna replacement pets. Robin, a small black Scottish terrier, was given by a friend, and at least one cat simply 'arrived' uninvited. Indeed, pets were steadily becoming part of the Bickleigh Vale experience, for most residents had a cat or a dog, and there was Edna's friendly old horse Garry (who had taken over from Adam), who was enjoying a long retirement.

The idiosyncrasies of pets, as well as owners, were part of the character of village life. Although this strange little cluster of housing was not really a village in the true sense of the word, it was beginning to look as if it had grown there naturally, like true villages should. There was more than a hint of *The Wind in the Willows* about the place, with Badger – or was it Toad? – driving off in rather a hurry through the Sonning gates. A friendly familiarity existed between the villagers, especially the permanent residents, but they did not live in each other's pockets. The whole idea of the layout of the subdivisions was that each cottage would be secluded once the gardens had grown. The fences may have been beautifully camouflaged but the inhabitants knew where the boundary lines were. It was not like Montsalvat in Eltham, Victoria, where a group of artists and their followers built homes and studios and even a church, and generally lived and worked together. Bickleigh Vale residents did not belong to 'a group', though there were a few common denominators: they were female, professional or retired, single or widowed, and usually of middle to mature age. Males were very welcome, but none actually purchased a cottage until a few years later. It's hard to say why. Perhaps there was a chauvinist reluctance to accept the controlling feature of Edna's covenant. Or perhaps there was something about the style of the place that didn't suit. Or perhaps Edna's personality was a little too forceful. Whatever it was, it didn't stop male friends and relatives from visiting.

By 1938 Edna was employing at least two more assistants: one to maintain the newly established gardens in the city, and one to assist at Sonning. Gwynnyth was busy taking over all aspects of rock plants, which meant that she was often working alongside Ellis Stones while he was putting the boulders for the rock gardens in place. These delegations of responsibility gave Edna a little more time to attend to other matters – not least the study of everything to do with house building. Edna's role as cottage designer was becoming more sophisticated, for she was increasingly addressing problems that would normally be solved by an architect. It was all very well to hand Eric Hammond a scrap of paper with a basic floor-plan of a one-room cottage, but these days she was being asked to design cottages that had several rooms and a staircase. Bearers, ventilators, gables, flooring – she had to know what she was doing. Consequently her bedside table was overflowing with publications about architecture and building construction. Perhaps she even dreamed of becoming an architect. And why not? She was teaching herself house design in the same way that she had taught herself garden design: through study and experiment. 'Architect' was a term she would never attach to her name but 'Cottage and Garden Designer' was definitely on the cards.

Edna had another dream at this time. It was a dream still connected to study, but it was far more exciting than the books on the bedside table. She desperately wanted to travel. She wanted to see all those places in Italy that she loved looking at in photographs, and she wanted to walk through all those gardens in Britain that she'd never taken notice of when she was a girl, and she wanted to experience the mysterious and exquisite culture of that extraordinary country called Japan. What treasures awaited if she could only save up her pennies and leap onto a ship and just *go*. And yet, it could not be, for practicalities and priorities, to say nothing of the lack of pennies, would always crop up to bar her way. For instance, in 1938 she was seriously talking about going to Japan, but then she found that she was in desperate need of a better car, so her pennies had to go towards that; and then her family was in need of her emotional support because Doris's husband suddenly fell ill and died and so she wanted to remain close at hand because of that; and then her new Sonning assistant turned out to be 'difficult' and it was agreed that she should depart, which was a relief to all concerned, but it still meant that Edna had to somehow cover those working hours; and then the matron from the Melbourne Orphanage bought a plot of land and wanted a particularly large cottage and Edna had to apply herself to that. And then there was the dark and troubling news about the increasing power of Fascism, and the awful prospect of another war, and so the thought of travel to foreign places did not seem at all appropriate, especially as her mother was prone to illness-inducing *worry* when her daughter was away for long periods and Edna did not want to trigger *that*. So she took herself to Sydney for a working holiday instead.

In January 1939, she packed her books and camping gear into her newly acquired Baby Austin, and she took to the road. The road to Sydney was still perilous and unpredictable, so it's likely that she also took a friend, though this is uncertain. What is certain is that she wrote to her dear mother to say that she was having a splendid time:

> 25.1.39
> Dearest mum,
>
> . . . I went for a drive all around Darling Point, poking in & out until we reached Rose Bay, we intended going to Vaucluse but just as we were driving on a sea plane came in & there was another expected in half an hour so we waited at the slip to see it arrive too. Rose Bay is going to be frightfully interesting with these sea planes arriving from the other side of the world. Huge new buildings are going up there on the coast to deal with this new form of travel . . .
>
> Still think I shall go to Flinders or somewhere for some bathing and that coastal wildness that I hunger for so much before starting work for I still have lots & lots of studying to get through before being fit to take on fresh jobs. . . .
>
> Took Blanche [Henson] through to Kuringai Chase but it's ruined down at Bobbin Head they've even knocked off Bobbin Head itself to make a footpath over it ! ! ! & there are hideous shelters with orange and red roofs everywhere. It makes me mad with rage all that they do to this <u>wonderful</u> place called Sydney, it's sacrilege & I'm dying to buy every vacant block of land to preserve its natural beauty. We don't realise that soon this exquisite beauty that is native to this place will no longer be here – it will all be ['improved'] out of sight. Oh! how unutterably sad it all is. One day I'll bust!
>
> Ever so much love dear, from Edna

Then she got down to the 'work' part of the holiday and visited a couple of clients and inspected a couple of sites and volunteered her services in the garden of her hosts. She would rather have sat in the garden and lazed, but people rarely let her forget what her occupation was, rarely let her be in a garden without asking for advice, without prompting for praise or help. She toiled over a few improvements, and when all was done she jumped into the Baby Austin and drove home.

Let's hope that she did indeed 'go to Flinders or somewhere for some bathing and that coastal wildness' before starting back at work. She had certainly earned a break.

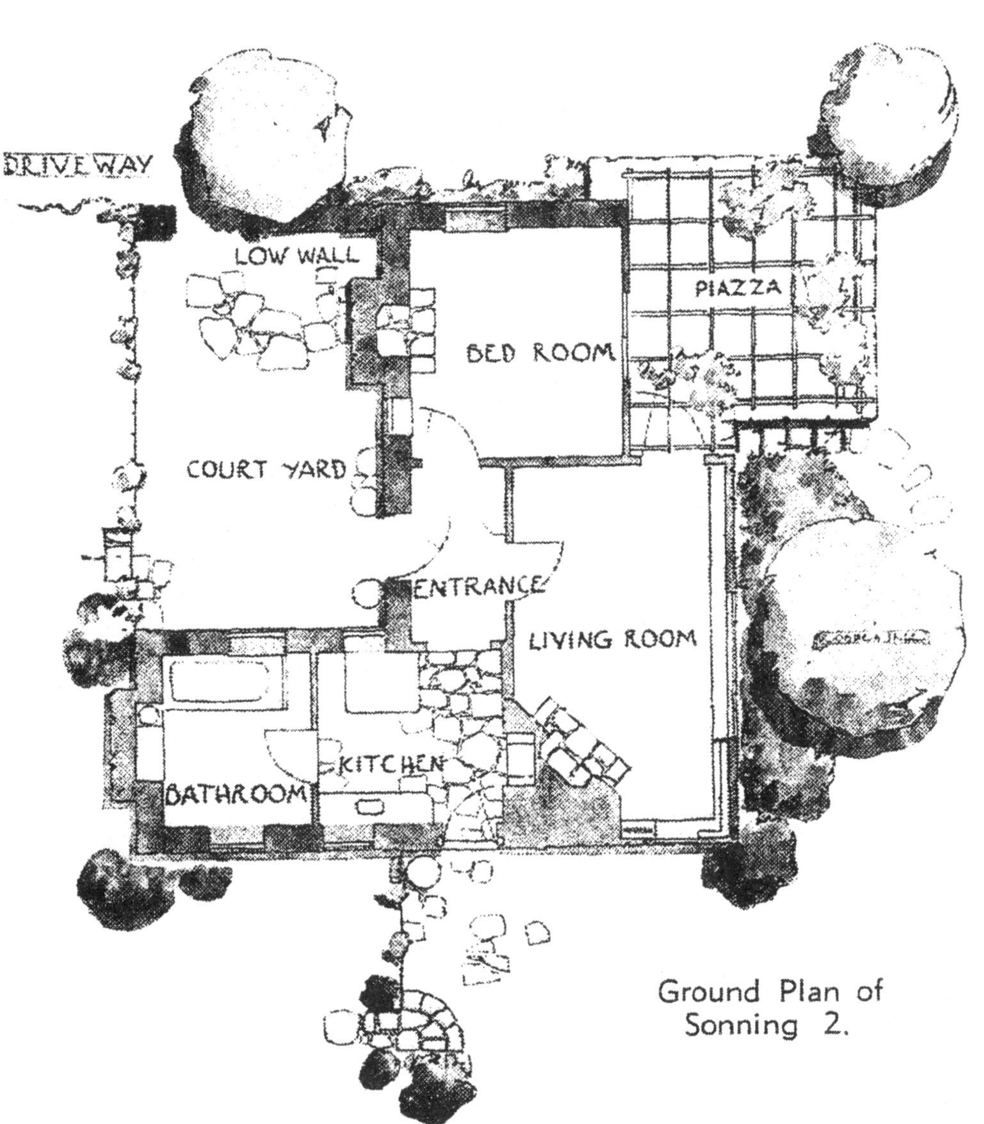

Ground Plan of Sonning 2.

Margaret Walling
at Sonning

Chapter 9

Flying high

In September 1939, the Australian Prime Minister, Robert Menzies, informed the people that Great Britain had declared war on Germany and thus Australia had also declared war: 'There can be no doubt that where Britain stands, there stand the people of the entire British world.' Mother Country or no, the news was not embraced with the same frenzy of patriotism that had arisen at the instigation of the 'first' World War. People's memories were not that short. Even so, there was a job to be done and people started preparing themselves to do it – though with the hopeful thought that 'it'll all be over in six months'.

The government moved quickly to introduce conscription in October 1939, while thousands of men started to enlist of their own accord. There was a flurry of excitement in January, when part of the 6th Division of the Australian Imperial Forces sailed off to the Middle East, and then there was a lull. There were songs about the Siegfried Line and rude jokes about Hitler, but otherwise, on the home front, Australian working life continued to roll along without too many changes. Petrol rationing would not begin until October 1940, while food, clothes and tobacco rationing would not begin until mid-1942. Consequently, the first few months of the war seemed relatively calm, or as Menzies put it: 'business as usual'.

So Edna continued with her business. She had various jobs on the go in Victoria, including the particularly difficult engineering challenge of a swimming pool set in a mountainously steep garden in the Dandenong ranges. There was also a big commission for a garden in Adelaide, South Australia, which she began in 1939 and returned to oversee in June 1940. She'd travelled by train for the first trip to Adelaide but drove over in her Baby Austin for the return visit.

These long-distance trips were another opportunity to get to know the landscape at close quarters. She loved travelling through the countryside. Loved the Australian landscape in all its variety and natural beauty – and she hated the short-sighted, greed-driven, mean-minded, destructive things that were happening to it.

Edna was well ahead of her time when it came to land conservation. All through the 1930s her articles had been peppered with pithy comments about the wanton destruction of Australia's beautiful landscape, with warnings about erosion and calls for better forestry management – and she reiterated these comments during the 1940s and beyond. Yes, there was a war going on, but Edna wanted people to realise that there was a terrible and lasting form of destruction going on in Australia's very own 'front garden'. As the war progressed, and those who had the means started moving out of the cities and into the country, she encouraged them to plant trees, lots and lots of trees: indigenous natives to replenish the bush, and others to harvest for wood. Native trees and shrubs and ground-covering plants had to be conserved and/or replenished at all costs – especially along the roadsides.

When a journalist visited Bickleigh Vale and interviewed the 'well known garden designer' in 1939, he asked her what she found most engrossing in her studies of landscape gardening and she surprised him by saying:

> Highway planting – to deal with arid and eroded roadsides; and in such a manner as to eventually conceal the hand of man . . . All the time I can possibly spare I give to the study of naturalistic roadside planting, for it is one of the most essential works to be properly undertaken in the future of this country. Tree planting methods suitable to suburban areas are most inappropriate to the open highway . . . It is painful to see meticulously spaced young trees at the side of a highway slowly but surely growing into monuments to those who unwittingly take the suburbs to the open country road.

But it was an argument that drew little interest. There really were other things to think about. Everyone knew someone who was packing up their kit-bag and going off to do their bit. Members of Edna's own family were among them. Cousin Edith's brothers had joined the navy, and Doris's son, David Oak-Rhind, had joined the air force. David had been studying architecture, but when his father died he took a job with his dad's old firm. Perhaps he was unhappy there, for he jumped at the opportunity to join the RAAF very early in the war. He was one of the first Australians to be sent to Canada, where he gained his wings. It all happened very quickly. By Christmas 1940, Pilot Officer David Oak-Rhind was in Britain embarking on operational training, and soon after he was in a Fighter Squadron flying over France and the English Channel. He sent his mother and aunt a photo of himself in his RAAF uniform: he stands, somewhere in England, on snow-dusted ground; his smile wide, his back straight, his wings clearly visible on the left side of his chest. It was his first experience of a white Christmas.

Doris's daughter Barbara was also doing her bit, for she had chosen to work on the land. There was no organised Land Army as this point but she knew there was a shortage of labour on a friend's property so she volunteered her services. She had the romantic notion that she would be riding the boundary line, but in fact she spent most of her time working in the kitchen.

Almost everyone on the home front wanted to *do their bit*, especially when there were loved ones 'over there' doing theirs. Edna's bit was fund-raising for the Red Cross. She had innumerable open days at Sonning, which sometimes included performances in her open-air theatre, and she raised and sold hundreds of plants from the Sonning nursery, and she posted off thousands of envelopes with seeds or cuttings, and gave talks on landscape design – all proceeds going to the Red Cross. Initial fund-raising went towards a new ambulance, but as the horrors of war increased, the fund-raising took on a different focus. As Edna described it in one of her magazine articles: 'Sonning is to be held responsible for the upkeep of at least one prisoner of war.' Such announcements were always followed with information about how people could purchase plants or be posted seeds or when the next Open Day would be. And people responded.

The beginning of 1941 was the very worst of times for Edna, and doubly so for Doris. David Oak-Rhind had only been flying a few weeks with his Fighter Squadron when he was reported missing in action over northern France. Goodness knows what this news did to his mother, but it certainly appears to have triggered a deterioration in the health of his grandmother, for Margaret Walling became very ill at this time. She took to her bed in her little cottage at Bickleigh Vale, and Edna and Doris and a trained nurse looked after her. A vigil went on for some weeks but she did not improve. Margaret Walling died on 7 May 1941 at the age of seventy-four. She was laid to rest at the Lilydale cemetery, just across the valley from Bickleigh Vale, in good company with Dame Nellie Melba.

Two weeks passed and then the fearful news came: it was official,

David Oak-Rhind had been killed in action, his plane shot down over the Channel. He had baled out, but didn't survive. In later years it gave Doris some comfort that his name was commemorated on the Runnymede Memorial in Surrey, 'one of the first of the few', but we can only imagine how she felt in 1941. Doris threw herself even deeper into the mysteries of Christian Science and the 'good works' thereof, and she knitted and she knitted as if her life depended on it. In other words, she carried on as usual but with an even greater degree of obsession. And in many respects Edna did the same.

It is late spring, and there is an Open Day, a fund-raiser for the Red Cross. There are Girl Guides and Boy Scouts standing at strategic corners all the way from Mooroolbark railway station. They stand in twos or threes, holding hastily painted signs saying 'To Sonning' – though it has to be said that not all of the signs are pointing in the correct direction. Most people have come by train, but there are a few cars roaring up the hill, and a special RACV coach is in the process of disgorging a number of people at the stone-pillared gate that is the entrance to Edna's driveway.

Almost all those stepping from the coach are women. Women in jaunty hats and light summer suits or frocks, their cheeks smoothed with cooling face powder, their mouths red with deftly applied lipstick. Women with slim leather handbags tucked under their arms and cardigans slung loosely around their shoulders. The hemline is just below the knee these days and stockings have seams, straight dark seams. There are a few servicemen in evidence, and a smattering of husbands, fathers, boys and girls, but it's mainly women who pass through Sonning's open white gate.

There's a trestle table set up just inside the gateway, with Blanche and a couple of Girl Guides in attendance. The table is covered with a starched tablecloth bearing a printed sign saying 'Croydon Red Cross

Society: Prisoner of War Fund – Admittance 3/-'. Blanche smiles as she takes people's shillings, and people smile back, though not so much at Blanche but at her two daughters. One is a baby in a pram and the other is a wide-eyed toddler, and both have rosy smiling chubby faces. They are beaming with good health and happiness and it is a 'beam' that seems to be infectious.

There are many visitors, but it's still possible to appreciate the view that greets the eye when rounding the curve of the driveway: wide sweeps of grassy lawn running away into clumps of native and exotic trees, with drifts of pale mauve irises at their base, the whole backed by a young forest of slender gums. It's enchanting.

Further along the driveway, half hidden by the greenery, peeps the newly shingled redwood roof of the cottage of Sonning. A stone chimney rises just above the roof line and the upstairs window is open, allowing curtains to flutter out on the breeze. The cottage looks as if it belongs in a fairy story – or it would if the way ahead wasn't guarded by a group of all-too-human Boy Scouts. The boys are pleasant enough, but they are beginning to tire of their unexciting task and are inventing silly games to keep themselves going. Even so, everyone is successfully directed down to the left, away from the cottage and through the garden and towards the nursery where there are a great many people viewing rows of potted plants, displays of jams and preserves and all manner of 'homemades'. People are picking over and picking through and buying or not buying and generally having a good fossick around. There is a gentle buzz of conversation with the occasional interjection such as: 'Over here!' or 'I say, Gwynnyth, do we have any more like this?'. The 'this' in question is a large cement pot of attractive design. It was created by Gwynnyth, or perhaps Edna, for they've both been making them for some time. The woman asking the question is Esmé Johnston, Edna's journalist friend, for all manner of helpers have been leaned upon to assist with the selling. Gwynnyth is busy overseeing the seedlings and pot plants but she raises herself to her full and impressive height and looks at the pot that Esmé indicates. She shakes her head, 'No, no more, sorry.' Esmé's customer is disappointed, for the one on show has already been snapped up by Mrs. Essington Lewis, one of the dignitaries supporting the Open Day, and none of the other pots seem to suit. Mrs. Essington Lewis is the wife of the 'big noise' at Broken Hill (BHP), and is doing her bit by spending her husband's money and lending her name to charitable functions. Another notable in the crowd is Mrs. Edith Lyons, the well-liked widow of Joe Lyons, the former Prime Minister of Australia. Rumour has it that she intends to stand for parliament, but for the moment she is intent on buying some of Lorna's homemade jam.

People are free to wander the Sonning garden – though Edna has learned from experience that certain people like to snap off bits of tempting foliage, so Guides and Scouts are stationed at vulnerable beauty spots with orders to politely deter. For those wanting a more detailed exploration, Edna is giving guided tours of the garden. She leads with a spade, Cook's tour fashion, and wears her best jodhpurs and blouse topped off with a brilliantly white pith helmet. She waves her spade like an over-sized wand and delights her audience with a commentary that mixes detailed knowledge with self-deprecating humour. She is currently standing next to a copse of silver birch and relinquishes her spade in order to pick up a bucket placed ready for the purpose. In a clear baritone voice, with neither the plum of the English nor the twang of the Australian, she explains how the silver birch trees came to be placed in such a natural-looking configuration. What better way to find a natural placement than to leave it to chance? Like a magician with 'nothing up my sleeve', she shows her audience that her bucket contains potatoes, five potatoes – there could of course be more but they should always be of an odd number. She turns and walks to an open space in the lawn and hurls the potatoes out of the bucket and into the air and everyone watches them cascade and thump and roll and rest. They have spread out in a natural and pleasing configuration, though one seems over-close to another and a woman in the group ventures to say so. Edna is adamant. Her silver birches would be planted exactly where the potatoes have landed – isn't Mother Nature just as haphazard, just as irreverent concerning the regulation distance of roots per square foot? There is a low murmur of discontent from one or two but Edna remains firm. She points her spade at the existing silver birch copse and all eyes follow the 'wand'. It's like looking into a fairy-tale forest, especially as there are three giant toadstools (one a birdbath) nestled to one side. The trees grow healthy and tall yet are quite close in places, their trunks sometimes forked, sometimes crooked or bent. In fact the trees almost appear unnatural because they look so unlike the usual 'straight up and well shaped' version so common in the suburban garden. 'How quickly one forgets what the natural shape of a tree really looks like,' says Edna, resting her spade, and her case.

The tour over, Edna heads towards the cottage in the hope of a tea-break. She takes a circuitous route via Lorna Fielden's garden, which is 'out of bounds' on this occasion and thus free of visitors eager to ask her just one more question. She has Sonning's roof-line in her sights when a little man in a bowler hat and high starched collar pops up from nowhere and squeaks, 'Where's the display of annuals?' Edna is still trying to formulate a polite reply when she hears Blanche calling from the back door of Sonning, 'You're wanted on the phone.' Blanche is walking towards them saying 'You answer the phone, dear, I'll help this gentleman.' And Edna gladly proceeds to her cottage where she finds Blanche's little daughters asleep upon the sofa, and a tea-tray with teapot and tea things all ready on the table, and the phone most definitely and firmly resting upon its cradle. 'Dear old sausage' says Edna softly. And she sinks into an easy chair and stretches out her weary legs, 'Annuals!'

Loved ones

ABOVE: Edna and Gwynnyth taking a break – perhaps they were enjoying the sensual pleasures of their small but treasured patch of thyme lawn. FAR LEFT: Cousin Edith at Sonning – she must have been a particularly jolly companion. LEFT: Eileen accompanied Edna on bushwalks in the early days.

RIGHT AND TOP: Two very different views of Blanche: a studio portrait, and in the driving seat of the Fiat with Margaret Walling just visible in the back. The snap was taken by Edna somewhere on the road to Sydney. LEFT: Edna with the beloved Brian Boru.

ABOVE LEFT: Lorna at Lynton Lee with her cat Teddy.
ABOVE RIGHT: Edna's multi-talented offsider Joan aka 'Twid'.

Comedy and drama are popular features of radio entertainment from 3AW. (Above) The Lee-Murray Players snapped during a rehearsal in the studios; the players being: John Storr, Esme Johnston, Theo Scales, Campbell Copelin, Catherine Neill, LEE-MURRAY, Austin Milroy.

ESME JOHNSTON

Esmé kept a record of her theatrical and broadcasting achievements in a scrapbook. These clippings come from *Radioprogram* 1935 and *Listener-In* 1936. Opposite: The opening and indeed closing sentences from Edna's 'St. Kilda letter' to Esmé aka 'Pony'.

7 MARYVILLE-STREET
ST. KILDA

My dearest Pony,

I wish my mind were readable by you by telepathy. The 'phone is always somehow inadequate; and letters are only letters. But I *did* love to hear your voice over the 'phone . . . Matters *begin* to be settled-down, although there have been so many preliminary doings, and the digging-in here has meant a good deal of moving-about, arrangements + general unavoidable what-nots. . . I WANT so much to see you & talk about yourself + myself. Heaven knows, though the 'phone is speech-with-you, Pony dear, I am diffident in more ways than one when talking that way — about keeping you too long, & about possible undesired listening-in. And to myself I never seem over the 'phone as the just-as-myself person though you do, — to me . . . [Please regard with lenience the appearance of

An intriguing shot taken by Edna's niece Barbara; the table setting has a certain gaiety but Edna seems pensive. Perhaps she was thinking about her move to The Barn. BELOW: Edna's renovations to The Barn included this inviting 'outdoor room'.

Later years

Edna's tailored clothes could be adapted to suit casual or more formal occasions – within reason. There must have been enough cloth in this instance to make jacket, skirt *and* waistcoat. BELOW RIGHT: Edna in the garden of The Barn in later years.

Edna tended to turn her photographs into birthday, Christmas and greeting cards. This one she entitled: 'At Maroochydore. The Maroochy River. Queensland.'

Flying high

A few months later. It is a midsummer afternoon and preparations are underway for a fund-raising performance at Sonning's open-air theatre. Miss Naismith and her ballet dancers are doing a last-minute rehearsal on the beautifully mown area of grass that is the stage, while Girl Guides are placing the last of the seating-mats on the terraces. They are elegantly curved terraces, with a steep rake that gives good visibility of the performance area. The sides of the stage are defined by bushes, which give the performers 'wings' to hide behind, and the whole is enclosed by a backdrop of tall gum trees. There is much activity on and around the stage, and quite a hullabaloo further away around the makeshift dressing rooms. The diminutive Miss Naismith commands her dancers to 'Step and step and twirl *together*', while a small band of musicians rearrange their seating and music stands, and Miss Webb, an elocution and drama teacher, warms her voice with a series of over-enunciated vowel exercises. It's a lovely day, not too hot, but there is a strong breeze and Miss Webb is concerned about the acoustics. She sees Edna fiddling with the assorted chairs that have been added to make an extra back row and projects her voice skywards, 'Miss Walling, can you hear me?' 'Yes Miss Webb, I certainly can!' 'Can you hear me now?' 'Yes' 'And n . . . ?' 'Pardon?' 'Thank you Miss Walling, that is all I needed to know.' And Miss Webb strides off into the bushes looking very professional.

Edna is wearing a suit today, a light sort of tweed, and her hat is of the Akubra variety. She has spent the last half-hour greeting the various dignitaries who have pledged their support, and has escaped from this task on the pretext of 'seeing how things are going'. She is deeply appreciative of the support, but some of these VIPs are awfully boring. She has left them in the capable hands of 'others' and skipped off through the garden, greeting friends and strangers as she goes. Some have brought a picnic basket, or at least a thermos, for the advertisement made it clear that 'refreshments will not be served'. Edna spots Margareta Webber and her friend Dr. Jean Littlejohn, and they wave and call her over. Edna developed a friendship with this pair when she created their garden, though she already knew Margareta through her 'Margareta Webber Bookshop'. Edna is looking a little anxious and Jean Littlejohn assures her that the atmosphere is splendid and that all will be well *whatever* happens. Edna laughs and reminds them to come back for drinks afterwards. She observes the little groupings of people as she makes her way back to the upper terrace, and senses that the atmosphere is indeed jocular and excited. People are pleased to be here.

Edna is unencumbered regarding the inner workings of the show, for Miss Naismith and Miss Webb have taken full charge of the production. However, it is mainly through Edna's contacts that the 'star turns' have been procured. For instance, Algeranoff, a character dancer with the Ballets Russes, is a friend, and Claire Mackinnon, a former Hollywood movie actress, is a friendly client. Algeranoff has agreed to dance, and Claire Mackinnon has agreed to turn up – an entertainment in itself. And then there's Doris Carter, a pal who was a hurdler at the 1936 Berlin Olympics and who is now a Flight Officer with the WAAAF. Doris Carter has agreed to introduce some of the 'items' and say a few words and – if all else fails – hitch up her skirt and hurdle over the audience (she's quite a gal, is Flight Officer Carter). There are many other splendid people involved, 'star turns' in their various ways, yet Edna is nervous. Nervous about the seating, about the weather, about the facilities, about the dressing rooms. This is the first time that her open-air theatre has been used on such a scale and she has no idea how it's all going to work. Yet it's much too late to worry. Miss Naismith and her dancers have cleared the stage and the musicians have settled and the Guides have laid all the seating-mats and the Stage Manager has released the Brownies – who are running, skipping and cavorting through the garden, ringing their fairy bells. The performance is about to begin.

The Brownies, Scouts and Guides run around the garden dressed as pixies, goblins and fairies, tinkling their bells and herding an amused audience towards the theatre. As the people settle, the sound of singing starts to filter from somewhere behind the trees. The sound grows louder and then schoolgirls from the Methodist Ladies' College choir file onto the stage trilling:

> Nymphs and shepherds, come away.
> In the groves let's sport and play,
> For this is Flora's holiday,
> Sacred to ease and happy love,
> To dancing, to music and to poetry . . .

The girls, all shapes and sizes in their school uniforms, sing beautifully, their eyes glued to the hands of their conductor who bounces her whole body with the beat. The song concludes and the applause is generous. By the time the choir is singing 'Begone, dull care, I prithee be gone from me' – dull care is indeed banished. A spell has been cast and there is enchantment in the air. The sun is kind, the breeze is light and the audience merry. Things might be frantic behind the bushes, but on stage, everything flows smoothly from one item to another. Miss Naismith's dancers – eight buxom young women wearing satin slips with long gauze over-skirts – present a delightful series of dances. The Guides and Scouts do a comic turn demonstrating the fire-fighting drill. The musicians play some charming numbers and somehow manage to keep playing when the breeze steals some of their sheet music. Miss Webb does a marvelous job with her cameo monologues, her powers of transformation a wonder to behold. Flight Officer Doris Carter recites a spirited rendition of Dorothea Mackellar's 'I love a sunburnt country', achieving an extra poignancy as she stands in her WAAAF uniform. Algeranoff, who used to partner Pavlova in his younger days, leaps onto the stage with tremendous gusto as Pierrot from *Le Carnaval*, instantly proving his star quality. He returns a little later as one of the Sisters from *Cendrillon* (Cinderella) and dances a humorous cameo wearing an overlong nightdress and silly bonnet. The audience love it and he receives much applause. And as the sun sets, and the shadows lengthen, Miss Webb returns to the stage with a group of her drama pupils. They perform the 'Wall Scene' between Pyramus and Thisbe from *A Midsummer Night's Dream*. It's wonderfully ridiculous, especially as Miss Webb plays the part of Pyramus – also known as Bottom:

> Thou wall, O wall, O sweet and lovely wall,
> Show me thy chink, to blink through with mine eyne!

Everyone cottons on to the playful punning with 'Wall' and 'Walling' and Miss Webb milks it for all she's worth. Edna laughs till she can hardly draw breath, which encourages more quips from friends seated about her. Mercifully, the scene comes to an end and the applause continues as the players, dancers, musicians and choir fill the stage and take their bows. Then all the performers withdraw and the clapping subsides and just as people begin to rise they hear the tinkling of fairy bells and a final reprise of 'Nymphs and Shepherds come away . . . sport and play . . . ' fading off into the distance . . .

The glories of the setting sun provide the final image for those who do not leave the terraces straight away, though the rumpus backstage dispels the last of the magic. There is mayhem for a while as people pack up and congratulate and give their thank-yous and say their goodbyes. Calm returns to the garden a couple of hours later. Now is the time that Edna and friends can sit around Sonning's courtyard and enjoy a drink and some simple fare: bread and cheese enhanced by pastries made by Lorna. Algeranoff, who is actually a very English Englishman, is holding forth with anecdotes about Pavlova. Most of those in the gathering are ballet enthusiasts and some would have seen Pavlova dance when she toured Australia. Edna in particular cherishes the memory; she loves the ballet, loves ballet music. There is no music playing at the moment, it is all conversation and the two recurring themes are 'the performance' and 'the war'. Doris Oak-Rhind is there, clicking away with her knitting needles and chatting with Algeranoff who looks so different in his conventional tailored suit. Algeranoff is a frequent visitor to Doris's home and it was through their friendship that Edna came to know him. Doris doesn't visit Sonning very often, country life does not appeal, but she helps on occasion, usually by bossing Edna about. Doris still manages to wield an older sister's authority, for Edna has never overcome her irrational desire to please her sibling. But Doris rarely offers praise. That's just the way she is.

Edna relaxes back in her chair, smoking an American cigarette and sipping her gin. She looks across at Doris, chatting and knitting and possibly even flirting, for Algeranoff has many charms and Doris is still a very attractive woman. No one discusses such things openly, but the private consensus is that Algeranoff is a 'masculine' man. He may be a ballet dancer but his interest in females appears to be 'straightforward'. Though of course nobody knows for sure, and Edna doesn't encourage gossip of that nature. There are things that are best left unsaid. Look at Margareta Webber and Dr. Jean Littlejohn, two brilliant women, sharing a home and going about their business. You don't talk about what goes on in the bedroom. You just don't . . .

Edna blows smoke into the air and looks up at the stars. 'What a day.' 'Yes, what a day,' echoes Lorna, who happens to be sitting next to her. 'We've raised a few more pounds for the POWs.' 'Several more pounds for the POWs.' They sit on, in a silent sort of reverie, observing the people around them. There's the urbane Marcus Martin, one of the finest architects in Melbourne, talking with the vivacious Esmé Johnston, who occasionally looks across at Edna. There's the bumptious Stephani Bini, a well-known radio producer, who chats with her shy young friend, Patricia Kennedy, a rising star in radio drama. There's Rosamund Dowling, looking trim in her army uniform, talking with Doris Carter, so tall in her airforce blue. Edna occasionally gives garden parties for people in the forces – just a simple afternoon tea, a place to relax and chat – and Rosamund and Doris help spread the invitation: men and women of all ranks welcome. A few Americans are beginning to attend, hence the American cigarettes. A burst of laughter comes from Ted Cranstone, the photographer, who is sharing a joke with Ethel Fielden, Lorna's cousin. Both have given Edna lessons in photography, for Ethel is a skilled amateur and Ted a professional. Both have taken numerous photographs of Sonning and the village, some of which have been used to illustrate Edna's articles. Edna much prefers Ethel's tuition because Ted Cranstone seems overly nervous, as if she might bite. True, she does bark at him rather, but bite? – never!

Margareta Webber steps into Edna's line of vision with a teasing 'O Walling, sweet Walling – Methinks we must depart' – and ducks just in time to dodge a cushion. 'You'll keep,' says Edna standing. Indeed, the time has come for everyone to depart, it's late and most have a long drive home. Off they go, offering lifts and sorting each other out, car doors slamming, engines starting, headlights beaming and then receding into the night. Edna closes the Sonning gate after the last car, Esmé's car, and stands for a moment listening. She hears the motor grumble into the distance, hears the reasserted sounds of the insects, the wind in the trees, the sounds of the night. As she walks back up the driveway she hears a sort of tinkling, a sort of singing. She knows that sound, it's the good fairy Lorna doing the washing up. Edna smiles and heads towards the kitchen.

Edna and Lorna had settled into a good companionship, especially since Lorna had fully retired from teaching at Methodist Ladies'

College. She now had much more time to spend on her cottage – and on Edna. The pair had developed a gentle understanding, they knew each other well and could get away with much joking and teasing without fear of offending. They were in tune, they knew what the other was thinking without needing to hear the completed sentence, indeed they began to complete each other's sentences. People who observed them together saw a closeness, a relaxed easiness, yet an ease that never seemed to include physical fondness. Hugs and kisses were never Edna's style, not in front of bystanders anyway.

What was she thinking and feeling at this time? Was she still sexually or romantically inclined towards Esmé Johnston? Was she repressing some of those feelings as too difficult to deal with? Did she see herself as androgynous, as the 'frankly boyish' persona that a journalist had once dubbed her, or was the image in the mirror telling her something else? She still had a fairly trim figure but the 'boy' was beginning to show signs of age. Interestingly, more and more women were wearing trousers to deal with their war work, so Edna's usual attire was becoming less conspicuous. Yet 'mannish' was probably the word that people used to describe her appearance, if not her manner. Idle gossips tagged her as a 'masculine woman', inferring that her sexuality was not quite the norm, but no one knew for sure. Decades later, when Gwynnyth was asked if Edna was a lesbian, she blushed and said that she didn't know about 'that sort of thing' then, she just didn't know . . . There are subtleties and inferences rather than clearly defined labels.

Affection appears to have been the central ingredient in the relationship between Edna and Lorna. They shared the simple pleasures: the sensual delights of the garden, the tastes of a well-cooked meal, the joys of an evening spent listening to classical music or to something special on the radio; or simply reading and conversing while sitting beneath the summer shade or in front of a cosy winter fire. Lorna's gentle presence probably gave Edna a welcome sense of constancy, for much had changed in her life. The loss of her mother and her nephew would have been by far the worst, but there was another loss that was difficult, and Edna didn't deal with it very well. Gwynnyth, her valued co-worker of over seven years, had married Ronald Taylor, a solicitor. This was all very joyous, especially as they'd settled in a new cottage at Bickleigh Vale. The disappointing part was that Gwynnyth had ceased to work for Edna. She chose to take freelance jobs instead, some of them with Ellis Stones. There were all kinds of understandable factors, but Edna was resentful. She had probably hoped that Gwynnyth would stay on and enter some kind of partnership; their skills were so compatible and she wanted someone to share the load. It was a selfish hope, especially as Edna wouldn't have handled a partnership too well – she liked teamwork but she was used to making the final decisions. Besides, the war had meant that there was less work, less prospects, and no one knew when, or if, that would change.

Apart from the practicalities, the real rub was that Gwynnyth's focus had changed: it was Ronald's interests and not Edna's that were her priority now. It was inevitable and entirely understandable – but Edna felt the loss, practically and emotionally, and there was a 'coolness' for a while.

The tension gradually evaporated, probably helped along by Lorna's soothing diplomacy, but things were never quite the same. Meanwhile, the village welcomed its first male resident in Ronald Taylor, Gwynnyth's husband. There was quite a large contingent of Gwynnyth's family in the village now, for her mother and sister still lived in Winty, and in due course her baby son and then daughter became part of the community – the first children to live in Bickleigh Vale. The Taylors moved closer to Melbourne in 1949 and their contact with Edna tapered away. Ronald Taylor acted as her solicitor from time to time but the connection between Edna and Gwynnyth was not sustained.

Despite the war, Edna still had plenty of work to do and she still needed the help of an assistant. One of the first of these was Beryl Mann, a real find; she had studied architecture before she'd done the course at Burnley and showed exceptional talent for landscape design – which is possibly why she didn't stay with Edna for very long. Beryl Mann took what she needed in the form of influence and training and moved on. This would be a repeated pattern with many of Edna's assistants – though very few would become as accomplished and recognised as Beryl. The separation was amicable; they had much in common and remained friends for years. Most of Edna's subsequent assistants were in want of training, and even these may have been hard to hold as the war progressed. Similarly, some of her male co-workers, men like Ellis Stones, were off doing war work. But in any case, as the news from the various battlefronts worsened, few people were thinking of having a new garden. The war had squashed many dreams and everyone had to compromise.

The one constant in Edna's working life was her regular *Home Beautiful* column – though even this was reduced because of paper and newsprint restrictions. She was now writing a monthly 'Letter To Garden Lovers' which allowed her to adopt a particularly familiar style. She inspired, cajoled and amused her readers, often signing off with 'Yours deciduously', or simply 'Yours'. Here's a sample:

May, 1942

Dear Gardeners,

Well, I'm very sorry to have to be faithless to the Honourable Edith Gibbs, but I can't help it, and the old girl will just have to take it because 'Silver Spray' IS ever so much better. This year the perennial borders had to be sacrificed, for the time and water spent on them previously had to go on to the 'Truck Garden', as we call the vegetable garden with deference to the good old Stars and Stripes. I felt so sad about it that I studiously avoided going into that particular part of the garden during the summer, but in the rain this morning I decided to inspect the ruins and was amazed to find that very little had actually died and there was a plant of Silver Spray flowering away as if it had received all the attention in the world! Well, if I could only have one variety of perennial aster, it would certainly be that one . . .

To my great joy I am finding that 'Sonning' is a wartime garden par excellence. Its appearance is really not at all bad, in spite of the fact that it receives little more than a tremendous spurt of the combined efforts of two women on Saturday mornings from 9.30 a.m. to noon! I'm a great believer in teamwork, and am quite sure two people get through more than double the work of one. It is impossible to keep all the shrub borders dug and hoed, so we have concentrated upon keeping the grass down and using the clippings and leaves as a perpetual mulch on all parts of the garden that are not lawn. Of course this is the best thing to do, war or no war, but it takes a war to make us realise it . . .

And now to food! And isn't it just too pathetic that nothing has yet been done to safeguard Australia against a food shortage. 'It can't happen here', seems to have been the swan song of some who have been asked to express their views. When I say nothing, I mean nothing by the government, which will no doubt eventually start a women's land army. The Y.W.C.A. Garden Army will help the vegetable shortage very considerably, but they can't introduce cows and pigs into their scheme . . . Where's that morsel of pork in the pork and beans tin coming from if they don't get busy on a land army? Heavens, they'll recruit the women when

> the shortage is really acute and then expect old Dame Nature to perform a miracle with her raw recruits.

And Edna was right. The government had been very slow to establish official organisations that catered for women's *paid* war work – be it in the forces, the factories or on the farm. Despite the increasing urgency, there was still some reluctance to allow females to take on traditionally male jobs. However, an Australian Women's Land Army was duly formed and raw recruits were rudely awakened to the joys and toils of agricultural work. Unlike some of her colleagues, Edna didn't become an instructor with the Land Army, or with any other organisation – not officially anyway. This was probably because the conformity of institutions didn't suit her. She preferred to contribute in her own way, as with her commitment to the Red Cross.

One day as Edna and Lorna were sitting and conversing, they started talking about writing a book. A book that would describe Edna's philosophy of the garden. It would have lots of Edna's photographs and maybe one or two of Lorna's poems. For Lorna was often writing poems inspired by the garden. It seemed like a good idea. Edna had a wealth of articles and notes and photographs to draw upon, and Lorna could help compile and type – and it would be fun to work on. Yet there was a catch. How could they think of creating such a lovely book when there was a terrible war going on? When gardens and even parks were being dug up and replanted with potatoes? 'Dig for Victory' was an increasingly urgent call now – and besides, there were paper restrictions.

Edna was an obsessive writer; she was always scribbling something on a scrap of paper or in one of her many notebooks: anecdotes, plant lists, descriptions, anything and everything that might come in useful for an article. One of these scraps of paper survives to show us how she tussled with the reasoning behind the idea of creating a book in wartime. It is written with a fountain pen and corrected in pencil and may have been an idea for the preface, a discarded idea for she slashed a line through it, yet kept it:

> It is war time & I'm writing a book about how to make a garden.
> 'It's no use doing it now' they said but with no avail – tap tap tap
> went the typewriter urged by the little voice that whispered –
> 'There will be mothers & wives & sweethearts & sisters with hearts
> to heal & there will be those who will be making gardens for the
> loved ones who will return tired and wounded and nerve-frayed.
> What can you do better than try to help in the creation of the most
> healing soothing & absorbing of all things in the world – a garden?'

Someone at Oxford University Press agreed with her and the book was published in 1943, with a second issue in 1944 and a third in 1946. The print runs were not huge but clearly people were keen to purchase a book called *Gardens in Australia: Their Design and Care*, by the one and only Edna Walling. It's easy to see why. The photography was superb, each picture a work of art with its grey/blue subtleties revealing the beauty of form, the grace of line, that Edna was describing in her prose. And her word pictures were equally charming, comprising short segments conveying a wealth of ideas for all aspects of the town and country garden. Dame Nature was the main muse but there was also a peppering of quotations from people such as Osbert Sitwell – 'green is the clue . . . ', Reginald Farrer – 'proportion, unity, restraint . . . ', and John Ruskin – 'the feelings of romance endure within us . . . '. And there were some of Edna's delightful sketches and plans, plus a poem by 'L. F.' (Lorna): 'It is a calm and fair retreat, / This sanctuary of fragrant growth . . . '.

It was a landmark book, for there had been nothing quite like it before. Previous gardening books had concentrated on horticulture, their flat and lifeless pictures echoing their dull pedantic advice. *Gardens in Australia* shone out as an elegant and inspirational departure from all those. Magazines tend to be temporary, but a book has a certain purchase in a household, a book is kept and borrowed and re-read. From this point on, Edna's philosophy of the garden began to take hold in the hearts and minds of the gardeners of Australia. Her recommendations for exotic and Australian plants, her advice on the use of sculpture, her suggestions for informal planting in a formal border, her ideas on landscaping the small garden, her particular joy in certain favourites like silver birch and Westmoreland thyme – were welcomed and used and dreamed upon.

The dedication simply said: 'To My Mother'; and the acknowledgements gave grateful thanks to 'my friend Lorna Fielden . . . for her patient assistance in compiling this book'. She also gave a general thank you to the owners of the gardens depicted in the photographs, and acknowledged Ted Cranstone's assistance with processing her films and for his photographic contributions – though without clarifying as to which of the photographs were *his*. It's likely that a small percentage of the photographs were taken by Cranstone and 'others', but Edna was never very good at being specific about such details. It's hard to know whether she avoided giving due credit on purpose or whether it all got into such a muddle that she lost track. It was probably a bit of both. Cranstone didn't seem to mind, for he continued to assist on subsequent books.

The fact that the owners of the pictured gardens were unidentified was probably due to a desire for privacy rather than muddle. Only those in the know would have recognised the many views of Sonning, or the three silver birches that grew in Doris Oak-Rhind's garden, or the various pools, steps and pergolas that graced the expansive gardens of Edna's most exclusive clients. The focus was on beauty, how to perceive it and how to achieve it, and the accent was on Australian conditions.

Editorial input was subtle. There may have been a few less exclamation marks than in her 'Dear Gardeners' letters, but there was no mistaking her warmly individual style. Thirty short segments with titles such as 'The Gentle Art of Pruning' and 'Landscaping the Window-box' (where a cigarette tin was suggested for the 'pool') conveyed what could be done when an artist was at work in the garden. The scientific skills of the trained horticulturist were shunned in favour of 'that divine something' found in 'the affectionate hands of those who personally tend their plants'. The book itself was also beautifully done, showing few signs of wartime restrictions. Much care had gone into the design, and the photographic reproductions were especially good.

When the war ended and the dust began to settle, Edna turned her attention to creating a second book. Lorna helped with the collating, Oxford University Press took on the publishing and *Cottage and Garden in Australia* appeared in 1947.

It was another delightful book, this time with its focus on cottage building and cottage garden making. The examples for almost all the photographs were the cottages at Bickleigh Vale, though once again only those who were in the know would have recognised this, for she didn't name the village or even Sonning. This was probably because she wished to engage the reader in a diversity of cottage-building possibilities. For instance, she presented details about building cottages by the sea or on a steep hillside, and she discussed various building materials, from stone to earth. The basic message was: you can build this yourself at a much cheaper price if you use local and recycled materials – and the end result will be much more attractive. There was a serious shortage of building materials at this time, so her mention of the lesser known mudbrick and rammed earth techniques was a significant inclusion. Many of her suggestions, especially for interior fittings, can be traced back to the ideals of the Arts and Crafts movement. In fact she quoted William Morris at one stage:

'Have nothing in your house that you do not know to be useful or believe to be beautiful'. It was a lofty order, but the interior views of Sonning demonstrated that Edna was sincerely attempting to live up to that ideal. Or at least, to live up to that ideal on the day the photographs were taken! One can hardly blame Edna for giving her home a thorough tidy and shine before exposing it to the public gaze, but the photograph of her office in particular looks strangely naked, without even a scrap of paper on her desk. Edna was not the tidiest of people, so it's likely that the usual disarray had been moved out of sight of the camera. Edna disliked taking posed camera shots of people, she preferred to catch them unawares, however the views of Sonning appear to have been carefully constructed – or perhaps the word is 'designed'. After all, the book was about design, and so the placement of the smallest detail – a cluster of flowers in a small pottery vase, the angle of a chair in relation to the window – was carefully thought out.

Constructed or not, the pages of *Cottage and Garden* gave a unique glimpse into Edna's home and, therefore, lifestyle. The effect is like peeping into some of the cottages in *The Wind in the Willows* – one of Edna's favourite and oft-quoted books. Badger, Ratty or Mole could have lived at Sonning – except that a strong Australian sunlight streamed in through the windows, and the open doors revealed the outdoor rooms of the piazza and courtyard. The kitchen was like a galley, with jars and tins neatly stacked, paraffin lamps hung on hooks, and blue and white crockery shelved on made-to-measure ledges. A wooden table had a chequered tablecloth, and upon this was a small vase of flowers and a simple setting of cutlery laid ready for one. A big black kettle stood on a cast-iron stove, while a copper bucket rested on the stone-flagged floor holding a quantity of ladles and wooden spoons. A very narrow staircase led to two bedrooms. Edna's little bedroom was an afterthought extension that could only be reached by walking through the slightly bigger guest bedroom.

Both rooms had single beds with rounded bed-heads, re-shaped from old cartwheels, and the patchwork quilt covers, and indeed all the fabrics, had a boldness about their design. Even the garage looked engaging, with its exterior suitably swathed in foliage and the Baby Austin almost 'grinning' from within. And of course the photographs of the garden suggested further enchantment.

Lorna's cottage of Lynton Lee received significant coverage in *Cottage and Garden* and there was even a photograph of 'The Mistress of Lynton Lee' herself, standing at an open window cuddling her cat. Lorna was the only human being featured in the book – or at least obviously featured, for Edna sometimes captured 'hidden' people in her photographs, virtually camouflaged amidst the shaded tones of the foliage that surrounded them. Lorna's cottage appeared to be more substantial than Sonning, the rooms were larger, and the furniture more solidly 'original' than some of Edna's recycled or improvised pieces. The style echoed Sonning, minus the more eccentric touches that gave Edna's cottage its 'character'. Lorna's spinning wheel was probably the most personal item to be revealed. It stood by a window that was especially low so that Lorna could appreciate the view when she was spinning her yarn.

Photographs of other Bickleigh Vale cottages served as further examples in the remaining pages of the book, and there were plenty of drawings and building plans to exercise the imagination. *Cottage and Garden in Australia* was dedicated 'To Father', and the acknowledgements listed the names of six photographers including Ethel Fielden and Cliff Bottomley, a professional photographer who had taken a cottage at Bickleigh Vale. A few verses of Lorna's poetry were included, plus a sprinkling of diverse quotations. These ranged from Kahlil Gibran's 'The Prophet' to four lines from Edna St. Vincent Millay, the latter accompanying a photograph of a stone fireplace with a wood fire:

> But the roaring of the fire,
> And the warmth of fur,
> And the boiling of the kettle
> Were beautiful to her!
>
> *Edna St. Vincent Millay*

A third book, *A Gardener's Log*, appeared a year later in 1948, again published by Oxford University Press. It was probably the easiest book for them to compile because it was based on Edna's 'Letter to Garden Lovers' (as seen in *Home Beautiful*) and carried fewer photographs than the previous two. Extracts from Edna's articles were roughly corralled into four chapters named after the four seasons, each headed by a little poem by Lorna. It was another delightful book.

It's interesting to note that Edna and Lorna were working on other publications at this time and that they were unsuccessful. Lorna compiled a slim volume of humorous ditties about the follies of gardening, and Edna tried very hard to find a publisher, but with no luck. Lorna published it herself in the end. Edna designed the cover, and wrote a glowing introduction and posted out numerous preprinted letters encouraging friends and acquaintances to 'buy for Christmas'. They also worked on a 'Cat Book' – photographs by Edna, verses by Lorna. The book didn't materialise, though the idea may explain why Edna took so many photographs of cats. Lorna's verses were sweet, icing-sugar sweet by today's tastes. Edna obviously enjoyed them yet she was careful to use a teaspoon rather than a ladle when it came to sprinkling them through the pages of her own works. Edna had a sweet tooth for poetry but she knew when enough was enough.

Edna's three books were a tremendous boost to her bank balance as well as her career. Her taxable income almost doubled when all three books were in the bookshops in 1948. A fragment from an accounts ledger reveals some figures:

INCOME FOR YEAR JUNE 1947–1948:

	£	s	d
Royalties	314	5	4
Professional services	348	8	6
Sales	42	19	0
Articles	22	11	6
Work expenses:	£	s	d
(car, wages, travel, commercial literature, etc.)			
total:	261	4	8

This was probably a peak year for royalties, and perhaps an average year for professional services and nursery sales. Edna's income without royalties was in excess of £400, which was good, though of course her work expenses reduced this figure by more than half. Her overall fee for a garden design ranged from £20 to £30, the amount based on the number of visits rather than a percentage of the total cost. Other 'non-work' income included payments from a couple of investments (£6 10s 9d) and the return of a loan (£109, details unknown). All in all she had about £1100 in the bank. Edna did not appear to have any debts so she was doing well, though she was not what we'd call 'well-off'. For instance, if she'd wanted to buy a new car at this time it would have cost her about £400.

The jam on Edna's bread and butter had been the extra cash she received for her journalism, though she was writing fewer articles at this time, or at least less for *Home Beautiful*. This may have been because she had a huge design job in New South Wales in 1948, and it may also have had something to do with the new *Home Beautiful* editor. Edna had worked with the previous editor, Bill Shum, for twenty years, but in 1946 he retired and a 'new broom' was applied to the magazine. Fashions and tastes were changing, and over the next ten years Edna's contributions to the magazine would steadily decrease.

Yet the wind of change was blowing a positive and invigorating breeze through Edna's life. She was in her early fifties, well-established, and still on the move. The village was still growing, her interests still expanding, and she could now add 'author' to her list of accomplishments.

All this success won her entry into the 1947 edition of *Who's Who*, a substantial achievement given her gender and profession. She was listed as a 'Landscape and Country House Designer'. This rather grand title was justified in that she had designed a few country cottages outside the Bickleigh Vale estate, and been asked to advise on the design of two housing clusters for Broken Hill Associated Smelters. Country house design was now a significant part of her job description. The standard format for a *Who's Who* entry included the listing of one's club. Edna could have joined almost any of the top-notch women's clubs in Melbourne but she didn't; her club of choice was the good old RACV. Interestingly, Edna listed her date of birth as 1896 instead of 1895. It was a tiny touch of vanity considering that most women fibbed about their age, there being less documentation to prove otherwise. In any case, Edna was born in December so it was hardly a lie. The fib was stretched a little further, however, as she got older. Her final driving licence gave her date of birth as 1898. It's a minor detail, yet it helps explain why subsequent records were inconsistent as well as inaccurate.

The 1940s had been a particularly difficult decade, yet Edna had survived and even prospered. Rather than easing back and resting on her laurels, she was keen to push forward and embrace change. She was exploring new possibilities for the garden, and she was on the verge of a new adventure. The timing of the adventure was perfect. She had lots of energy, a bit of spare money, and had found the ideal mate to help her transform yet another extraordinary dream into a sparkling, rather unusual, reality.

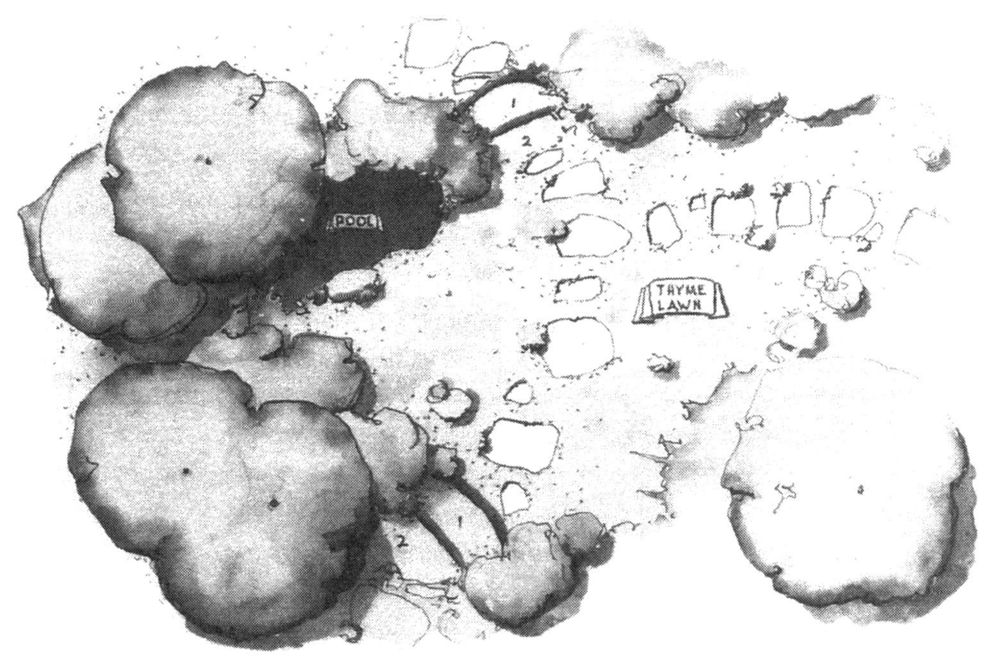
POOL
THYME LAWN

The Great Ocean Road

CHAPTER 10

The open road

For someone who spent so much time working with the soil, it's little wonder that Edna was drawn to the sea when she had the chance of a holiday. It was the sea that called her when she hungered for a rest. The sea, and some coastal wildness where the waves' roar would cleanse the mind and refresh the body. Where some quiet cove could offer bathing and beachcombing. Where hours could be passed just gazing at the view. One of Edna's favourite escape routes for such pleasures was the Great Ocean Road which travels south-west of Melbourne, hugging every cliff bend on its way to Anglesea, Airey's Inlet, Lorne and beyond. Edna had been going to that area for holidays ever since the early 1920s and had longed to have her own bit of land down there, her own little holiday shack. But it seemed an impossible dream. And then in 1947 she heard about a ridiculously steep plot of land that was for sale near a place called Eastern View, a tiny hamlet between Airey's Inlet and Lorne. Lorne was the larger of the two townships but they were both very small communities, this being years before they became widely popular.

The plot Edna purchased was on Big Hill, aptly named for its girth and height. The area had suffered from drought, and fire was always a possibility, but the hillside was well-wooded when Edna took it on. The trees were mainly ironbarks with a sprinkling of blue gums, shrubs, rock ferns and lichen-patterned rocks that had a pink tint to them. The rugged terrain would present awful difficulties when it came to access, let alone building, but the view, ah the view of the sea was breathtaking! Edna named her plot East Point. In years to come, the Great Ocean Road would have a lookout for tourists at the hairpin bend that was beneath East Point, for it was the perfect place to have a panoramic view of coastline and ocean.

The difficulties of building at East Point were daunting, even for Edna, and so she looked for a builder to take on the major part of the job. Yet the builders she spoke to were reluctant. It wasn't an attractive proposition from their point of view: everything would have to be walked up the hill until a road could be made, not even a tent could be pitched until some ground was levelled, and it was a long way from Melbourne. There also seemed to be a moral problem. According to Edna, those few builders who were actually willing to take the job were prevented from doing so by their wives. The wives were not at all happy about their husbands going off to a remote place 'with a couple of women'. It seems an odd comment, but then, this was the 1940s. These rejections did not matter in the end, for the 'couple of women' – Edna and her young assistant Joan Niewand – found that they were much happier doing the work by themselves.

When Edna wrote about the process of creating East Point she mentioned various friends in passing, but it was Joan Niewand who was the most consistent work-mate. Edna was supposed to be teaching Joan about gardening, but neither teacher nor apprentice hesitated when it came to skipping down to the coast for a few weeks of backbreaking building. Friends (male and female) lent a hand, but it was Edna and Joan who brought East Point into being.

First they had to dig into the face of the hill. Joan did the digging-out with pick and crowbar, Edna did the donkey work with shovel and barrow. Excavation unearthed all sorts of rocks that were ideal for building, but then Joan hit her pick into boulders. Immovable boulders, exactly where Edna imaged the living-room would be. Fortunately these boulders had interesting and even useful shapes. One had a convenient ledge that allowed it to be used as a passable armchair, another had some indentations, perfect for whatever it was that would one day find its home there. Each new problem became an occasion to adapt and invent. Improvisation was the key, and conservation was the policy. If a precious sapling was in the way of a straight line, then the line would have to have a chink in it. The shape of the building was 'revealed' rather than made, sculpted rather than imposed. Retaining walls and paved areas were reasonably true and level but the stone steps seemed to have a mind of their own. They looked irregular, and they were irregular, but walking up and down felt absolutely right. The curve and flow seemed in tune with the body. This was the kind of stonework that Edna adored. Finding the right place for each stone. Collecting them and sorting them and finding them just the right place.

She was not happy doing the carpentry work, however, especially if Joan was excavating something interesting. Yet the carpentry was a priority because a frame was needed for a roof because a roof was urgently needed to catch the rainwater. The nearest creek was a long walk away and so tank water was essential. Almost all the materials used to build East Point were recycled or found, but the water-tanks were new and the plumbing and plumbers paid for. Edna drew the line when it came to putting up pipes and gutters.

Edna and Joan welcomed help with the really difficult tasks, like getting the water-tanks up the hill (a friendly widower assisted with this), but they were reluctant for friends to give a hand during the major building process. Friends, lovely though they were, wanted to relax as well as help and this interrupted the duo's determined routine. Friends might work for a couple of hours then suggest they all go for a walk. A walk! Edna and Joan wanted to keep going. Walks, if they had to have them, were cunningly turned into expeditions that proved productive. A stroll down to the beach would be a chance for beachcombing. There might be a plank of wood down there, or a fish box that would do as a little table. Friends would find their stroll turning into a haulage operation as they staggered back up the hill with their load. It was nice that people took an interest, but Edna and Joan found that it was easier to get on with it themselves, in their own way. Friends were encouraged to come when the major work was finished.

East Point took shape as a two-level building. The ground level included a kitchen-living room area complete with stone 'armchair'. Cave-like, it was partly enclosed by solid rock, and partly open to the elements. This extended to the outdoor terrace, a stone paved area complete with stone workbench, fireplace and additional features such as a rock that was perfectly shaped to hold a bar of soap and a nailbrush. The upper level was fairly conventional in structure (walls, windows, doors), and consisted of a bedroom and a wet-weather cum fire-danger kitchen that had cupboards and a tiny stove – a boon to the person making early morning tea. They called their creation a Chalet and painted it the palest shade of pink.

The place soon became habitable, though there was always a long list of things to be done – an access track for cars, a car turn, a proper roof for the dunny – but nothing that couldn't wait. The Chalet was a fully functional holiday home, give or take a few details. A haven with a view.

There was even a view by night, for the Airey's Inlet Lighthouse could be seen far off to the left. When the day's work was done, or when the light was fading, Joan would begin cooking the evening meal. By the time they'd finished eating and Edna was doing the washing up, darkness would be all around them. They'd settle down in the cave-like sitting room and listen to music and watch the night. The silver of the stars, the steady wink of the lighthouse, the flickering fire casting shadows round about. Edna would roll a cigarette or perhaps fill a pipe, for pipe-smoking was one of her relaxing rituals. There would be insects, there would be the rustle of the breeze in the trees, and when the record on the wind-up gramophone came to its scratchy end, there would be the sound of the sea coming from the darkness below . . . A nightcap, a quick wash, a brush of the teeth, and so to bed.

They had ex-army canvas stretchers to sleep on when they camped there in the early days: the sort that groaned when you turned over and sometimes split down the middle during the night. They had an ex-army canvas tent as well: the sort that leaked if you touched it when it was raining, and which shrank rapidly in the sunlight, to the point where it would fall over if the guy-ropes hadn't been loosened. The tent probably belonged to Edna's ex-army friend, Rosamund Dowling, one of the few who braved the difficult conditions – elements and work ethic – when East Point was taking shape. Not that Rosamund was especially practical, she had no idea how the tent should go up for instance. Edna wasn't too sure either, so the first attempt was 'interesting'. The tent probably became a good standby when extra friends came to stay. For they did come to stay, once the roof was on and the major work done. It was a good getaway, as long as you enjoyed being *very* close to Nature.

Years later, Edna wrote about her experiences of building East Point in a memoir entitled *The Happiest Days Of My Life*: a significant title, given that those days were spent far away from Bickleigh Vale. She hoped to publish the short memoir as a book with photographs, but this didn't eventuate. The memoir is a charming and somewhat romanticised account of what must have been extremely hard work as well as happy days. Reading between the lines it appears that Joan Niewand was still very much the assistant at this holiday home, happy yet still undertaking many of the duties that she was responsible for at Sonning. For instance, Edna's memoir indicates that Joan (who had the rather odd nickname of 'Twid') was the chief cook:

> The simple fare that Twid dished up was always delectable and satisfying, and at times surprising! I noticed with interest, that the most fastidious of visitors ate up with relish what she put before them!! Of course there was always a special serving for Skipper [Edna's dog]. What I greatly appreciated was the fact that I was never expected to go into Lorne or Airey's Inlet merely to shop for food. If food was not mentioned when we went in for urgently required building material, well it was just too bad. Twid's inventive mind came into play and she would concoct something with which one would be not only satisfied, but enthusiastic!

Edna did the washing-up. She also brought Joan the occasional breakfast in bed. Edna's photographs of Joan at this time show a happy young woman, clearly enjoying life. Edna and Joan had a special kind of loving friendship. One that rose above the in-built hierarchy of boss and assistant. Joan was in her early twenties while Edna was in her early fifties, so perhaps the age difference helped rather than hindered their ability to get on. Joan worked terribly hard, but she wouldn't have persisted if it hadn't been fun. Working with Edna wasn't a job, it was an exhilarating, fascinating and often exhausting 'experience'.

There was time to play, time to rest, time for simple pleasures:

> On wet days we could lie in bed and watch the antics of the tree creepers on the ironbarks and the frolics of the wrens and the grey

> mountain thrush. How we adored that bird! And I'm reminded of the little ringtailed possum that had taken up his quarters on a cross beam that was left exposed in the doorway to the kitchen.

Friends recognised the philosophy that lay behind the building of East Point, but neighbours could be less sensitive:

> We always felt the great charm of our view was enhanced by seeing it through the trees and we almost fell out with our neighbour because he never came up without trying to persuade us to "cut down those trees that are spoiling the view". We only had to walk along a little track to get a more extensive view if we wanted it.

The neighbour in question was Mr. G.F. Smith (Lieut. Col. retired). He had distinguished himself during the war, but had found it difficult to resume life as a banking inspector. He'd taken his wife and four children down the coast to live, and had built the family home on the lower region of Big Hill. The Smith house was an inventive creation, with bits added as the children grew. Edna was on good terms with the Smiths and popped down to visit them quite often. Their argument about the trees versus the sea-view was an ongoing discussion rather than a full-on dispute, or at least this is how Alistair Smith remembers it.

Alistair Smith was the second eldest son, a teenager who was quietly fascinated by Edna's ideas. He liked Edna, and used to walk up the hill to see her. Sometimes he'd hear lovely music wafting through the trees. He'd ask Edna what it was and she'd tell him Mozart or Beethoven or some other favourite – which is how he came to discover the joys of classical music. Alistair was interested in carpentry and Edna suddenly decided that it would be great fun if he helped her build the little add-on kitchen next to the bedroom. He was daunted by the rag-bag pile of building material he was to work with, and amazed at how well it all turned out. Edna and Alistair began to have deep and meaningful talks. He was discontented and didn't know what to 'do' with his life. Edna suggested he pack a bag and head north to Queensland and have adventures. She thought he needed to get away from his parents and go off and explore. He took her advice, and believes that it was the best thing he could have done. He returned to Big Hill after many interesting experiences and set about creating a new type of café with his two brothers. The café was called The Arab and became famous for its unique bohemian style and its real espresso coffee. It opened in Lorne in 1956 and was an immediate success.

Holidays at East Point could only last so long. There was 'real' work waiting at Sonning. Design jobs were pending, the Sonning garden required maintaining, and Edna's knowledge of native plants needed extending. Her passion for the Australian countryside had gradually led her to an astonishing revelation: Australian gardens should be characterised by Australian plants.

Edna had always been open to using at least some native plants in her designs – if the architecture was appropriate. The significant shift in her thinking concerned her appreciation of exotics. She was so imbued with the Australian landscape that exotic plants were beginning to look out of place. She told her *Home Beautiful* readers in 1945 that she regretted her youthful exuberance for putting:

> . . . Birches and Poplars in places where Gums and [Australian] Cypress Pines would have been much more congruous and beautiful. Now as I go tottering down the hill I see in Lombardy Poplars and all their suckering tribe only pitiless reminders of my own past miss-deeds!

There had been minimal research into Australian plants so there were few publications to help Edna expand her knowledge. It was a wonderful excuse to mount her own exploratory expeditions. She'd take the 'scenic route' to country jobs, and make special trips to places like the Grampians and Mount Kosciusko. She'd gather specimens of unknown plants for later identification, she'd take photographs, make notes, and enjoy herself. Study of this kind wasn't work, it was pure pleasure.

One or two friends would join her on these excursions, but her most frequent companion was her assistant. Joan Niewand was part of the 'we' when Edna told her *Home Beautiful* readers about her first trip to the Grampians:

> January, 1947
>
> *Dear Gardeners,*
>
> We've just returned from the Grampians and how could I write of anything else! I don't mind admitting that when we came upon the wildflower garden on top of that mountain . . . tears rolled down . . .
>
> Wandering up and up the mountainside you begin to wonder where the wildflowers are, not that you're not enjoying the little familiar violets and innumerable other plants that brighten the climb, but you know it is going to be something to take your breath away, and that every step is bringing you nearer and nearer. Suddenly we see a baeckia [heath-myrtle] and then more and more of them, and we think we are there, but go on wandering along the track of washed sand which is so lovely to walk upon, and skirting a mass of sandstone boulders we come face to face with thousands of baeckias and the shell-pink boronia. I just sat down and gazed and gazed. To have seen anything so exquisitely

> beautiful before one dies seemed to be all that mattered! I shall never forget that soft pink cloud of flowers amongst the lichen-patterned, rosy-hued sandstone.
>
> How friendly those rocks are, how unaustere. That's what I loved about the Grampians . . . On and on we wandered, threading our way through a veritable sea of baeckia and boronia that covers the plateau at the top of this mountain. I didn't know it was going to be like this. I didn't know this glorious garden would be on top of the world. It's so remote, and you are so glad, for somehow you feel it's safer up there! It was a dull day, mountain mists drifted over us, and though we wanted photographs (had we not come to the Grampians especially for pictures?) it didn't matter, we were so terribly lucky to be there.

She was careful to give the correct botanical name for the plants she'd seen, yet she didn't want her readers to feel she was assuming the status of expert:

> I know so little about native plants that one has to be most cautious when writing about them, but I never want to become a fanatic as regards Australian plants, and shall never attempt anything beyond a knowledge of those I really love.

Even so, the number of plants she *really loved* kept increasing – as did her desire to learn more. Her enthusiasm was infectious. Expert botanists like Thistle Harris (whose name Edna relished) became friends, and even collaborators. Edna was so excited when Thistle Harris's *Wild Flowers of Australia* came out in 1938 that she drove to Sydney just to meet her. The meeting must have gone well for Thistle included some of Edna's garden plans in her next book.

Revered gentlemen would write kindly letters in answer to Edna's scrawled questions. Some would even visit Sonning and assist with plant identification and nursery experiments. One such helper was Mr. Percival St. John, a modest gentleman with an encyclopaedic memory.

Percival St. John (1872–1944) was a botanist who had worked at Melbourne's Botanic Gardens for fifty-four years. He was also the leading authority on all matters relating to the eucalypt. Edna was fond of Percival St. John, and an avid supporter of his work. She stated publicly and bluntly that it had been an everlasting loss that Mr. St. John had not been chosen as the Director to succeed Guilfoyle.

St. John was in very poor health by 1944, but he was still eager to pass on information regarding native trees. He was also keen to congratulate Edna for her courageously outspoken article in the *Herald*. The article was called 'Mutilated Landscapes' and criticised landscaping decisions that had altered aspects of the Botanic Gardens and the Shrine of Remembrance. St. John's letter of congratulation was written with difficulty – he died a couple of weeks later – yet his especial blend of support and knowledge clearly shines through:

> 14a Naples Rd.
> Mentone
> July 27th 1944
>
> Dear Miss Walling
>
> What a pity that my condition prevents a visit to Sonning so that I may help you for a month, may be able to do so yet, one never knows.
>
> I saw the article 'Mutilated Landscapes' and congratulations to you, although you let them down lightly, I lectured on that spot, in much harder terms . . .
>
> In the spare moments, when feeling better, I made a list of Native (Vict.) Trees. Would you believe that we have at least 70 species fit for any garden, plantation or avenue . . .

> Will show you a journal on Forestry . . . They [in West Australia] have exported Sandalwood to China etc. valued at [over four million pounds]. They are producing an oil distilled from Sandalwood, far superior to that produced in Mysore, there is a rapidly increasing demand for the W. Aust. product. This species is difficult to regenerate, it is a parasite.
>
> With my best wishes and congratulations
> Your sincere friend
> P. R. H. St. John

Edna would have been extremely sad when Percival St. John died. He was a good friend.

Edna's enthusiasm for native plants did not mean that she suddenly started creating all-native gardens. One of the drawbacks to creating all-native gardens was that only a limited range of native plants had been cultivated to thrive in garden conditions. Nursery owners were slow to develop a reliable range of Australian plants because so few customers were interested in buying them – and those who did were often disappointed because the common and wrong assumption was that native plants would look after themselves. It was a self-perpetuating cycle: customers didn't buy them so nursery owners didn't develop them so customers didn't buy them. This situation only began to change in the post-war period when a handful of specialist native-plant nurseries came into being. Edna's growing interest in designing native gardens coincided with the increasing availability and range of healthy nursery plants. Once she had the wherewithal to make native gardens she began to encourage people to have native gardens.

Times were changing and technologies improving yet having a new Edna Walling garden was still an intense process for all concerned.

Planning a garden was like shaping and reshaping a huge sculpture. A sculpture that had to please both the artist and the patron. A sculpture that would one day require a small troupe of workers with a clear set of instructions so they could bring the imagined shape into being. A process that became unpredictable as soon as work began. There could be all manner of surprises hidden beneath the surface: a layer of rock for instance. A topographical problem needing a clever solution, aesthetically as well as economically – and quickly – for often as not, there would be a band of workers waiting for orders.

These intense situations were not assisted by Edna's own unpredictability. One client, Margaret Carnegie, remembered a difficult couple of days when her new garden almost didn't get made. Edna had completed her preliminary visits to the Carnegie homestead in Holbrook, New South Wales. She'd drawn the plans, received the go-ahead, marked the layout of specific features including the extensive ha-ha and the low stone walls; indeed all preparations were concluded. Margaret Carnegie recalled that there were two gangs of workmen, ready and waiting on the morning that work was to begin; and that her husband, Douglas Carnegie, was in overall command:

> Douglas, a Rat of Tobruk just out of the army, had planned it all like a military operation. Mr. Hammond and his men had arrived from Melbourne, the bulldozers were waiting to sculpt the earth under Edna's direction, while our men, with loads of huge boulders and rocks which they had brought down from the hills on a makeshift sleigh, were standing at the ready, when a telegram arrived from Edna: "Sorry, arriving a day later."

Douglas Carnegie was furious and insisted that his timetable proceed as stipulated. Edna was equally furious when she arrived next morning to see that Carnegie had not only taken the role of military commander but also started the earth-moving without her. She was deeply affronted. From her point of view the creation of a garden was the absolute opposite of a military operation – it was art, and she was the artist. She quipped most pointedly that the ballet does not begin without the prima ballerina. That the curtain does not go up until said ballerina is in position. The Rat of Tobruk was not about to relinquish command to a 'mere ballerina' and the two looked set to clash. There was even a possibility that the ballerina would walk off the stage. Then Margaret Carnegie had the presence of mind to calm the moment by offering Edna a mid-morning sherry. It must have been a powerful drop because the ballerina and the commander got on famously from then on!

The Carnegie garden was a big job, especially given that it was in New South Wales. Edna had both Eric Hammond *and* Ellis Stones as team-leader stonemasons working on the low stone walls and ha-ha, setting the standard and providing the training for the local workmen to follow. Ellis Stones stayed on for the next three months to oversee the completion, which gives an idea of how much stonework there was to be done. The Carnegies had wanted a predominantly native garden and Edna was delighted to oblige. The year was 1948 and so Edna was able to order the plants she wanted from the newly established native-plant specialists: Dulcie and Bernhardt Schubert. Mr. Schubert duly arrived from Victoria with a truckload of native trees and shrubs and proceeded to plant them according to Edna's plan. Edna would have been especially interested in Schubert's planting technique for he had developed a unique method involving sawdust rather than soil. Ellis Stones would have been a keen observer also. He was developing his own landscape business by this time, and was eager to use native plants in his designs.

True to form, Edna's parting comment to Margaret Carnegie was: 'Never water. If you do you will have to continue'. The Carnegies followed the instructions and didn't water, but over the next three years they found they were losing an increasing number of native shrubs so they changed their tactics and began a watering regime. This stopped the losses – but started an ongoing commitment.

Practical difficulties aside, the Carnegie garden matured into a magnificent example of graceful harmony – uniting homestead, garden and surrounding paddocks.

The post-war atmosphere brought Edna fresh commissions. These were mainly in Victoria but there were also trips into South Australia, New South Wales and even Queensland. Most of the time she travelled by car but very occasionally she went by aeroplane. Air travel was still unusual so it was a thrilling experience to be so high above the landscape. She perceived the view as looking rather like a vast painted plan: roof-top and tree-top, paddock and mountain range, and the wriggling line of a waterway following the contour of the land.

Arrival at some of these country properties was not always as exhilarating as Edna had hoped. The bulldozer and the chainsaw were now affordable, transportable beasts. Excellent tools in the right hands, horribly destructive in the wrong. Some country clients liked to clear their land in anticipation of Edna's arrival. They'd leave her with a 'nice flat surface' to work on, devoid of undulations, vegetation, top-soil and rocks. Edna could plead for a native area if she arrived in time, but her pleading wouldn't necessarily be successful.

Consultation was an important element of her job. She worked hard to please her client *and* to create the design she felt would be best for the plot. One country property had a badly eroded front paddock and Edna suggested that the area should be dammed back and made into a lake to solve the problem. It was a very bold idea, especially as it meant that the front driveway would have to be relocated. Yet the client agreed and the end result was superb. But not all clients saw things her way. Consultation was an intricate dance of negotiation, a cordial series of movements towards aesthetic and economic agreement. Consultation included an element of compromise, but only to a point. There came a time when Edna could afford to turn down a commission if the compromise was too great.

Edna made fond friendships with many of her clients but there were a few that she couldn't abide. We get an inkling as to her private thoughts regarding such clients by dipping into a letter she wrote to her sister. The letter concerns the Nicholas family along with an incidental connection with the pianist Hephzibah Menuhin. The letter was undated but was probably written in the 1950s because she refers to Hephzibah Menuhin's recent concert tour. Hephzibah had once been married to Lindsay Nicholas, son of George Nicholas, who'd made his wealth from 'Aspro'. Hephzibah married Lindsay when she was eighteen and moved from California to live on Lindsay's remote sheep station in the Western District of Victoria. Edna's letter recalled the scandal when Hephzibah left Lindsay for another man. Polite society had been in an uproar, but Edna had felt sympathetic. She knew the Nicholas family, and understood *why* Hephzibah needed to escape:

> Only one who knew those crashingly boring people as I did, who worked for them from time to time [during the 1920s and 1930s] could understand how she could not possibly survive going on living there and with young [Lindsay] Nicholas. Funny that I should have struck his brother up here [near Mooroolbark] – pleasant enough but hopelessly dull. They had a piece of land that was – well arid is the only word for it BUT the wild flowers loved it and were springing up in abundance 'Gosh! <u>aren't</u> <u>you</u> <u>lucky</u>!!' I almost screamed when I saw it:- I wish you could have seen his wife's expression who was not only brainless but bad tempered. I'm sure she would have liked to have said 'Are you mad??' – Anyway, my vision of a most interesting wild flower garden wasn't their cup of tea so I collected my initial fee and departed in peace,

> thankful to get away from that soul crushing atmosphere. I drove off remembering the days when I couldn't afford to be so uppish and gleefully increased my speed.

A clash of taste or a sense of incompatibility would have cut both ways of course. Few would have called Edna a soul-crushing bore, but she was hardly an angel. Her enthusiastic forcefulness wouldn't have suited everybody. Even her most devoted clients, those who commissioned her services each time they moved house, knew that a certain amount of inner fortitude was required when she arrived.

The 1950s saw further developments in Bickleigh Vale village. Some of the original cottages changed hands, others had extensions added, and a small number of new cottages were built – all under Edna's guidance. Some of the villagers were not necessarily owners but renters. Rosamund Dowling, Edna's ex-army pal, was probably one of these, though she may not have paid rent as such. Edna was pleased to let friends occupy dwellings such as The Cabin, and Rosamund stayed in one or other of the cottages over a period of seven or so years.[*] Cliff Bottomley, a friend and professional photographer, purchased his plot in the mid-1940s and lived in the village for decades. He tried

* Edna's relationship with Rosamund Dowling seems mysterious. The Electoral Register gives Rosamund Dowling's permanent address as Sonning from 1945 to 1949, and as Lyndon Lee [sic] c 1952. She also had an address in Toorak and ran her own electrologist (hair removal) salon in the city. Dowling was a 'problematic' friend. Edna once compared her to the disturbing good/evil Rachel in Daphne du Maurier's *My Cousin Rachel.* Edna compiled a portrait album of her friends and Dowling's photograph is unique in the collection in that it is strangely abstracted. She is out of focus and ghost-like, seemingly Edna's comment on her character.

to persuade Edna to lift her covenant at some stage. He thought it was too restrictive and would reduce the value of his property – but of course Edna didn't agree. Lorna Fielden decided to sell half her block of land, the half that included Lynton Lee. The overall size of the place seems to have been the reason, though decreasing funds may have been a factor. The garden was very large to maintain, and she had never asked for the extra attic bedroom that Edna had been so pleased to give her (Lorna felt that an extra bedroom encouraged extra guests). Lorna moved into Winter Sweet, a tiny dwelling that was built on the remaining half of her land. Edna designed Winter Sweet and created an all-native garden to go with it, the first of its kind in the village.

Edna, meanwhile, was beginning to see Sonning's garden with different eyes. The sight of so many exotic plants was not as appealing, and the garden as a whole was demanding to maintain. Another disturbing feature was that her home was attracting a number of uninvited visitors. Her books had made her increasingly popular, indeed *Gardens in Australia* went into its fourth reprint in 1948. Her journalism, speaking engagements, occasional radio broadcasts, all served to keep her in the public eye. She received fan letters from all over Australia, and even from overseas. Edna enjoyed such letters and answered them personally, but she did not enjoy it when enthusiasts came calling. The sign on Sonning's gate said 'No Admittance Except By Appointment' but the curious were undeterred. Skipper (her 'bitsa' watchdog-with-attitude) would mount a loud challenge which gave Edna time to rush to a bolt-hole or hide behind a tree, but this was hardly ideal!

These difficulties may have caused Edna to think about moving from Sonning, but it was Joan Niewand's departure that really gave her the push. Joan decided to leave Edna's employ, which meant that she vacated The Barn which meant that Edna had another place to live. It also meant that Edna lost a remarkable off-sider.

Joan decided to move on in about 1951, probably because she intended to marry. Edna would have been very sad to see Joan go, yet delighted to see her happy. Joan probably had mixed emotions too, for her affection for Edna ran deep at this time. Edna rarely kept personal letters, but she did keep one particular letter from Joan. In fact she carried it in her wallet for so many years that part of it wore away. The letter was written during the Christmas holiday of 1949, when Joan was at her parents' home in north-west Victoria. Joan wrote a delightful, uncomplicated account of country life, from the foibles of various relations to the absurdities of the Christmas Concert. The tone of the letter displays a fresh innocence, typical of its time and place. It also shows signs of deep affection, which is surely why Edna kept the letter so close. Joan's opening endearment was to: 'My most beloved one', and the closing carried all her love plus thirty-one kisses. It was not a 'love letter' by any means, but it was a loving letter, and Edna was clearly touched by it.

The loss of Joan's daily companionship left a gap in Edna's life. An uncomfortable, distressing gap. Joan had looked after Edna for five years. It would be difficult – in fact it proved impossible – to find a replacement.

So The Barn stood empty, and perhaps its emptiness started Edna thinking. The grounds were relatively easy to maintain (mostly native trees and grasses), the location was more private. It would need renovation and a new access road – changes that didn't come cheap – yet the move seemed to make sense. Edna took the plunge and subdivided the Sonning plot. The north-easterly strip, the part that included The Cabin, was separated from Sonning by a sensitively drawn surveyor's line and sold off.

Renovations to The Barn went ahead. Edna's living, sleeping and working areas were on the ground floor, her bolt-hole cum darkroom was in an outbuilding. The central drive-through, originally an open access for horse and car, was enclosed at both ends with large concertina-type glass doors – closed in winter, open in summer. The unusually low eaves caused problems of height in the side-room extensions, but only for tall people! The loft was given an outside stairway, landing, and stable door. Edna built the new brick chimney herself, timing her descent from the ladder to coincide with the music playing on the wind-up gramophone – Tchaikovsky's Fifth suited the task best. The final touch was to paint The Barn the palest shade of pink, the same colour as East Point. Edna recommend this warm off-white colour as most suitable for Australian country cottages:

> With pink houses the bronze-green foliage of pear trees and the grey-green of gum trees can be very lovely, but the pink must be *very* pale.

The pink was very pale, and the whole effect nicely appealing. Edna moved into The Barn during 1951 and Sonning was sold thereafter. The Barn – or 'Good-a-Meavy' to give the place its rarely used but official name – would be Edna's home for the next sixteen years.

Selling Sonning, and then living near the new Sonning owner, must have been difficult. Yet clearly it had to be done. Edna needed to make life easier for herself, practically and financially. Yet profit was never her motivation. She'd only sell to a like-minded buyer. Such people usually had less money than the 'wrong-minded' type.

Subdivision was a sign of the times. Substantial gardens, some of them Edna Walling gardens, were being halved and built over in the suburbs; and the suburbs, old and new, were expanding. Edna couldn't stop the march of progress but she did protect the integrity of her village. Subdivision lines were dictated by the lay of the land, not by strictly measured blocks; and the protection of her covenant still held good. In any case, people who lived at Bickleigh Vale wanted to retain its beauty. That's why they'd chosen to live there.

The march of progress brought improved modern conveniences: machines that cleaned or froze or cooked or mowed. The Victa Rotomo could clear the 'jungle growth' from your new block of land in half a day, then keep your new lawns 'velvet smooth' thereafter. Australia's own Holden could transport you through the increasingly car-friendly city and take you further and faster along the new highway for your country picnic or camping holiday. Everything was speeding up, and the blind force of it all deeply concerned Edna. Issues of ecology and conservation were always on her mind as she travelled the countryside, and the changing look of the actual roads she was travelling were a particular concern.

Charming country roads were being replaced by wider, straighter, more efficient roadways. Indigenous trees, shrubs, and seed-rich topsoil was being destroyed and replaced with standardised highway planting. Edna was not regressive; she knew that roads had to be improved and new highways built. It was the manner in which this was being done that was the worry. She wanted Australian roads to reflect the native flora of the area – to reflect the local ecology. She wanted the journey to be interesting and attractive as well as safe and efficient. She wanted to warn against the American and German superhighway models that were straight, fast and deadly boring. And she wanted to share the enjoyment and knowledge that she'd gathered over many years of travelling and exploring the south-eastern states. All these wants found their home in her fourth book: *The Australian Roadside*, published in 1952 by Oxford University Press.

> Those of us who love Australia so often seem to love the least spectacular thing about it; the old Stringybarks and Messmates, and the Tea-trees, with their small and invariably white or pale pink flowers. We smile with the utmost pleasure at the sight of

> a gnarled old Red Gum, exclaiming 'What a perfect specimen!' though it leans almost to the ground and has a huge crown that is no perfect dome, worn at the craziest angle!
>
> Could anything be more inspiring than the towering Mountain Ash, Spotted Gums, Sydney Blue Gums and Mountain Grey Gums, or more interesting than their distinguishing barks and their odd little seed cases?

Edna's text and black and white photographs were an ode to the great and small wonders of the Australian landscape. Her words and camera captured a vanishing Australia. A rugged, majestic, old and bold Australia. It evoked the smell of gum leaves, the feel of paperbark, the sound of kookaburras; and way off, in the far distance, the rumble and trundle of bulldozers.

Edna's book captured an Australian countryside essence. It explained how this essence could be respected and protected as well as enjoyed and utilised. She was critical of contemporary highway-making practices yet positive (and to a small degree prophetic) about the practices of the future:

> In the highway of the future the two tracks will be separated sufficiently to allow their maximum adaptation to the natural topography. That is to say they will neither be one broad road permitting two traffic lanes, nor will they be side by side with an artificial centre strip for planting, but two separate and distinct one-way roads divided by a piece of natural country varying in width according to the topography. This has been called the 'fitted highway' . . .
>
> [W]e have all been witness to an appalling amount of unnecessary destruction of natural beauty, and the pitiful sight of torn-up plants and churned-up top soil in the vicinity of new highways.

> It is plain that someone responsible for the protection of the roadside refinements, the trees, the flowers, the mosses, rocks and grasses should be on the scene at the very outset; working with surveyors, setting out that which is to be protected and that which is to be transplanted to places where the grade has been lowered or raised. Future road-makers will display their intelligence and experience in such a manner that there will be a minimum of destruction.
>
> Men show their greatness more by circumnavigating flowers and mosses than they do by sailing over them with bulldozers . . . It is the landscaper's job to conserve and to re-create the natural scene. This requires, before all else, a thorough knowledge of native plants, and a taste for Nature's informal way of doing things, as against man's assertive formalism.

Edna's book was not as popular as her earlier works, but it proved to be an important and enduring publication as time went on and views gradually changed. It would be many decades before ecologically driven ideas found formal support in Australia, and longer still before the words 'conservation' and 'ecology' were upon the lips of 'intelligent road-makers'.

Edna dedicated *The Australian Roadside* to her nephew, David Oak-Rhind, the RAAF pilot who had died during the war. And she acknowledged Joan Niewand's sterling assistance:

> To Joan Niewand I owe my admiration and thanks for collecting the specimens; two of each are collected, a numbered tag is attached; they are pressed and brought home, and one set sent to the herbarium. She kept the record of my photographs and spent hours in the dark room making pictures from the negatives, typed the script (a task that can be infuriating with some writers) and made interminable cups of tea.

Edna also thanked Lorna Fielden for her 'checking of the script and captions'. Such acknowledgements are another reminder that Edna could not have achieved all that she did without good support.

Edna had at least one other book on the go at this time, one that the botanist and author Jean Galbraith helped her compile. Jean Galbraith was yet another expert that Edna had befriended through her researches. The new book was called *Flowers by the Wayside* and followed Edna's search for wild flowers along coastal roads and mountain tracks throughout the south-eastern states. It was another lovely book but unfortunately she couldn't find a publisher. Letters of rejection were a new experience for Edna, one that she would have to get used to. She compiled several books during the following years, some with Jean Galbraith and the illustrator Moira Pye, some with the help of other friends, and some all on her own (with the eternal help of Lorna) – and all were rejected by various publishers. Perhaps her writing style was becoming dated, and surely her topic, as far as ecology and conservation was concerned, was ahead of its time.

Book publishers may not have been willing, but newspapers and journals were happy to publish the occasional article on native plants. One such journal was *Walkabout*, and it's interesting to note that one of her 1953 contributions was focused on the trees to be found in southern Queensland. Queensland, or more specifically the coastal area just north of Brisbane, had captured Edna's imagination.

Various impulses had prompted Edna to travel north. She was very keen to extend her knowledge of indigenous species, she had a couple of commissions there, and her niece was now living in southern Queensland. Barbara had married C.E. Barnes and moved to Canning Downs, his property near Warwick. A trip to Warwick to visit Barbara and family in about 1950 whetted Edna's appetite for further exploration.

Edna fell in love with Queensland. Or at least she fell in love with the area known as the Sunshine Coast. She discovered Buderim, a sleepy township on Buderim Mountain. Lookout points from Buderim offered stunning views of mountain ranges, sub-tropical forests, clear-water rivers, long white beaches and far-off islands. She could see the Glass House Mountains to the south, the Blackall Range to the west, the expanse of the South Pacific Ocean to the east, and the white sandy beaches of Mooloolaba and Maroochydore below – and hardly any of it spoilt by development. The landscape, the vegetation, the wild-life, the insects, the seed pods – it was all extraordinary and fascinating.

The Sunshine Coast won Edna's heart. As early as 1954 she was asking an acquaintance at the University of Brisbane to send her a list of recommended nurseries, *and* to look out for places where she might settle. The acquaintance was pessimistic about the latter: 'Mostly these days it's a matter of take what you can get'. The observation proved correct. Edna's search for a suitable place (one that she liked and could afford) took a very long time.

It's difficult to know how serious Edna really was about moving to Queensland so early in the 1950s. Did she really want to leave The Barn and East Point so soon after making them her home? Did she really want to leave her circle of friends, her centre of employment, her village? It took many years of thinking and vacillating, but she did make the move eventually, so the idea wasn't a passing fancy.

Edna's new-found passion for Queensland may have had something to do with her disenchantment with suburban developments around Melbourne and especially Mooroolbark. Bickleigh Vale was becoming more beautiful by the year but the landscape around it was turning very ugly. One of the most heartbreaking sights that greeted Edna each time she drove home from a long trip away was the number of roadside trees that had been cut down during her absence. Indigenous trees, ancient and young, would have been cleared in the name of road-widening or developing. It was depressing to see such destruction, such *unintelligent* planning.

Yet how wonderful it must have been to turn off the main road and turn into the leafy oasis of Bickleigh Vale village. To drive along the gently curving lane, to catch glimpses of the various cottages nestled amongst the green on green. To arrive at The Barn, to be greeted by the dog and cat, to unload the Holden, to make a cup of tea, to ease into an armchair, to observe the signs of welcome left by Lorna: the newly-picked violets in the pottery vase, the loaf of bread, the jug of milk. To know that her pets had been looked after, and that a hot meal would be waiting in Lorna's little cottage when she was ready to pop down . . .

No wonder Edna kept changing her mind about moving to Queensland. Who would protect the best interests of Bickleigh Vale and East Point? What if she didn't cope with the climate or couldn't find any like-minded friends? What if she couldn't persuade Lorna to move to Queensland with her? There were so many uncertainties. How was she to find her way?

Interlude: a dog's tale

Edna and her assistant were on their way to a job in New South Wales. It was pouring with rain and getting dark and they were desperately looking for somewhere to camp for the night. They entered a little township called Adelong and spotted an old blacksmith's shed that had a simple lean-to veranda. It was better than nothing so Edna swung the Holden alongside.

They pulled their swags out of the van and only then did they notice that the shelter had an occupant. Curled up in the corner was a dog, a black and white middle-sized long-haired dog, with floppy ears and a stumpy tail. He looked forlorn and did no more than flutter his short tail in half-hearted acknowledgement.

It was a chilly night, and by the early hours Edna was so cold that she went to the van for an extra rug. She thought the dog looked cold too, so she found a cover for him as well. His tail waved a little 'thank you', and they settled down again to sleep. The rising sun brought a fine warm day and the three enjoyed breakfast together. The dog was enthusiastic and gentle, and not nearly as sad-looking as he'd been the night before.

The owner of the old smithy wandered across from the main house to greet his visitors. Edna assumed that the dog belonged to the household but not so. He'd appeared a few days earlier, maybe left behind by people passing through. It was a shame, he was a nice dog, but what was one to do?

They thanked the man for the lend of his lean-to and packed their gear into the Holden. Edna climbed into the driving seat and the dog jumped in beside her. She hesitated: she liked the dog and wondered about keeping him. She didn't have a dog of her own any more. Skipper, her aggressively loyal watchdog, was no more. He'd been overzealous with his protective behaviour and bitten a child – a misdemeanour for which he could be forgiven but not excused. Edna had been forced to ask a friend to put a bullet through his head. The whole affair had been ghastly. Another dog was out of the question. Besides, she had an ancient cat that couldn't possibly deal with a new dog in the house. She pushed her four-legged friend out of the van and slammed the door.

He ran beside the van as she drove off, and tried to keep up as she accelerated. She could see him in the rear-view mirror. A dot in the road getting smaller and smaller.

The image caused an ache in her heart for the whole day. She finally decided to send a telegram: 'To the Blacksmith, Adelong. Please feed stray dog until our return in ten days. Writing.' She sent money for food, and then another telegram to say that their return would be delayed by three days. When they eventually drove back into Adelong they wondered if the dog would still be there. Yet there he was, sitting by the blacksmith's gate, ready and waiting and wagging his stumpy tail. He even answered to his new name: Tony.

Tony went home with Edna and was given a memorable welcome by the old cat: the dog bounded up, the cat scratched his nose, the dog knew his place.

Tony proved to be a good friend, and a hopeless watchdog – watching, greeting, and never barking. But Edna had no regrets. Tony was heaven sent, and that was that.

Self-portrait with the Rolleiflex

CHAPTER 11

Shifting ground

Edna's prime position as landscape designer extraordinaire was gradually overshadowed during the 1960s. Connoisseurs still ranked her as a top talent, but there were many more landscape designers running the race. In fact there were so many calling themselves landscape designers that the 'properly' qualified amongst them began to push for a regulated institute – later called the Australian Institute of Landscape Architects (AILA). Edna was invited to join this group when it was in its infancy, but she declined. She joked that she'd 'be an anachronism in *any* institute', but in truth she had no reason to join. She had no desire to attend their meetings and no need for the AILA tag of approval. She said she'd rather pay her dues by working on her new book *Architecture in the Garden*, in other words: something really *useful*.

Interestingly, Ellis Stones and Eric Hammond did join the institute, though as affiliates. Full membership of the AILA was only for those with formal qualifications.

Formal qualifications never impressed Edna. Either you had the magic touch or you didn't. She could detect natural ability a mile off, and when she saw it she encouraged it. Some of her student–assistants developed careers in landscape design or horticulture, and she influenced a great many to 'find themselves' over the decades. Ellis Stones is the prime example, but there were many young women and not a few young men whose lives and careers were influenced by Edna. Ironically, it was the males rather than the females who went on to establish long-term careers. Marriage often interrupted career progress for women – it certainly stole away two of Edna's best assistants – and there was always the added challenge of gender inequality: less pay, less opportunity. There are shining exceptions, notably Beryl Mann, but most of the outstanding success stories belong to the men that Edna encouraged.

Men such as David Higgins, Glen Wilson, Rodger Elliot and Gordon Ford. Young men who were taught or influenced by Edna and who went on to establish impressive careers. There was a clear line of mentorship: Edna provided the initial inspiration and Hammond or Stones provided the all-important on-going employment. Formal qualifications had very little to do with it.

Edna was full of dreams and schemes, not only about where she might settle, but also about future projects: her next book, her next travel adventure, her next action in the ongoing campaign to protect Nature from the next man-made onslaught. Acts of conservation were increasingly important to her now.

She had become a conservation warrior, an ardently outspoken defender of the Australian natural landscape. She wrote to newspapers, councils, politicians, organisations. She spoke to anyone who would listen. She didn't simply complain, she also suggested alternatives. She submitted an alternative plan to the proposed car park and restaurant to be built on Mount Dandenong for instance.

Her blueprint included an elegant viewing terrace, walking paths and a one-way tourist road. She said the point was to enjoy the mountain, not to drive up a main road and stare at the city from a car park. She made many loud protests concerning many issues: to save trees, to save wildlife, to save environments, to protect, protect, protect.

There were also clandestine activities. Edna would 'adjust' certain impurities in the ecology of an area by weeding out saplings that didn't belong. She would even go off on midnight raids if she knew of a new piece of misguided roadside planting that needed attention. She'd have a torch, a spade, and a box of seedlings, and she'd pull out the offending articles and replace them with something much more sensible.

Close friends were sometimes pressed into 'active service' and one of these was Esmé Wilson (née Johnston), the broadcaster and journalist Edna had known since the 1930s. Esmé had remarried and now lived near enough to go off on Edna-adventures at short notice. One particular jaunt took Esmé and Edna on a moonlit ride to Mount Dandenong to investigate what was planned for the site – and perhaps to do some 'unofficial replanting' on the way.

Popular opinion was generally against her, but Edna never tired of making her point. Only a small percentage of her letters made it to the press, but when they did get published they caused a flurry of response. She was accused of 'sentiment gone astray' over a tree-lopping issue, but the architect Robin Boyd came to her defence. He wrote a column in *Architecture* that not only supported her views but recognised her exceptional talent: 'Miss Edna Walling, perhaps the only landscape designer here, wrote a letter to *The Age* full of regret for the destruction of the great blue gums on the highway at Lorne, the once wonderful holiday resort on the south coast . . . the blind futility of the destruction of Lorne's trees is surely hard to beat.'

Robin Boyd wrote those words in 1952, a time when Edna probably *was* 'the only landscape designer here'. Some ten years later, 'here' was a very crowded place.

Edna was beginning to feel alien everywhere she went. Everything was changing so quickly – the city, the suburbs, the country, even the concept of outer space. Some of the changes were impressive, but many were disheartening. She was appalled by Australia's involvement in the war in Vietnam for instance, and sickened by the re-introduction of conscription. Edna didn't declare her politics, but it's likely that she was right of centre in her younger days and increasingly left of centre as she grew older. By the 1960s she was taking an interest in Aboriginal issues and the development of the new wave of feminism; and she was circumspect regarding the scaremongering associated with Communism. She strove to keep an open mind, though of course she had her prejudices and lapses. She loathed the idea of television for instance and was disdainful of its 'popular entertainment'.

Edna had never taken much notice of fads and fashions, but the popular culture of the 'swinging sixties' seemed particularly alien to her. Even familiar lifestyle magazines like *Home Beautiful* looked a world away from what she knew. The lack of comprehension worked both ways. Edna's writing style and her black and white photography did not suit the new-look glossy magazines. The new breed of editor found her distinctive individualism 'problematic' rather than charming. Even her extraordinary village scheme was seen as quaintly folksy – if indeed it was known of at all.

Edna was undaunted. She kept sending off articles and photographs and no amount of rejection would dissuade her from trying again. She was a compulsive creator, an obsessive writer. Sleep didn't come easily so she wrote through much of the night. One of her new projects was to write biographical sketches. Anecdotes about Melba, about the early days at Burnley, about her childhood in Devon. She sent one of these to *Woman's World*, along with a photograph of herself. The editor showed interest in the sketch but rejected her photograph as too unconventional.

The photograph in question shows Edna looking down at the

viewfinder as she holds the camera steady. She wears a linen shirt and a dark sleeveless jumper and the metallic parts of the camera catch the light. Her face shows calm concentration as she looks at the viewfinder. Her hands look strong and sturdy. The 'eyes' of the camera's double-lens seem to take the place of Edna's own eyes, for clearly she had no intention of looking up at the mirror when she was ready to click the shutter. It's an intriguing image, full of multi-layered reflection. One's attention is drawn to Edna's face, then to the point where she is looking, then to the camera's 'eyes', which hold your gaze. The overall effect is powerful and fascinating. It's also a rare glimpse of Edna in middle age. Edna with a thickening waist, unruly wavy hair streaked with silver-white, and deepening lines on her calm concentrated face. She must have liked the experiment for she repeated it periodically, at five- or ten-year intervals. Sometimes making eye contact with the mirror, sometimes almost smiling. A record of herself, taken by herself. A photographer in charge of her own image.

How did Edna come to take the self portrait? Was she bored with the paperwork in her office and tempted to play with the light and shade in the room? Her new (second-hand) double-lens Rolleiflex was her dream camera. It was the Rolls Royce of cameras, extremely expensive and superlative in every way. Its precision mechanism had to be explored, which is perhaps why Edna came to take a photograph of herself in front of a mirror. An unusual step for a person who resisted being photographed.

One imagines that she dusted off the long mirror before placing it just so. That she stood in front of it for some time, looking at her image in the viewfinder, adjusting and adjusting. That she pressed the shutter and wound the film at least a couple of times before the experiment was complete. That she was pleased with the one negative that came out well. A good unconventional, unorthodox self-portrait.

Edna showed but few signs of slowing her pace. She continued to design gardens, though she was more selective about what she'd take on. Irresistible projects were still undertaken, especially if they were in Queensland. Edna waxed lyrical about Buderim Mountain, but she was still undecided about whether to move there permanently. The decision would have been easier if she could have persuaded some of her friends to make the move too. Her photographer friend Ted Cranstone and his wife did make the move, but she had less luck convincing those who were closer to her heart. Lorna Fielden for instance. Lorna's main reason for resisting Edna's many and varied proposals was that the humidity would be too much for her. Lorna's devotion to Christian Science meant that she avoided direct mention of physical frailties, but advancing years must have been an issue. After all, she was in her late seventies. Edna, meanwhile, would reach her seventieth birthday in December 1965.

Once upon a time she produced elegant watercolour plans and did much of the building and planting with her own hands; now she tended to restrict her workload to consultancy. She did pencil sketches and as much as she could by phone and correspondence, recommending a chosen few to carry out the construction. She didn't have a permanent assistant, but Moira Pye, her illustrator friend and sometime collaborator on hoped-for books, generally went along for the ride.

Ellis Stones was the garden designer that Edna usually recommended when she didn't want the job herself – not that he always had time. His landscape design business was flourishing and he was a very busy man. He was the same age as Edna yet rapidly becoming the new 'top name'. Edna admired Stones's placement of boulders but she didn't like his overall design style – it lacked finesse – but that never stopped her from recommending him. Eric Hammond remained her contractor of choice, though he was a very busy man too. Hammond was expanding his business with his sons and working on a diverse range of projects, some of them of his own design.

Edna felt uneasy about Hammond's diversification. She'd worked with him for almost forty years. He knew all her methods, all her tricks. Was it fair if he reproduced her techniques when working with other designers? Edna didn't think so. Her techniques and ideas were her trademark, her bread and butter. She did not want to see them duplicated by all and sundry, especially if they were not truly understood, not thoughtfully interpreted. She felt compelled to write to Hammond and state her case:

> I feel sure that you will not misunderstand me when I ask you not to give too much away in your association with other landscape designers.
>
> Having been practically the sole contractor of my jobs during almost a lifetime of work you have been in a unique position, and I would not like our happy association to be marred by any feeling of resentment on my part for the sake of a mere word of appeal . . .
>
> It must always be remembered that ideas are one thing and their right application is another. You will, I know, also realise that discrimination in the matter of the recipients of these ideas, and experiences is rather important to me.

There were many more landscape designers than there used to be, but few with exceptional ability. Edna honestly felt that her talent was 'a gift from above', a precious God-given artistic gift. She did not want this very personal commodity compromised by misapplication or inferior reproduction. Edna wrote her letter to Hammond in 1959 and they continued to work together long after – so the problem must have blown over. It was not that Edna didn't want to share her ideas.

Sharing her gift was the reason for her God-given existence. Writing, speaking, demonstrating – it was all part of the process, but a process she wanted to be in control of.

One of the people that Edna was very keen to share her gift with was a young man called Brian McKeever. Brian McKeever lived at Bickleigh Vale for five years when he was a teenager in the 1950s. He didn't know Edna during this time but he was certainly influenced by the environment she'd created. He went on to become an architect. When the chance came to purchase Downderry (the cottage that Edna had built for her mother), Brian and his wife leapt at the opportunity. They moved into the cottage in the early 1960s and, finding it far too small, began planning an extension. It was Brian, rather than Edna, who worked on the architectural plan. Brian made sure that he kept faith with Edna's style, and took care that the splendid trees growing near the cottage would not be affected. The restrictions made it a difficult assignment, especially as he was designing the house for a growing family. He had a good rapport with Edna, but it was an anxious moment when he handed over his design. She looked at the plan for a long time, smiling, frowning, chuckling, and then finally said with a twinkle in her eye: 'What about the morning sun?' A few adjustments were made and the extension went ahead; and a fine extension it was too.

Brian and Edna had a special friendship. They'd meet quite regularly and settle down for a long talk about architecture, which inevitably led to associated topics such as philosophy and religion. These were generalised discussions rather than deeply personal exchanges. Personal questions were not part of the equation. Edna also developed a friendship with Brian's wife Jan, and with the much photographed baby Bridget. It was a happy association all round, and a providential one. Edna knew that Brian McKeever would be the perfect person to oversee architectural developments in the village – *if* she ever moved to Queensland.

Edna's health was reasonably good, though her legs wouldn't take her for long walks any more. She was still driving her Holden van, though not as confidently. Trips to her holiday place at East Point had become rare because she hated driving through the centre of the city, and a minor car accident in Queensland added to her sense of anxiety. Long trips without a co-driver were out of the question, which meant that journeys to Queensland had to wait until she could find someone to undertake the drive with her. Her old friend Blanche Marshall made one of these trips in 1964.

Driving with Blanche must have reminded her of the old days when she always had a friend-cum-offsider to rely on. Blanche had 'been there' for Edna and believed in her vision of a village in the 1920s. Indeed, The Barn had been built for Blanche and marked the first stage of the transformation. Blanche had remained a good friend over the years, though her commitment to family and pharmacy had inevitably reduced her involvement with Edna's doings. A long drive to Queensland may or may not have been Blanche's idea of fun, but she knew her old friend needed support, and so she gave it.

Edna was beginning to show signs of frustration at having to carry the full weight of all decisions on her own. Most of the time she was happy to be alone, but there were fleeting moments when she allowed herself to think otherwise. As she told her niece Barbara:

> Often I wish I were in double harness & pulling <u>with</u> someone [-] & then the inner voice says 'you be grateful you're not living with the wrong person – <u>that'd</u> drive you mad!'

These 'double harness' thoughts may have been inspired by a new friendship with two women who had a special living/working long-term partnership – the kind of partnership that Edna may have hoped for, if she'd ever found the 'right' person to share the load – and her life – with. The pair were the landscape architect Mervyn Davis (Mervyn being the Welsh name she was christened with), and her all-round partner Daphne Pearson. It was Mervyn Davis who'd tried to persuade Edna to join the Australian Institute of Landscape Architects, and indeed Mervyn had initiated the first push to get the institute started. Mervyn's pushiness had put Edna off, but then she met Daphne and her attitude changed. Daphne was delightful and Edna was enchanted.

Mervyn and Daphne were in their late forties when Edna came to know them. Daphne was English and the couple probably met in the mid-1950s when Mervyn went to Durham University to gain formal qualifications in landscape architecture. Daphne had a background in horticulture – and much more: she was a professional photographer, she knew how to fly a light plane, she'd worked at a number of interesting jobs – and she was a war hero. Daphne's moment of heroism occurred when she was a medical corporal at an RAF base. A plane crash-landed as Daphne was going home from her shift. She ran to the scene, dragged the injured pilot away from the burning plane and protected him from the blast when the plane exploded – she stayed with him even when he told her there was a full load of bombs on board. It was such a brave act that she was awarded the George Cross, becoming the first woman to receive the honour.

Edna thought Daphne was adorable and happily told Mervyn how lucky she was to have such a partner. She was eager to get to know Daphne and looked forward to the time when she could take her photographic portrait – making no mention of taking Mervyn's portrait! Mervyn and Daphne were able to tempt Edna to attend the occasional lecture in the city. Perhaps Edna enjoyed the sight of Daphne as much as she appreciated the lectures, for she told Mervyn after one occasion: 'I thought she looked so lovely last Saturday I couldn't take my eyes off her.' This was an honest and unabashed appreciation – with just a touch of envy. Daphne was probably flattered and clearly Mervyn wasn't threatened, for the three became good friends during the 1960s. Mervyn and Daphne would be invited to The Barn for 'a sherry and a sandwich', or Edna would go to their flat for a meal or a five o'clock drink.

Mervyn Davis proved to be a significant supporter of Edna's work. She had a special interest in the history of Australian landscape design and encouraged Edna to write about her work, and to describe some of her most outstanding gardens. It was through this interest that the three came to visit 'Mawarra', an exceptionally fine Edna Walling garden at Sherbrooke in the Dandenongs. Edna felt that 'Mawarra' was probably her finest achievement. She described it as a 'symphony in steps and beautiful trees' and predicted that it would 'weather into greater beauty as the years went on' – and indeed she was right.

Edna wrote a few pages about her gardens for Mervyn, but she was busy with other projects and the account remained incomplete. She did, however, give Mervyn a number of her original garden plans to study. It's unclear whether this was a loan or a gift, but it was a fortuitous act, for Mervyn took great care of them and eventually placed them with the State Library of Victoria. Perhaps Edna knew or hoped that Mervyn would put the plans to good *use*. After all, it was better than leaving them for the silverfish to nibble.

There was a certain amount of muddle and chaos accumulating in The Barn. There were possums in the attic, cobwebs in the coffee cups, and dusty piles of 'things' awaiting Edna's attention. Progress towards Buderim was frustratingly slow, yet Edna knew that she had to achieve some kind of move, even if it was only for the winter months. The draught that blew through The Barn brought a chill to her bones, even in summer; and the ugliness of Mooroolbark's housing developments brought a sadness to her soul.

There were times when Edna felt downhearted, days when she felt particularly grim. Yet she wouldn't allow herself to be despondent for long. She worked hard to see the positive, and she drew strength from her faith in God. Her faith, as with everything else in her life, was a self-devised construct. She was not a Christian Scientist, though she took what she needed from that religion, as indeed she took from all manner of spiritual, philosophical and even political thought. She created her own little book of supportive and spiritual sayings. Things she'd read or heard and particularly liked were carefully copied into the pages of an old diary. The majority of the quotes were from Christian Science publications or the Bible, yet there were many other sources including quotes from Goethe, Shaw, Wilde, and one particularly wry snippet from Gershwin: 'It aint necessarily so'. Edna filled at least three old diaries in this way over the next few years, little books with kid leather covers that could be carried in a pocket and opened at any page.

Faith and persistence began to pay off, but only in fits and starts. The good news was that Edna achieved her dream of turning her holiday place at Big Hill into a protected reserve. A couple of organisations rejected her unusual proposal, but the Bird Observers Club of Melbourne willingly agreed to accept the land and preserve it as a sanctuary for flora and fauna. They even arranged to erect an entrance gate and notice board to that effect. The bad news was that a bush fire swept across Big Hill and burned East Point to the ground. Only the water-tanks and the stonework survived. Ironically, Edna had just visited the chalet to clear the last of her things. She hadn't seen it for a long time and was pleased to see how well it had stood up to the elements.

It was Edna's third experience of a house fire. There had been her childhood home in Plymouth, the first-built Sonning, and now the house she'd built with Joan Niewand – the house that inspired her to write 'The Happiest Days Of My Life'. All was not lost, for the vegetation grew back and the birds and other wildlife returned. But it was a sad end to a particularly happy experience.

The more difficult Edna's circumstances became, the more she sought sustenance from God. As she wrote to her cousin Edith:

> Every time I feel a bit appalled I remind myself 'I am not alone' – how do people manage without God?

One of the quotes in her little book of spiritual sayings became particularly significant. It became a mantra of hope and faith in the move to Queensland:

> Behold I see an angel before thee to keep thee in the way and to bring thee into the place which I have prepared. Ex:23:20.

Yet after months and years of looking, no angel and no place seemed willing to appear. Edna grew despondent and sometimes believed that the move simply wasn't 'meant'. Then everything changed and Edna added the words 'TO "BENDLES"' above her angel mantra in red ink. An angel was looking after Edna after all.

In 1965 she was invited to buy Bendles, a simple weatherboard cottage in Buderim. The house belonged to her friends Ted and Vera Cranstone, who had been inspired to move to Buderim after hearing Edna's euphoric descriptions of the area. The Cranstones had lived in Bendles while their new house was being built, and when they were ready to leave they offered the cottage to Edna. A generous benefactor then appeared in the form of Aubrey Bowen, a client and friend who greatly admired Edna's achievements. Aubrey Bowen invited Edna to accept a long-term loan (or gift) so that she could purchase Bendles without having to sell The Barn. This meant that she could move to

Buderim knowing that she had a secure base to return to if things didn't work out on the mountain. *Behold, I see an angel!*

The move to Bendles was not a simple or quick procedure. In fact it took Edna three more years to sort everything out. There were renovations to organise for Bendles, legal and money matters to untangle – Edna was drawing the old age pension by this time and had to explain her financial affairs in detail every time she changed them – and there was the subdivision of The Barn. She decided to subdivide the last of her Bickleigh Vale land into four half-acre blocks. The Barn itself was not to be sold until she'd settled in Buderim for sure. Then there was the sifting and sorting of possessions . . . Each time she drove to Buderim she loaded the Holden with 'useful things', yet each time she returned it seemed as if The Barn was just as full and chaotic as ever.

Edna was a hoarder, or perhaps 'recycler' might be a kinder term. Her large attic had been a wonderful depository for items, as had her various outhouses. It wasn't all junk. She had a marvellous collection of garden tools, a darkroom full of photographs and equipment, and her attic held boxes of back-journals, papers, books and 'things' (including possums). All had to be looked at before it could be sorted, and of course the looking became fascinatingly absorbing and so the sorting never seemed to get done.

Money matters worried her a great deal. She was appreciative of Aubrey Bowen's financial assistance, yet eager to assert her independence and repay at least some of the loan. Yet selling off her half-acre blocks wasn't easy, especially as she would only sell to the 'right' kind of buyer – the ones who never had quite the 'right' amount of money. Her dear friend and bookkeeper, Lil Drew, kept reminding her how tight the cash flow was – new photographic materials had to be forsaken if the Holden van needed repairs. A haphazard cash flow meant that renovations to Bendles could only be done in fits and starts. And of course these weren't your run-of-the-mill renovations. They were renovations that were clever, quirky, and specific, which meant that they required a particularly understanding kind of tradesman, and would cost more than your average kind of job.

The Cranstones tried to be helpful, but Edna found their assistance meddling. Ted Cranstone had been Edna's garden photographer during the mid-1930s, and had also taught her photography. But he knew nothing about design as far as Edna was concerned. In fact she seems to have found him irritating. Her private nickname for him was 'old belly-ache'. The one person that Edna found genuinely helpful was Barbara Barnes, her niece in Queensland. Edna's letters to Barbara were bursting with enthusiasms, frustrations, progress reports – and requests. Barbara responded with equal vigour, as far as she could. Barbara was busy managing Canning Downs, the family's horse stud and farming property, while her husband was in Canberra being the Minister for Territories. The other difficulty was that Canning Downs was over three hours' drive from Buderim, Barbara could hardly 'pop over' and see how things were going. Yet Barbara helped her aunt in a multitude of ways. In fact Edna might never have managed the move to Bendles at all if it hadn't been for her niece – and her benefactor Aubrey Bowen.

Doris Oak-Rhind could have helped her sister financially. But then Doris always felt that she was poor, even though she *knew* she was rich. Acts of monetary generosity were alien to her, yet she would willingly knit a jumper, or make yet another alteration to her sister's best and only tweed skirt.

Edna knew that she would miss a number of people when she headed north, and this prompted her to create a special photograph album. It was part keepsake and part social record. Friends, family and admired acquaintances were pressed into having their portraits taken – Daphne being top of the list. The project expanded over time and she eventually called the album her 'Book of Famous People'. Not everyone in the book was truly 'famous' yet the finished collection included an extraordinary array of interesting and often gifted men and women – plus the occasional child and four-legged friend.

Pets were a sore point for Edna. Her old dog Tony, and very old cat, James, both died during the mid-1960s and she resolved not to have any more animals. It was a sensible, practical decision, but she missed the company very much. Then the Cranstones asked her to take on two adult cats that had somehow made themselves 'sitting tenants' at Bendles, and of course she said yes. It was the thought of the cats as much as anything that drove her to get things organised.

Edna announced that she would be moving to Bendles in 1968 – ready or not (and indeed it was not). The announcement seemed to push Lorna Fielden to a sudden change of heart. Lorna would, after all, move to Buderim *if* Edna found her a nice little cottage, well situated and close to the shops. It was easier said than done of course, but Edna was delighted that Lorna had chosen to join her after all. It made her departure from Bickleigh Vale somewhat easier.

The fateful day came, and Edna cried and laughed and cried and smiled as she tied the last of her things to the over-laden Holden. She had a young co-driver and various 'helpful' people trying to persuade her to reduce the load, but she was determined to take the lot. She knew in her heart that she'd never be back. A small crowd waved their last goodbyes as the Holden tottered along Bickleigh Vale Road. People cheered and waved and wondered as the strange cargo trundled into the distance. Edna was on her way at last, leaving piles of unfinished business in The Barn. All the sifting and sorting had overwhelmed her in the end. She instructed her estate agent to have it all thrown out when she'd gone. Much of it was rubbish, but there were hundreds of photographs and negatives in the dark-room, drifts of papers and jumble in the attic, scatterings of postcards and newspaper cuttings pinned to the walls. Maybe of value, maybe not. Edna couldn't be bothered with it. She'd moved on.

BRONZE FIGURE
POOL

Self-portrait at Bendles, Queensland

Chapter 12

'On this mountain it is always green'

The people of Buderim must have been aware that they had a new 'character' in their midst. An unconventional woman with a strong personality, forthright nature and ready laugh. A mature woman with white hair and an interesting array of hats. An interesting woman who wore slacks and who seemed to possess only one skirt. A determined woman who turned a nondescript wooden box of a house into a surprisingly attractive abode.

Buderim people were very friendly, but few could offer much in the way of stimulating conversation. Not the sort that stimulated Edna anyway. This didn't bother her unduly; it was the day-to-day organisation of her life that concerned her more. She was used to having someone around to help with things, and without such a person she was inclined to get in a muddle. As she told her cousin Edith:

> You see I've always been so spoilt with people doing things for me

> & now I'm alone. Mind you I like being alone I'm never lonely
> but there does seem a lot to do – & these two adorable cats
> don't do a thing!!

'A lot to do' included domestic chores and creative projects; it also included ongoing alterations to Bendles, the search for a house for Lorna, and various garden designs for people in Buderim. Domestic chores were a bore when there were so many other things to do – so they didn't always get done.

Letters to friends was another priority, many of them written in the early hours when she was unable to sleep. Her mind was overactive while her body was beginning to let her down. She rarely complained about it, so friends may or may not have known that she'd suffered a couple of mild strokes. They were minor setbacks and she recovered well – but they made her even more aware that she must achieve as much as she could in the time she had left. And achieve she did. By mid-1969 she'd found a perfect cottage for Lorna to live in – and she'd found a willing publisher for one of her books. A letter to cousin Edith gives us an idea of how she was feeling about it all:

> Bendles,
> Buderim P.O.
> Q'land.
>
> [no date, c. 1969]
>
> No, my dear girl, you certainly were not abrupt in your previous letter which I first apologise for never answering – or did I? I have a tray full of letters awaiting answers which sounds very remiss but I never seem to be without an awful lot to do, which of course is better than not having enough to do.
>
> It's this way, the Lord gives me so many ideas, an article

or something or other, a letter to the paper or something like that & then I'm everlasting trying to cope with cartons & cartons of notes for half finished chapters for future books. Incidentally you will be interested to hear that MacMillans the publishers are going to reprint my 'A Gardener's Log' in time for Christmas so lets hope it sells well. The jacket will be a coloured shot of Bendles' garden, all other illustrations will be fresh ones otherwise it will not be altered. 'Gardens in Australia' is only available second-hand & at 17$! . . . perhaps if the Log sells well the publishers will consider a new edition of this book. I've a lot of new pictures for that of gardens that didn't appear in the original.

The only additions I've made are a tiny office which has a large drawing board hinged to the wall AND a bed for my midday siestas from 2 to 4! Also a smart little darkroom. Regrettably I don't get the time to get into it what with the household chores & the garden & going out a bit – not socially, I hasten to add, I sidle out of all invitations, they bore me stiff, there just isn't time to waste.

I feel sorry for my old friends back in Melbourne this winter must have been unbearable, & up here simply lovely.

It's grand having Lorna Fielden living up here. I fixed up a dear old cottage for her not far away. She sold her Mooroolbark house & has been here about 6 months I think, I'm no good at remembering dates.

The colour photograph for the jacket of *A Gardener's Log* was taken by Ted Cranstone. It featured a bedraggled Monstera, a tropical plant Edna disliked and later got rid of. Perhaps the Bendles' garden was still under construction, for there was no attempt to show the pleasing stone walls that gave shape to an otherwise modest corner block. Edna's new Foreword for the book was written in her typically relaxed style, almost as if she was catching up with an old friend, which she was in a way:

> It is now two years since I came to live on Buderim. I had bought a funny little house with two magnificent jacaranda trees, a poinciana and an old mulberry tree behind it and grass right around it.
>
> What more could one want I thought? I shan't need a garden except the little bits around the foundations when the alterations and additions are completed. I shall enjoy growing some flowers for the table there . . . O yes, this garden of mine is not going to be a fashionable one of native plants; much as I love natives. My garden will be stuffed full of as many of the old world flowers I can find that will thrive happily in this rather humid climate.

The promotional notes on the flyleaf of *A Gardener's Log* were suitably complimentary:

> The reissue of this book provides a rich mine of information for the new gardener and will be a pleasant reminder to the more experienced ones that in their midst, to quote from Mr. R.T.M. Pescott's Introduction, 'is a landscape designer who has created a new concept of horticulture which could reasonably become the basis for a universally accepted style of Australian landscaping'.

Mr. R.T.M. Pescott was the Director of Melbourne's Royal Botanic Gardens – which does not necessarily mean that Edna valued his opinion! She disliked being associated with the word 'horticulture' (she always accented the 'horti'), but she must had been pleased with the general tone of Pescott's Introduction. After all, he said that she was one of the first landscape designers to see a way of combining Australia's natural landscape with the best of old-world styles:

> It was this wealth of vision, combined with the uncanny ability to be unorthodox when the occasion demanded, that made Edna Walling one of the first to realise that such a combination was not only possible but desirable.

It was a timely statement of recognition. Pescott had acknowledged Edna's remarkable contribution to the development of the Australian garden – while she was still alive to appreciate it! The book came out in hardback in 1969 and cost $4.50, a bargain considering Edna's second-hand publications were now fetching almost $20. Edna didn't rest on her laurels. She worked hard to see at least one more book into being before her demise. Yet she knew her chances were limited, especially when Macmillan published Ellis Stones' first book, *Australian Garden Design*, in 1971. Stones was now being lauded as one of the most influential garden designers in Victoria. Some even suggested that Stones taught Edna more than she'd taught him – though Stones was *not* one of them. Stones formally dedicated his book 'To Edna Walling who started me on my career'. He also sent her a copy inscribed with a heartfelt: 'Without you this book would never have been written'. Edna appreciated the gesture, though she couldn't raise much enthusiasm for the book.

Edna kept working away at various projects: letters to the press, chapters for books, garden designs, even the possibility of creating a new village (she'd also wanted to create a village at Big Hill, but decided a sanctuary would be better). She was indefatigable. She maintained a sense of curiosity, persistence and wonder, day after day. There were moments of despair of course. She knew her health was deteriorating. Gardening gave her headaches and her legs were weak, but it was the wanton vandalism of the natural environment that really saddened her. Everywhere she looked there was a horror story, globally and locally. She wrote to Daphne Pearson bemoaning the new housing in Buderim, saying it looked like cardboard cartons all in a row. She longed to rescue a patch of land:

> I'd love to save one little bit & create a village . . . It seems to me a bad sad world – or rather era, with so much disregard of beauty rampant.

Yet there was much to enjoy on the mountain, not least the company of good friends. Lorna was just up the road, and another good friend, Madge Rogers, had moved to Buderim from Mooroolbark. Even Esmé Wilson had moved to Tweed Heads, just south of the Queensland border. Edna and Esmé were able to see each other occasionally, and they maintained a regular correspondence. Here are a few extracts from some letters to 'Dear old Sausage' as Edna called her:

> I'm on the last lap of a fairly large job for the most difficult old boy who has nearly driven everyone mad. I've had to tick him off once or twice which he's not used to . . . [we've] become quite good friends in consequence.
>
> . . . ye Gods, what a storm! Last night I draped myself over the stable door watching the heavenly display . . . clouds backlit with sheet lightning and fork lightning dancing across in front . . .
>
> Jean, the girl with the lovely hands, is coming to help me with the blasted housework . . . the cobwebs were getting a bit much, and the mental uplift she's given me has been miraculous. . . . Better get a bit more sleep now because Elsie and I are going cow-manuring tomorrow . . . Five a.m. and the sound of a little bantam rooster makes me inordinately grateful for living within such sounds . . .

> . . . Steve [the black cat] and I are sitting on the balcony watching the tiny blue butterflies fluttering over the plumbago which is climbing a trellised post so sweetly . . . and here comes one of those delightful showers although the sun is shining. I do love the way it does that . . .
>
> Lorna's little Bird Orchard's quite one of the most interesting jobs I've done – I must be improving. But I do need a secretary . . . If I hadn't always been so strong it wouldn't have been such a blow to be suddenly old and feeble . . .

The time came when Edna needed to employ various people to help her manage things. She engaged an assistant, Mrs. Mavis Morris, to attend to her paperwork, plus a gardener and a cleaner to control the weeds and the cobwebs. The arrangement proved satisfactory, especially in the case of Mavis Morris who, though inexperienced, quickly taught herself to type and soon became adept at deciphering Edna's handwriting.

News concerning developments at Bickleigh Vale filtered through occasionally. Sonning had changed hands and Edna was particularly happy with the new owners, though she was staggered to hear that the asking price had been twenty thousand dollars. She had asked Brian McKeever to look after developments in the village, but occasionally building plans were sent directly to her. One such was from a cottage owner requesting what must have been an inappropriate extension. She was furious and sent the plans straight to Brian with a curt note drawing his attention to the name of the designers on the blueprint: 'Ringwood Homes Planning & Drafting Services'! She sincerely hoped that Brian would attend to the matter. Brian surely did, but generally speaking, it was a difficult situation to control. Owners wanted to extend and modernise their cottages according to their own needs and tastes. Edna's covenant could curb excesses, but only to a point. Compromise was inevitable, yet the overall style of the village held good. The lanes remained unsealed, and the cottages still nestled amongst the trees – though it was probably fortunate that the trees were mature, for the rooftops were getting taller.

All was going reasonably well at Bendles, but then Edna's need for assistance suddenly intensified. She was hospitalised following a stroke in January 1972. Her niece Barbara Barnes and her benefactor Aubrey Bowen did their utmost to ensure that she received what she needed – whether she argued against it or not! She was proudly independent and found it difficult to accept financial help, particularly from Aubrey Bowen. Yet without such assistance she wouldn't have been able to live at least semi-independently when she came out of hospital – and Edna was determined to return *home* when she'd recovered sufficiently. Lorna was a wonderful comfort through the ordeal, though she was quite frail herself, being in her early eighties by this time. Friends, young and old, came willingly to Edna's aide. The cats (Steve the girl, Tiger the boy) were not forgotten. Mavis Morris organised a feeding roster, and obeyed when Edna insisted that the front door be left wide open so that the cats could come and go as they pleased.

The extra help with finance meant that Edna could enjoy daily visits from a much-liked physiotherapist when she returned home. It also meant that she had to endure a much-*disliked* live-in housekeeper. It took a few months, but Edna's will prevailed. An alternative arrangement was made and the housekeeper was sent packing.

Edna was 'wobbly' as she put it, yet eager to resume her interests and daily routine. She wasn't ready for visitors, however, especially from interstate:

> I'm fed up so you had better wait until I feel stronger before coming up . . . Mavis drives me anywhere & does all necessary shopping . . . I have plenty of sleep & reading, in fact it must be a pretty dull time with me! I don't encourage visitors other

> than Madge Rogers & my several close neighbours.
>
> Lorna comes down every Sunday to lunch which she brings. Aren't I lucky that she is living at Buderim? She is such a wonderful person.
>
> I'm dying to see you but better wait until I'm better. Tiger & Steve send love and kisses. Lots of love,

She gradually regained her strength, and by the beginning of 1973 was feeling less 'wobbly'. Her typed-by-Mavis letters gave little indication of her physical deterioration. She was the same vigorous Edna in spirit, but her body was frail. She looked like a little old lady, especially since she'd found a hairdresser who permed her hair in the way that every other little old lady permed her hair. She was not becoming conventional in her old age, far from it, but she was less likely to appear distinctly 'different'.

Edna made a new will in February 1973. She'd made all sorts of lists as to who was to receive what of her few possessions, but in the end she kept it simple. She left Bendles and the contents therein to her niece Barbara, the royalties from her books to her sister Doris, and any monies remaining in her bank account to her assistant Mavis – and that was that.

Time was running out. She pushed and pushed to get another book published, and worked away at new ideas. She knew there was a new trend towards conservation and she knew she had something important to contribute. Yet in truth she didn't have the energy to follow her ideas through. She knew this too. Rather than abandon a good idea, she'd send the outline to someone who might be able to 'do something' with it: friends like Jean Galbraith and Thistle Harris, who advised and assisted as best they could. But Edna's good ideas needed an awful lot of work, too much work, especially when there was little likelihood of publication.

Edna wanted a 'last hurrah'. One more moment in the spotlight when she could say, with forceful clarity: look at the natural beauty that is here, and look after it. It was a sincere message, a vitally important message, and she was frustrated that she wasn't able to deliver it.

Yet Edna did get a last hurrah. It wasn't of her own making, and it wasn't about conservation, but it was a significant moment in the spotlight. It came from an unexpected quarter: Beatrice Bligh, gardener and historian. Beatrice Bligh had already written *Down to Earth,* a book that told the story of her struggle to create her award-winning Australian country garden, Pejar Park. Edna had helped to design the garden during the 1940s – though Bligh had 'forgotten' this fact subsequently. Beatrice Bligh's new book, *Cherish the Earth*, was the first to explore the history of the development of the Australian garden – and Edna's contribution was given due recognition.

Bligh celebrated Edna's achievements. She said that Edna became 'an inspiration and outstanding guide after World War II'; then she placed Edna's writing and design in historical context:

> Unlike some writers of today, she did not advise growers to concentrate on natives to the exclusion of exotics, but suggested a mixture of ideal plants for the climate . . . With energy and enthusiasm Miss Walling made garden plans and gave advice on all kinds of horticultural work. Hers was very much a lone voice at the time, carrying out a crusade for the improvement in style of the Australian garden, and her books were unique of their kind . . . The influence of her Australia-inspired garden designing was felt throughout the whole country. When the popular first editions went out of print, and the author retired, the much-needed crusade for better Australian gardens came to a standstill. Only in recent years has there been an attempt to produce books of good style . . . but those that have appeared have not captured the peculiar Walling magic, and few have the same universal appeal.

Edna may have read those splendid words with a wry smile, given that publishers continued to turn a blind eye. And she probably baulked at the word 'retired', for she'd never officially done so. Yet it surely gave her pleasure to know that her work hadn't gone unnoticed, that she was more than a footnote in the scheme of things.

Edna's time on the good earth was coming to an end – and she knew it. Liberty was gradually denied her. She could not drive, she could not walk far, and she was not in total charge of her affairs. Yet she made the best of it – as this letter to a friend demonstrates:

> Both Lorna & I are very grateful to be away from Victoria so tragically dry & Lorna was always so nervous of bushfires. On this mountain it is always green & there is no fear of fire, & we both enjoy the fact that English flowers grow & thrive here & we don't have to grow tropical plants, which neither of us like. I wish you could see Lorna's little house & garden which is so sweet, but we both deplore not being strong enough to garden now-a-days.
>
> Dorothy Edwards my physiotherapist who comes every day, is a perfect delight, a lovely sense of humour & we are perfectly in accord in the garden where she does quite a bit of planting for me.
>
> I sold my car to my friends the Roger's, who kindly drive me to Lorna's on a Sunday. I am so glad I didn't have to sell it to a stranger because I was rather fond of that Holden.
>
> So I'll say good-bye. Lots of love & good wishes . . .

Edna suffered another stroke in June 1973 and was taken to a private hospital in Nambour. A few weeks went by and only a partial recovery seemed likely. Edna was strong enough to make it clear that she would *not* contemplate entering a nursing home, though it was also clear that she could not remain in a private hospital indefinitely.

It was a difficult situation for her family and friends to resolve – but then it resolved itself. Edna had been struggling to keep alive, but as Mavis Morris described it, one evening she just gave up. She died on the night of 8 August 1973, aged seventy-seven.

There was an unmemorable service at the Brisbane crematorium, and Edna's ashes were placed in Buderim cemetery. A tiny metal plaque near the exit gate marks the spot. Some thoughtful soul planted a native tree close by: a vibrant tree that bursts forth with intricate copper-coloured flowers in the summer – a *Grevillea robusta*. What better name of tree could there be for such a one as Edna?

A Contemporary Edna Walling garden

Chapter 13

Star burning bright

'Edna Walling' is now a very big name, albeit in a relatively small garden-interest 'pool'. Her outstanding contribution as a leading landscape designer, garden writer, photographer, native-plant enthusiast and conservationist has been recognised in all mediums. There have been celebratory books, articles, television and radio programs, new discoveries of Edna Walling gardens, plants named in her honour, National Trust and Heritage classifications, protective zonings, exhibitions, web site listings – and an outdoor theatre performance. Edna has earned and won a prominent place in Australian garden history.

Edna's contemporary presence is strong. It's as if she never really died, but simply transformed herself into an earthly spirit. Walk around any of her gardens and that spirit, that sense of Edna, can be found. Her gardens may have been changed, or cut in half, or had terribly ugly features imposed upon them, but stand somewhere near a mature tree, or a low stone wall, and contemplate, and her work will weave its magic spell.

If Edna had lived just five years longer she would have seen Bickleigh Vale recognised by the National Trust as a classified landscape. If she'd lived twenty years longer she would have witnessed a phenomenal growth of interest in her work.

Initial interest was stimulated by two significant new works: *The Edna Walling Book of Australian Garden Design* (1980) which combined selections from Edna's first three books, and Peter Watts's landmark biography *The Gardens of Edna Walling* (1981). There was also a renewed interest in the 'cottage garden' at this time and so the cottage garden/wild garden aspect of Edna's style was suddenly in vogue. More Edna Walling books began to emerge: gorgeous books like *The Garden Magic of Edna Walling* (1988) which contained quotes from Edna's writings and sumptuous photographs in silver grey and colour. Added to this, authoritative writers such as Howard Tanner were giving Edna's work (both publications and designs) due recognition in books about the development of the Australian garden. Then came the foundation of Australia's Open Garden Scheme in 1987, which meant that some of Edna's magnificent gardens could be experienced first-hand. Bickleigh Vale was included in the Open Garden Scheme as early as 1988, and the village became a regular place of pilgrimage thereafter. Meanwhile, Trisha Dixon and Jennie Churchill had been exploring, photographing and recording as many Edna Walling gardens as they could trace, and their first book on the subject, *Gardens in time: in the footsteps of Edna Walling*, was published in 1988. All of the above publications went into repeat editions. One of Edna's previously much-rejected manuscripts, *On the Trail of Australian Wildflowers*, was published in 1984, and three of Edna's original books – *Country Roads: The Australian Roadside* (1985), *Gardens in Australia* (1999) and *A Gardener's Log* (2003) – were reissued. It was a stellar rise to popularity, and her star still burns bright.

If Edna had lived a decade longer she would have lived to see the beginning of this resurgence. Lorna Fielden lived to see it, or at least the start of it. Lorna moved back to Melbourne in 1975 and was probably quite surprised to be contacted by a young man called Peter Watts who wished to interview her. Peter Watts was a Garden Research Officer with the National Trust (Victoria) and was researching for a book about Edna in his 'spare' time. Lorna's recollections of Edna's early life were sketchy, but she was able to pass on some very useful contacts.

It was through Lorna that Peter Watts met Blanche Marshall. Blanche was an old woman with a bent spine by this time. She told Peter Watts that she'd been Edna's bookkeeper, and that she'd burnt all of Edna's letters just a month before – she'd had a clear-out so there'd be less for her daughters to deal with when she was gone. Fortunately she'd held on to a few items, an article or two and some tiny photographs of Edna, Blanche and Margaret Walling on the road to Sydney in the 1920s. She was also able to show him her Edna Walling garden and the watercolour plan that went with it, for Blanche still lived at the same address. Interestingly, she did not choose to show him her little green diaries, with their brief but accurate entries as to dates, names and places. These diaries would be kept, however, and revealed to later researchers after Blanche had 'gone'.

Peter Watts contacted a great many people, anxiously aware that some of them would not be around for much longer. He met Olive Mellor who'd taught Edna at Burnley, Joan Jones who'd been head gardener with Melba, Gwynnyth Taylor who'd been Edna's longest serving assistant, Ellis Stones, Eric Hammond, and so on. Contacts led to more contacts and he discovered clients and gardens and plans. He uncovered vital puzzle pieces, clues that would have disappeared otherwise. Even Esmé Wilson's unpublished biography of Edna found its way into his hands. He gathered information for five years, and then he wrote his landmark book: *The Gardens of Edna Walling*.

The book explored Edna's life, analysed her design styles, and contained pictures of her gardens and plans – many of them in colour. It was a revelation to see the delicacy of Edna's watercolour plans, to see photographs of existing gardens, mature, and full of grace. Peter Watts's book was recognised as a pivotal work, and received widespread acclaim.

Blanche Marshall lived to see this publication, but Lorna Fielden did not. Lorna's last few years were difficult, not because of her health but because she couldn't make up her mind about where she wanted to live. Perhaps she saw Buderim with different eyes after Edna's demise. She loved her little cottage but was dismayed by the sight of five new houses being built on the next-door block. She lived in Melbourne for a couple of years, but wasn't happy there. Finally she moved into a nursing home in Caloundra, not far from Buderim. By an extraordinary coincidence, or perhaps through spiritual simpatico, Lorna died exactly four years after Edna's death, to the day and the month: 8 August 1977, just short of her ninetieth birthday.

Her ashes were placed next to Edna's in Buderim cemetery, and a second *Grevillea robusta* (silky oak) was planted close by. Two trees, two lives, forever interconnected. A beautiful and fitting memorial.

Fashions in garden styles come and go, yet most people can still be seduced by an Edna Walling landscape. There's something about the beauty, the line and contour, the sense of reverie one feels, just being there, breathing it in . . . Edna's spirit lives.

Edna's spirit lives, and long may that be so, yet we have not travelled all this way – from Plymouth Harbour to Buderim Mountain – to end this story with an ethereal spirit wafting through a garden. We will end this story with a very much alive Edna, and some gentle recollections from three people who knew her.

Lorna Fielden's niece Judy was a child in the 1930s and remembers the early days of Bickleigh Vale when she spent weekends with Aunt Lorna. She remembers Edna as a gruff fantastical person, a sort of wizard in baggy trousers who spoke with a growly voice and smoked a little pipe. Judy would hide in the bushes and follow this weird apparition around the garden – and run like hell when Edna suddenly turned and headed in her direction. Judy remembers rushing through the wild undergrowth, sitting ever so still by the pond and watching the fairies dance on the surface of the water, being sent by Aunt Lorna to the weird one's cottage with a bowl of pudding and custard . . .

Barbara, Edna's niece, has childhood memories of an easy-going aunt who encouraged creativity. An aunt who gave her a small drawing-board and paints so that she could do what Edna was doing, and who gave her a little parcel of land at Sonning so that she could build herself a cabin if she wanted to. Barbara remembers her aunt as someone who dressed for practicality, who was always crisp and clean, whatever she was wearing. That it was Aunt Edna who taught her to drive, who took an interest in what she was doing, who woke her in the mornings with a burst of Beethoven or Bach, who wrote delightful letters, who said exactly what she thought and didn't bother with idle chatter. When Barbara was married, Edna gave her a little section of land next to her own plot at East Point – though she took it back again later when she wanted to turn it into a reserve! Barbara remembers that Edna could be impatient at times, but never ill-tempered, never ill-mannered, and not at all boastful.

Alistair, the young man who helped Edna build the kitchen at East Point, remembers Edna's uniquely inventive way of doing things. For instance, the car-turn at East Point was literally a 'car-turn'. You came to the end of the track and drove onto a platform that could be turned around so that the car faced the other way. It's uncertain how long this turn-table lasted, but Alistair remembers seeing it in action. The dunny door was another unusual creation. It turned on an off-centre swivel rather than by hinge, a mechanism that provided a two directional sea-view, if you left if ajar. He recalled that all sorts of people were drawn to her enthusiasm, and that she had the knack of putting their enthusiasm to good *use*. A local bloke would find himself offering to bring her a pile of old building timber for instance, because they'd happened to have a chat about recycling. Alistair remembers Edna as a cheeky rather than forceful person. If she wanted to make a point she'd do it with subtlety, with a half smile and a twinkle in her eye. Though he also suspected that she could be very tough if she wanted. He recalls that her red hair was turning white, that her face was lovely, not beautiful but lovely; that she had fine English skin with a touch of ruddiness about the cheeks, and that her hair always stuck out at odd angles from beneath her hat. That she wore trousers, and liked to wear a colourful cotton neckerchief. That she wore a strange mixture of clothes, yet somehow managed to make the combination fit together with a stylish flourish. That if you put her in a field of wheat with her arms outstretched you could mistake her for a scarecrow. That she could look mannish in appearance but that she wasn't masculine in manner, neither masculine nor feminine. That she was always telling him things – useful, practical things. That she had a young friend. An attractive young woman who didn't say much, but who always seemed to be there in the background . . . This is what Alistair remembers.

Memories and anecdotes, facts and documents – these are the elements that have formed and shaped this story of Edna's life. Edna once said that a person's garden was an indication of their taste, and indeed character. Edna liked her gardens to conceal as well as reveal; it kept the onlooker curious. Trying to describe Edna's life has been like trying to describe one of her gardens: there are glorious formal expanses with a distinctive poetic style, wild undulating areas with interesting pathways, tempting gateways, and dark mysterious pools.

A note about Edna Walling's gardens

THE FOLLOWING EDNA WALLING SITES HAVE BEEN CLASSIFIED BY VICTORIA'S NATIONAL TRUST:

Bickleigh Vale Village, Mooroolbark (in 1978)
Corymbia Citriodora – lemon-scented gum avenue, main driveway, Cruden Farm, Langwarrin
Durrol, Mount Macedon Rd, Mount Macedon
Folly Farm, Falls Rd, Olinda
Langi Flats, (north garden), Toorak Rd, Toorak
Little Milton, Albany Rd, Toorak
Mawarra, Sherbrooke Rd, Sherbrooke
Mount Macedon Gardens Area – which includes gardens by Edna Walling

THE FOLLOWING ARE REGISTERED WITH HERITAGE VICTORIA:

Bickleigh Vale Village (in 2004)
Little Milton, Toorak
[Blanche] Marshall Garden, Carlsberg Rd, Eaglemont
Cuming Garden (Woodbine), Kooyong Rd, Toorak
Habbies Howe Homestead, Dropmore Rd, Dropmore – has Edna Walling connections
Warrock, Warrock Rd, Casterton – has Edna Walling connections

Bickleigh Vale Village is listed on the Register of the National Estate; it also has a protective zoning under the Upper Yarra Valley and Dandenong Ranges Authority. Yet restraint has come too late in certain cases. Some of the village cottages have reached mansion-like proportions and have modern swimming pools and double garages eating into the somewhat altered gardens. The above protections should ensure that further developments are kept in character. Further Edna Walling listings are currently under consideration.

The G. H. Mitchell Garden, Medindie, South Australia, is listed on the Register of the National Estate.

Some Edna Walling gardens are occasionally open to the public.

Contact Australia's Open Garden Scheme for information:

www.opengarden.org.au
Phone: 03 54284557
national@opengarden.org.au

Endnotes

Key archival sources

Barbara Barnes, niece of Edna Walling, private collection.

Burnley Archives, held at the Institute of Land and Food Resources, University of Melbourne, Burnley College.

Peter Watts, private research material.

State Library of Victoria, La Trobe Collection.

Introduction

PAGE xi: Suzanne Spunner, *Edna for the Garden*, performed by the Home Cooking Theatre Company, 1989.

Chapter One: Prelude

PAGE 3: The story of the fire comes from a variety of sources threaded together, major sources are: Gwynnyth Taylor née Crouch:– Interview in ABC video recording – *Edna Walling Lives*; Peter Watts notes from interview given 8 June 1977; Walling, articles in *Home Beautiful*, January 1936, pp. 32–6; March 1940, p. 7; July 1940, pp. 19–21; also unpublished Walling memoirs in Peter Watts research material, Barbara Barnes private collection and State Library of Victoria.

PAGE 5:Edna gave her *Home Beautiful* readers regular updates concerning The Cabin's structure, contents and even whereabouts: *Home Beautiful*, February 1928, pp. 48–9; May 1928, pp. 26–7; November 1933, p. 34; January 1936, pp. 34–5 – so it wasn't entirely private!

PAGE 8: Garden tour as experienced in *Home Beautiful*, January 1930, pp. 33–6, Walling, 'A Garden Of Changing Scenes', plant names quoted from article.

Chapter 2: Devon heart

PAGE 14: The 'frankly boyish' comment appeared in *Everylady's Journal*, January 1927, p. 14.

PAGE 14: Walling, 'As Far Back As I Can Remember', p. 1.

PAGE 15: Walling, 'Memoirs with Education', p. 6.

PAGE 16: ibid., p. 1.

PAGE 17: Margaret Walling's first name was Harriett, the same as her mother-in-law; she seems to have adopted her middle name after marriage, perhaps to avoid confusion. Edna's middle name was Margaret.

PAGE 18: They had lived over the ironmonger's shop for about eight years; by March 1905 the Wallings were living at 1 Melville, Compton Park Road, Mannamead, Plymouth.

PAGE 18: Based on Edna's own account, 'As Far Back As I Can Remember', pp. 1–2.

PAGE 24: Walling, 'As Far Back As I Can Remember', p. 5.

PAGE 24: ibid., pp. 2–3.

PAGE 25:Edna mentions the village of Sonning in *Home Beautiful*, July 1940, p. 21.

PAGE 25: Jekyll, *Children and Gardens*, p. 1.

PAGE 26: The three-volume Country Life Library publication *Gardens Old and New*, 1901–7, described nearly 200 stately gardens in Britain. The Deanery and Jekyll's own Munstead were among them, as were Bicton, Sydenham and Saltram.

PAGE 26: The school was bombed in World War Two and all records destroyed, yet another instance of Edna's papers going up in flames. The school still exists.

PAGE 27: Walling, 'As Far Back As I Can Remember', p. 6.

PAGE 27: ibid., p. 6.

PAGE 28: Johnston, 'The Girl Who Loved Donkeys', suggests William had a business contract with the New Zealand company, p. 2.

PAGE 28: William related this 11/11/1911detail to his Melbourne colleague John Renwick; Peter Watts research material.

Chapter 3: Postcard from New Zealand

PAGE 31: Johnston, 'The Girl Who Loved Donkeys', p. 2 gives Aeawa as the spelling but no such ship existed; *Arawa* seems correct.

PAGE 32: Baeyertz, *Guide To New Zealand – The Scenic Paradise Of The World*, p. vii.

PAGE 32: Dame Joan Hammond's family had a similar experience; they arrived in Christchurch in 1912 but went to Sydney soon after because of these difficulties. Hammond, *A Voice, A Life*, p. 14.

PAGE 33: Walling, 'As Far Back As I Can Remember', p. 7.

PAGE 33: Kaituna is 12 km west of Masterton in the southern part of the North Island; Edna spells the name as Kituna in 'Memoirs with Education', p. 5 but Kaituna seems correct.

PAGE 33: Walling, 'Memoirs with Education', p. 5.

PAGE 33: Letter from Edna to Barbara Barnes, 8 April 1965; Barbara Barnes private collection.

PAGE 34: There was a strong Christchurch Arts and Crafts movement for instance, particularly amongst women. See Calhoun, *The Arts and Crafts Movement in New Zealand 1870–1940.*

PAGE 35: Edna boarded the *Wimmera*, without any other members of her family, travelling from Lyttelton to Melbourne via Hobart, arriving 28 July 1915;
Inward Overseas Passenger Lists: NZ Ports 1852–1923 VPRS 7786.

Chapter 4: Australian Soil

PAGE 38: The 1900s had brought increasing opportunities for women to work in industrial, retail and clerical areas.

PAGE 38: Arundel Flats was erected in 1911 and had tenants from 1914, the flats may have been a hybrid: part serviced, part self contained. The building is no longer there.

PAGE 39: Walling, 'Father: Education'.

PAGE 39: Matron Jane Bell was the inspirational matron in charge of training at the Royal Melbourne Hospital, 1910–34. See Adam-Smith, *Australian Women at War*, p. 22.

PAGE 40: Walling, 'Father: Education'.

PAGE 40: Australia was not as industrialised as Britain so there was less 'men's work' as such; nursing, nurturing and fundraising were the common demands on women, often unpaid.

PAGE 41: Doris was formally admitted into the First Church of Christ, Scientist, 2 December 1919. Aileen Goldstein (sister of Vida) was the Clerk who signed the certificate.

PAGE 41: The suffragist and horticulturist Ina Higgins was also a member; Bomford, *That Dangerous and Persuasive Woman: Vida Goldstein*, p. 49.

PAGE 42: Walling, 'As Far Back As I Can Remember', p. 8. The Burnley principal in 1916 was E. E. Pescott; in 1917 it was J. P. McLennan.

PAGE 43: Burnley Archives, Peter Watts research material, and Pullman, 'Olive Mellor'. See also Shepherd, 'Six Melbourne Landscape Designers – All Women'. In theory Miss A. Knight, the Fruit Preserving Instructress, was the first female staff member, presumably without qualifications.

PAGE 43: The Burnley school is still there, and after many changes of name, it is now part of the University of Melbourne.

PAGE 46: Olive's step-brother Eric was Director of the Singapore Botanic Garden 1925–42.

PAGE 46: There is no record of who taught Landscape Design classes, who took them, or what they consisted of. Students keen to learn appear to have sought further training elsewhere – e.g. Millie Gibson née Grassick.

PAGE 47: Walling, 'Australian Gardens. Jacket', p. 1.

PAGE 47: Peter Watts notes from interview with Olive Mellor née Holttum, 1978.

PAGE 47: Ina Higgins (1858–1948) would have been Olive's role model; after being one of the very first to train at Burnley she became a professional landscape gardener and horticulturist. She was also a feminist and a Christian Scientist and worked closely with Vida Goldstein. Given the Christian Science connection, it may have been Ina Higgins who suggested the course at Burnley to the Wallings.

PAGE 48: Olive suggests that Edna studied at Royal Melbourne Institute of Technology known as The Working Men's College in 1916; evening classes at this time included Architecture, Metallurgy, Art, Applied Art etc.

PAGE 48: Grassick did start teaching in 1918 but Olive's breakdown was probably in 1920.

PAGE 50: Walling, *Gardens in Australia*, p. 1.

PAGE 50: Walling, 'As Far Back As I Can Remember', p. 8.

PAGE 50: Walling, 'Father: Education'.

PAGE 51: ibid.

PAGE 51: Walling, 'Australian Gardens. Jacket', p. 1.

PAGE 52: George Russ emigrated from England in 1899, and was at Burnley from 1910 to 1936. Winzenried, *Green Grows Our Garden – a centenary of horticultural education at Burnley*, p. 50.

PAGE 52: Burnley Archives. See Patrick and Scott, 'Emily Gibson'; Shepherd, 'Six Melbourne Landscape Designers – All Women'; Winzenried, *Green Grows Our Garden*, p. 52.

PAGE 52: Winzenried suggests Edna was a Head Girl (p. 52) but I've found no records to substantiate this.

PAGE 52: Reeves, 'Millie Gibson Blooms Again', p. 6; Winzenried, *Green Grows Our Garden*, p. 52.

PAGE 53: Will Grassick had been a structural consultant to architects Alec Eggleston and W. B. Griffin c. 1914; Reeves, 'Millie Gibson Blooms Again', p. 6.

PAGE 53: Bertha Merfield (1865–1921) exhibited her art work regularly in Melbourne during 1900–20; Australian Artists File, State Library of Victoria.

PAGE 53: Meldrum's School was set up in 1913 in opposition to the Australian Impressionist School. Clarice Beckett was one of his students.

PAGE 54: Vernon, 'Griffin and Australian Flora'.

PAGE 54: By 1920 William Walling's office was in Bourke Street, six doors away from Max Meldrum's studio. Perhaps the Wallings were aware of his work – and his school.

PAGE 55: Miss Katharine Crawford of East St. Kilda and Frank Dodgshun of Hawthorn; Frank's father was a warehouseman, Katharine's mother states 'householder' as occupation. Burnley Archives.

PAGE 56: Pullman, 'Olive Mellor'. Olive probably had the breakdown she refers to in the Peter Watts interview in 1920 rather than 1918.

PAGE 57: Walling, 'As Far Back As I Can Remember', p. 8.

Chapter 5: Ladies who lunch

PAGE 62: Edna was elected to the committee on 13 August 1918; see *The Home Gardener*, September 1918, p. 173.

PAGE 62: *The Home Gardener*, June 1917, p. 134.

PAGE 63: Ina Higgins co-established a women's training farm at Mordialloc in 1915: Bomford, *That Dangerous and Persuasive Woman*, p. 153. Her brother was Henry Bournes Higgins, politician and judge; her sister Anna was amongst the first women to enter university; her niece was the author Nettie Palmer.

PAGE 63: Elma Denham (1891–1971) was the author of *Australasian Catechism of Carnation Culture* (1917), one of the earliest gardening books written by a female and specifically devoted to the carnation. Aitken and Looker, *Oxford Companion*, p. 181.

PAGE 64: Eileen Wood (1892–1988) attended Burnley in 1910. An orphan, she was educated at Fintona and MLC. She did some volunteer work for the Red Cross during WW1; her interests included arts, crafts, horticulture, dressmaking, bush walking and Christian Science. She married H. Bamford in 1922 aged thirty.

PAGE 64: Calder, *A Far-Famed Name: Braithwaite of Preston*, pp. 61, 123, 153, 169. The Braithwaites lived at 'Northallerton', close to the tannery in High Street, Preston. They moved to 1 Chesterfield Avenue, Malvern, in 1928.

PAGE 65: Bertha Merfield was a founding member of the Arts and Crafts Society of Victoria (1908) – as was Rodney Alsop.

PAGE 65: Ruth Alsop (1879–1976) took up articles with Klingender & Alsop c. 1908 to c. 1916; Willis and Hanna, *Women Architects in Australia 1900–1950*, p. 9. Rodney Alsop suffered poor health, especially asthma, and died in 1932 aged fifty-one. Miley, 'The Decorative Art of Rodney Alsop', pp. 78–80.

PAGE 65: Dorothy Alsop née Hope Lockyer, see Aitken and Looker, *Oxford Companion*, p. 17.

PAGE 66: Miss I. Frances Taylor (c. 1895–1933), was creator and editor of *Woman's World*, first published December 1921, with Edith Alsop a prominent illustrator. Katharine B. Griffith (journalist) married William U. Ballantyne (warehouse director) in 1919, aged twenty-six.

PAGE 68: Walling, 'Father: Education': Edna earned about 40s a week in her early days as a gardener; the average weekly wage was about 74s.

PAGE 69: Jekyll's smaller books cost about 12s. Edna's 1919 reading list would have included Australian, American and British authors (Luffman, Wharton, Mawson, Farrer, the list is very long), Burnley and other Melbourne libraries would have been her primary source.

PAGE 69: *Woman's World*, August 1922, p. 10.

PAGE 72: See Harriet Edquist, 'Arts and Crafts Gardens in Melbourne and their Legacy' in Whitehead (ed.), *Planting the Nation*, p. 113. The Burnley School garden, designed by C. B. Luffman, would have been another strong influence.

PAGE 73: W. Butler noted the absence of walls in his lecture 'Garden Design in Relation to Architecture', p. 93.

PAGE 73: The holiday was probably spent around Flinders, one of Edna's favourite spots; Flinders is where she saw the inspirational wall; see Walling, 'Gardens by the Sea', *Home Beautiful*, June 1926, pp. 46–7.

PAGE 73: Walling, 'Australian Gardens. Jacket', p. 2. In other accounts Edna simply says she took herself into the city and spoke to a couple of architects who gave her a chance. The 'brother architect' in question is unclear though there are various possibilities: the date of first meeting is unknown but Edna was friends with Marjorie Butler, whose brother, A. R. Butler, and uncle, Walter Butler, were both architects; Edna also knew the Alsop sisters, and the office of Alsop and Klingender was open to employing women. Katharine Ballantyne was not related to the architect Cedric Ballantyne as has sometimes been assumed.

PAGE 74: Male garden designers are not featured in the magazines in this era, one reads of named architects, unnamed garden contractors – or Edna Walling.

PAGE 74: *Woman's World*, August 1922, pp. 10–11; it's almost certain that Frances Taylor wrote the article.

PAGE 74: ibid.

PAGE 75: The 'ideal' pergola was at the Capuchin Convent, Amalfi, see Jekyll, Garden Ornament, p. 294; the same picture is also featured in Jekyll's Gardens for Small Country Houses, 1912. Edna gave a greatly enlarged copy of this picture to her friend Blanche Marshall. The Oak-Rhind garden was designed in 1928. Edna's most glorious Italian pergola is in the Boortkoi garden, Western District of Victoria (1937). Dixon and Churchill, Vision pp. 82–7

PAGE 76: Millie Grassick had to pay a fee to work with Milner White & Son, UK. See Reeves, 'Millie Gibson Blooms Again', pp. 7–8.

PAGE 77: *Real Property Annual* became *The Australian Home Builder* quarterly in 1922 and *Home Beautiful* monthly in 1925.

PAGE 77: *Real Property Annual*, July 1921, Griffin's article is on pp. 36–7, Edna's is on p. 39.

PAGE 77: Monthly articles from July to November 1924; also for *The Home Gardener* from October 1924 to September 1925.

PAGE 78: *The Garden and the Home*, August 1924, p. 28.

PAGE 78: ibid., October 1924, p. 28.

PAGE 78: ibid., October 1924, p. 28.

PAGE 79: ibid., November 1924, p. 25.

PAGE 79: ibid., September 1924, p. 38.

Chapter 6: Love

PAGE 81: Walling, State Library of Victoria. From an undated letter to Doris Oak-Rhind (c. 1950), unfinished and thus not posted. It was perhaps kept because it contained potential memoir material; Edna later extracted the Olwyn story and typed it up, with few changes, as 'A Friend Arrives'.

PAGE 81: ibid.

PAGE 82: People with 'anti' views were not necessarily wowsers; they were combating the enormous social suffering connected to alcoholism, unwanted pregnancies, illness, poverty and sexually transmitted disease.

PAGE 83: Walling, 'Father: Education'.

PAGE 83: Interviews with Barbara Barnes, March 2001.

PAGE 83: Douglas, *Two Loves*.

PAGE 83: For example, Dane, *Regiment of Women* (1915), Lawrence, *The Fox and other stories* (1922); see Foster, *Sex Variant Women in Literature*.

PAGE 84: Vita Sackville-West's journal was written in 1920 and published in Nicolson, *Portrait of a Marriage*.

PAGE 84: ibid., p. 33.

PAGE 84: ibid., p. 136, letter from Vita to Harold.

PAGE 86: Eileen Wood married Henry Bamford in February 1922 and they moved to Tasmania. My thanks to the Bamford family for these details.

PAGE 87: Edna bought Lot 26, measurement: 2 acres and 36 perches; net annual value £3, rates 6s., Shire of Lillydale Rate Records, 1921. Edna completed the payments by November 1927, for her Certificate of Title is dated 14 November 1927.

PAGE 87: *Woman's World*, December 1921, p. 31. This cluster of cottages must have been fairly near Mooroolbark, which was 20½ miles from Melbourne.

PAGE 88: ibid., p. 32.

PAGE 88: ibid., p. 32.

PAGE 88: Margaret Walling's basic domestic duties would have been done by a paid 'home help'.

PAGE 89: Walling, 'As Far Back As I Can Remember', p. 9.

PAGE 90: ibid., p. 10.

PAGE 90: Johnston, 'The Girl Who Loved Donkeys', p. 5; Peter Watts interview with Mrs Joan Jones née Anderson, 6 March 1977. 'Trousers Lane' was Edna's original Sonning driveway. It was and is accessed via Pine Road. The nickname gradually faded from use.

PAGE 91: Walling, 'An Adventure in Rural Development', *The Australian Handbook*, Winter 1939, p. 10.

PAGE 91: Doris and Alfred Oak-Rhind had two children: David born 1920 and Barbara born 1924.

PAGE 92: Alice, like other members of the Houghton family, owned various pockets of land in the area. Edna revised her occupation in the Rates Records to 'Landscape Architect' in the mid 1930s (a term she almost never used elsewhere). 'Home duties' seemed to be the stock answer for women – whether true or false.

PAGE 92: Walling, 'An Adventure in Rural Development', *The Australian Handbook*, Winter 1939, p. 11.

PAGE 93: Rate Records: Edna's rates changed from 7s 6d to £1 during 1923 and the word 'house' was added in the 'buildings' column.

PAGE 93: *Home Beautiful*, March 1926, pp. 23–4.

PAGE 94: ibid., p. 24.

PAGE 95: The phone listing came under Kilsyth as there was no Mooroolbark exchange in 1925; it was not a continuous service, the operator worked 9–6 weekdays and 9–1 Saturdays.

PAGE 97: The Griffith property was at Myrniong, Victoria. Especial thanks to Richard Aitken for sharing his information on Ballantyne.

PAGE 97: They used their real names but also wrote as 'Walltyne' and 'EW and KB' and perhaps other pseudonyms, so the number of articles is uncertain; see footnote on page 76 for known details.

PAGE 97: The article was 'Landscape Gardening in Victoria by Miss Edna Walling and Miss [sic] Katharine Ballantyne' featuring gardens for: Mr & Mrs Anderson, Linlithgow Rd, Toorak, and G. G. Sergeant Esq., 'Riverswood', Warrandyte, Victoria. The photographer was Adamson. *The Home*, December 1924, pp. 37, 70.

PAGE 97: Rate Records 1926. Katharine (and presumably William) Ballantyne maintained a house and land at Mooroolbark for several years. Katharine's city movements remain a mystery.

PAGE 97: The address directory lists Hammond as a fruit grower in nearby Kilsyth from 1921 to 1925, though from December 1923 he was advertising himself as a Landscape Gardening Contractor in *The Home Gardener*, with a city address in Windsor (near South Yarra where the Wallings lived). Either way he was not far from Edna's activities.

PAGE 98: Peter Watts interview: Blanche Marshall named Blamire Young (1862–1935) as a friend of Edna's; *Home Beautiful*, September 1933, p. 5, has a poem by Ida Blamire Young accompanying a photo of Sonning's garden.

PAGE 98: See Fink, *The Art of Blamire Young*.

PAGE 99: The mutual friend was Miss Ethel S. Leon, a nurse who became a chemist; she had owned a plot of land at Mooroolbark, selling it in 1923. Possibly a feminist, she was a member of the Women's Centenary Council which produced the 1934 *Centenary Gift Book* in which Edna contributed a chapter.

PAGE 99: Wren made his initial wealth through illegal gambling, starting with the Collingwood Tote in the 1890s; he became highly influential within ALP politics.

PAGE 99: Especial thanks to Helen Marshall for these details, interview 2 December 2002 and subsequent correspondence.

PAGE 100: Blanche obtained her motoring licence by driving a policeman around the few streets of Beaufort, in western Victoria.

PAGE 100: *Woman's World* January 1928, p. 39. The 509 appeared in 1925 and was the first Fiat to be mass produced. Edna had the 22 horse power, 4 cylinder Tourer model, capable of reaching 50mph/78kph.

PAGE 100: Perhaps it was a thirtieth birthday present: 4 December 1925; William Walling's father died in 1925 so it's possible that there was a small inheritance.

PAGE 103: Edna added to her land in 1926 bringing her plot to 3 acres 3 perches; her rates went from £1 to £1 15s.

PAGE 103: *Home Beautiful*, March 1926, p. 24.

PAGE 105: Louis' parents lived next door to the widow of the landscape painter Louis Buvelot (1814–88); when Louis was born (1890), Madame Buvelot asked the Marshalls to name him after her husband.

PAGE 107: Helen Marshall, family archive.

PAGE 107: *Home Beautiful*, May 1928, p. 26.

CHAPTER 7: BILLY VALE

PAGE 109: Peter Watts interview: Blanche specifically named Sir Frank Packer and Melba as clients who had not paid for services rendered.

PAGE 110: Walling, State Library of Victoria. In 1927 Melba's Head Gardener was paid £3 15s and the two under-gardeners £2 15s each per week; interestingly Edna paid Blanche £4 per week.

PAGE 111: Walling, State Library of Victoria, and Walling, 'Melba Called', Barbara Barnes private collection. Edna presented her exhibit in tandem with Michael O'Connor, the stone garden furnishing designer, c. 1927.

PAGE 111: *Everylady's Journal*, January 1927, p. 14; and see Mimi Colligan on Alice Anderson in Lake and Kelly (eds), *Double Time: Women in Victoria – 150 years*, p. 306. It would have been interesting to make an ongoing comparison between the two women, but tragically Alice Anderson shot herself – apparently accidentally – in 1926.

PAGE 111: Peter Watts communication with Joan Jones, 1977. Melba's gardener had also cut down her beautiful old elms when she was away, replacing them with a cypress hedge which she loathed.

PAGE 111:Burnley graduates Betty Begg and Mollie Shannon did a stint as under-gardeners with Melba, they later set up their own nursery and landscaping business in Kew c. 1928–32, Aitken and Looker, *Oxford Companion*, p. 84. Edna's friend Eileen Bamford was Mollie Shannon's cousin, so the interconnections are extensive.

PAGE 112: Peter Watts communication with Joan Jones, 1977; my communication with (relation) Peṭo Beal, 2002. Joan Jones née Anderson: 1906–94.

PAGE 112: *Home Beautiful* May 1933, pp. 39–40. Melba died in 1931.

PAGE 113: Blanche's diary, 28 September 1928, Helen Marshall family archive.

PAGE 114: For a rough comparison of costs: in c. 1926 it cost £218 to add a small supper room, cloak room and porch to the Mooroolbark local hall.

PAGE 115: There are two Bickleigh Vales in Devon. Edna may also have known the other pretty village, north-east of Dartmoor.

PAGE 115: Blanche's diary, 6 and 7 August 1928, Helen Marshall family archive; Johnston, 'The Girl Who Loved Donkeys', p. 12. Edna also designed a fountain for the zoo's new aviary and a Nursery Garden, 1928. Eric Hammond was the building contractor.

PAGE 117: Monks, *Elisabeth Murdoch: Two Lives*, pp. 90–117 gives an account of the Cruden Farm renovation; correspondence Elisabeth Murdoch, May 2002.

PAGE 117: Blanche's diary, 16 January 1929, Helen Marshall family archive.

PAGE 118: Blanche diary: re Edna 19 January 1929; re Louis 31 July 1926, Helen Marshall family archive.

PAGE 119: It has been likened to a scaled-down version of 'Tara' from *Gone With The Wind*. Monks, *Elisabeth Murdoch: Two Lives*, p. 108.

PAGE 120: Edna usually had her watercolour plans copied (in black and white); many of these, including three for Cruden Farm, are now held in the Picture Collection of the State Library of Victoria; see Walling website: Plans.

PAGE 121: Elisabeth Murdoch can't remember where the suggestion came from but thinks it might have been Russell Grimwade, see Monks, *Elisabeth Murdoch: Two Lives*, p. 117; however, Edna did use native plants where appropriate in her early days, e.g. the Frankston garden for Mrs Hamer designed in 1927, see Dixon and Churchill, *Gardens in Time* p. 22.

PAGE 122: See Dixon and Churchill, *The Vision of Edna Walling*, pp. 140–5 for a detailed list of gardens; and see Walling website: Plans.

PAGE 123: 'Your Garden Design: A Special Lay-out and Some General Hints' was the first in the series, appearing in *Home Beautiful* in July 1926, pp. 63–4; such plans appeared every two or three months initially, then more sporadically during the 1930s.

PAGE 123: Monks, *Elisabeth Murdoch: Two Lives*, p. 109; Keith Murdoch and his executives also took a salary cut plus reduction in annual bonuses.

PAGE 124: It's impossible to be accurate, so many plans are missing or undated, but of the plans held by the State Library of Victoria: there are fifteen dated 1930 and only three dated 1931 – whereas there are twenty-two dated 1928.

PAGE 124: *The Home*, January 1930, p. 60.

PAGE 124: Peter Watts notes from interview with John Renwick c. 1979; Renwick joined Toledo Berkel in 1926 and said it was a large concern with offices in all states. In 1932 William Walling established a business partnership with John Renwick: Walling, Saunders & Renwick, 416 Bourke St., agents for scales; Toledo Berkel disappears from the Melbourne Directory listing at this point.

PAGE 124: When old enough, all four Oak-Rhind children were made to attend Christian Science meetings, until each rebelled.

PAGE 125: Blanche married Louis B. Marshall in 1929 and they purchased a house in 1936.

PAGE 127: Walling, 'Adventure in Landscape Gardening', *Home Beautiful*, November 1930, pp. 24–5. The O'Shanassy reservoir was constructed in 1928.

PAGE 127: Tanner and Begg, *The Great Gardens of Australia*, p. 45. Griffin also worked on subdivisions in Heidelberg and Mornington in Victoria, but these were less adventurous, see Watts, *Edna Walling And Her Gardens*, p. 28.

PAGE 128: James, *Border Country, Episodes and Recollections of Mooroolbark and Wonga Park*, p. 56.

PAGE 128: Coved ceilings allowed for lower exterior walls which saved on costs of framing, plaster and paint; see Walling, *Cottage and Garden*, p. 121. Most of Edna's builders disliked the unorthodoxy and begged for the walls to be higher – to no avail.

PAGE 128: Walling, 'A Romantic Cottage. Further Adventures at Bickleigh Vale', *Home Beautiful*, June 1934, pp. 10–11.

PAGE 128: Eric Hammond's initial quote for building the Hughston cottage was £390, specification written 8 September 1933; Barbara Barnes private collection. Cottages built by 1934 were called Hurst, Chagford, Downderry and Mistover, the first three probably named after English villages; see *Home Beautiful*, June 1934, pp. 10–11 and April 1936, pp. 30–1.

PAGE 128: The survey for the subdivision was completed on 5 March 1933; especial thanks to Richard Aitken and the National Trust of Australia (Victoria) for the detailed information contained in the classification report for Bickleigh Vale Village dated 7 April 1994.

CHAPTER 8: BURNING THE CANDLE

PAGE 132: Blanche told Esmé Johnston that Edna helped her to 'discover' classical music; Johnston, 'The Girl Who Loved Donkeys', p. 10.

PAGE 132: Edna possessed a piano and even an organ at one point, but it's unclear when or how these instruments arrived.

PAGE 133: Edna's letters and notes to her mother reveal a caring and solicitous daughter. Eight such letters were kept by Margaret and subsequently kept by Edna; Barbara Barnes private collection, now with State Library of Victoria.

PAGE 133: Letter dated 20 April 1933; Burnley Archives, Burnley Horticultural Past Students' Association (BHPSA) folder, 1930s. The 'bachelor' accommodation sounds very like the loft in Blanche's The Barn.

PAGE 133: Burnley Archives, BHPSA folder, 1930s.

PAGE 134: ibid. Letter from Edna 21 March 1934; it's interesting to note that Edna's printed letterhead for this letter includes the statement: 'Represented in New South Wales by Allison Bluett, 194 Queen's Road, Woollahra, Sydney'. A.R. Bluett was a city solicitor, with a Miss J. S. Bluett sharing the same address. The statement disappears from subsequent printed stationery, but clearly Edna was spreading her contact network interstate.

PAGE 134: Gwynnyth Crouch's plan appeared in *Home Beautiful*, May 1933, pp. 56, 58.

PAGE 134: See Sue Forrester's biographical sketch of her mother, Gwynnyth Taylor née Crouch (1915–98) on the Walling website

PAGE 135: Walling, 'Open Air Theatre At Sonning', *Adelaide Advertiser*, 7 July 1936. State Library of Victoria.

PAGE 135: Peter Watts interview with Gwynnyth Taylor, c. 1977.

PAGE 136: See Middlemis, 'Garden Design in the West – Edith Cole', p. 21.

PAGE 137: Copy of original letter provided by Shobha Cameron. Edith married Sydney Cameron in 1941; she raised two children and died in 1999.

PAGE 139: See Dixon and Churchill, *The Vision of Edna Walling*, pp. 68–71 for details about the H. J. Youngman plan.

PAGE 139: ibid. pp. 82–7 for the A. Manifold plan; the garden has been well cared for and survives to this day.

PAGE 140: See *Home Beautiful*, April 1936, pp. 30–1 where C. Bottomley and D. Wade are credited for two of the seven photos of the village; the other five have no credit and may have been taken by Edna.

PAGE 141: Burnley Archives, BHPSA folder, 1930s.

PAGE 141: Edna became a friend of Marcus Martin. He liked her work, and she (rather than he) designed the gardens for many of his houses, including his own in South Yarra; see *Home Beautiful*, July 1933, pp. 8–9. Other architects known for their garden design in the 1930s included Cedric Ballantyne, Walter Butler, Rodney Alsop and Desbrowe Annear (though the latter two died in the early 1930s).

PAGE 141: Letter from Joan Jones née Anderson to Peter Watts, 11 June 1977. She returned to Melbourne in 1930, and after a short period of working and teaching in Melbourne moved to Narbethong near Healesville, where she took over The Hermitage.

PAGE 142: Millie Grassick married E. Gibson, an agricultural writer and widower, in 1934; the Gibsons moved to a farming property where they established a large garden. E. Gibson died in 1944 and Millie sold the farm and resumed her profession. Edna designed a garden in Heidelberg for F. Grassick, Millie's brother, in 1936, presumably because Millie was no longer in Melbourne.

PAGE 143: Olive criticised Edna for giving the wrong information about a species of grass in *Home Beautiful*, June 1940, p. 41. Edna didn't respond, not in print anyway! See Aitken and Looker, *Oxford Companion*, pp. 405–6 for details about Olive Mellor's publications.

PAGE 143: Edna was published in the *Adelaide Advertiser* from c. 1933 to 1937 and her most regular contributions were in 1936. Two of Edna's *Sydney Morning Herald* articles appeared in the *Women's Supplement* on 26 April and 3 May 1934. Edna also contributed chapters to anthologies e.g. Frances Fraser and Nettie Palmer (eds), *Centenary Gift Book*, Robertson and Mullens, 1934; and W.A. Shum (ed.), *Australian Gardening Of To-Day*, Sun News-Pictorial, c. 1940.

PAGE 144: Enda's annotated copy of *Messiah* was discovered in a secondhand bookshop in 1994 and is now in a private collection.

PAGE 145: *Home Beautiful*, January 1936, p. 36.

PAGE 146: ibid., pp. 32–5.

PAGE 146: Edna had been a regular visitor to MLC, for she had designed parts of the garden and assisted with a tree-planting scheme, so it's possible that Lorna and Edna had met at MLC.

PAGE 147: Walling, *Cottage and Garden in Australia*, pp. 33–4.

PAGE 148: Thanks to Judy Hodge for information about her aunt, Lorna Fielden (1887–1977), phone interview 24 May 2001; also to Barbara Barnes and MLC archives.

PAGE 149: *Home Beautiful*, June 1943; Walling, *Letters to Garden Lovers*, p. 209.

PAGE 150: One or two lots had *not* been owned by Whisson and Edna acquired some of these later on.

PAGE 150: Village-dwellers now included: Mabel and Ethel Love, who had moved into Glencairn; Chrisma Wahlers, who had bought a cottage but then changed her mind and sold a year later to Grace Wilson, who seemed much happier and stayed on; and there was Lorna Fielden and Margaret Walling; and the original pioneering purchasers Emily Hansen, Grace Houston and of course Blanche (and Louis) Marshall. Most of the initial owners used their cottages as weekend retreats.

PAGE 150: National Trust of Australia (Victoria) classification report, Bickleigh Vale Village, 1994.

PAGE 151: 'First Fig', *A Few Figs from Thistles*, 1923. Esmé Johnston quoted this poem in her unpublished biography of Edna, 'The Girl Who Loved Donkeys', c. 1975, p. 69. Edna was fond of the poetry of Edna St Vincent Millay.

PAGE 152: Grateful thanks to Susan Halley for bringing her great-aunt's papers to my attention. And to Michelle Adler for sparking the serendipity.

PAGE 152: *Home Beautiful*, February 1931, pp. 8–11.

PAGE 152: *Home Beautiful*, June 1933, pp. 32–5.

PAGE 155: January 1937 is the only period when 7 Maryville St. was changing owners and when Esmé Johnston was living in nearby Brighton.

PAGE 158: Johnston, 'The Girl Who Loved Donkeys', has been a useful reference for this book, as endnotes will attest. She almost always wrote under her maiden name.

PAGE 159: The Marshall house was set on an angle, as opposed to facing the street, which suggests that Edna influenced the architectural design; she'd advocated angle siting since the 1920s for it took advantage of sunlight and ventilation, and was more interesting, e.g. see *Home Beautiful*, October 1925, p. 49. The Marshall plan is in Dixon and Churchill, *The Vision of Edna Walling*, pp. 78–81.

PAGE 160: Latreille, *The Natural Garden – Ellis Stones: His Life and Work*, p. 28; and see Aitken and Looker, *Oxford Companion*, pp. 570–2.

PAGE 160: For example, in *Home Beautiful*, December 1938, Edna named Ellis Stones and Gwynnyth Crouch as her co-workers on an Arts and Crafts Exhibition exhibit; she acknowledged Stones again in *Home Beautiful*, January 1941.

PAGE 161: One of these new cottages, Badger's Wood, was for Misses Annie Peterson and Olive Foreman, both of The Hermitage, a school in Geelong, Victoria. Peterson became the sole owner by the end of 1937.

PAGE 161: Letter from Edna to her mother, 17 October 1937; Barbara Barnes private collection, now with State Library of Victoria.

PAGE 163: Letter from Gwynnyth Crouch to Edith Cole, 7 July 1938; especial thanks to Shobha Cameron for sharing her Cole, Walling and Cameron family archives.

PAGE 164: Letter from Edna to her mother, 17 October 1937; Barbara Barnes private collection, now with State Library of Victoria.

PAGE 164: Letter from Gwynnyth Crouch to Edith Cole, 7 July 1938; Shobha Cameron family archive. The matron was Miss Davies.

PAGE 165: Letter postmarked Gordon, NSW (north-west of Sydney); Barbara Barnes private collection, now with State Library of Victoria.

PAGE 166: ibid. Edna's hosts/friends were Blanche Henson and her husband, and Iris Henson. Edna appears to have known Blanche Henson when she lived in Melbourne.

Chapter 9: Flying high

PAGE 170: The swimming pool was for Edith Hughes-Jones of Olinda. Edna drew on the professional advice of an engineer as well as the practical know-how of Ellis Stones for this job.

PAGE 170: The garden was for Mr & Mrs G. H. Michell in the Adelaide suburb of Medindie and is now listed on the Register of the National Estate. Edna created other South Australian gardens, and had planned a large project for Sir Edward Holden at Inman Valley, but he died before it could be implemented.

PAGE 171: Article by W. Whitford Hazel, *The Sun News-Pictorial*, 10 November 1939. Walling, State Library of Victoria.

PAGE 172: *Home Beautiful*, August 1942; Walling, *Letters to Garden Lovers*, p. 183.

PAGE 173: This Open Day description is informed by a multitude of sources. The events of the day are imagined but the names and associations are factual.

PAGE 175: Mrs Essington Lewis and her party visited 'the now famous village at "Sonning," the artistic home of our leading landscape gardener' on 12 November 1939, *The Sunday Sun*; Walling, State Library of Victoria.

PAGE 175: Enid Lyons replied to a letter from Edna in 1940 and it appears that she visited Sonning on more than one occasion. She became an MP and was appointed a Dame in 1943. Walling, State Library of Victoria.

PAGE 177: This theatre performance is imagined but the names and associations are factual.

PAGE 177: Edna designed an outdoor theatre for Irene Webb's garden in Hawthorn in 1930.

PAGE 178: Edna purchased many books from the Margareta Webber Bookshop in Little Collins Street. Webber's lifetime partner was the exceptional Dr. Jean Littlejohn, specialist of the ear, nose and throat. They shared a home at St. Leonards Court, South Yarra, for which Edna created the garden in the late 1930s. Interestingly, Webber attended Burnley for a term in 1920.

PAGE 180: Algeranoff (born Harcourt Essex in London in 1903) joined Pavlova's company in 1921 and they toured Australia in 1926 and 1929; he toured Australia with various companies in the 1930s and 1940s, and settled in Victoria in the 1950s.

PAGE 183: It was Neil Robertson who asked Gwynnyth the question; he also engaged me with anecdotes about Margareta Webber and Jean Littlejohn, interview 22 November 2002.

PAGE 184: Gwynnyth and Ronald Taylor married in 1940 and took up the second plot that Mrs Louisa Crouch had purchased when she bought Winty c. 1938. The Taylors appear to have managed the design and building of their cottage themselves – within the guidelines of the covenant, i.e. Edna's approval.

PAGE 185: Beryl Mann, 1911–82, studied architecture at the Gordon Institute in Geelong during the 1930s, and received her certificate from Burnley in 1935, having studied part-time. She was Highly Commended for her entry in the *Home Beautiful* Garden Layout Competition and her plan was published in January 1940, p. 13; it bears a strong resemblance to Edna's style.

PAGE 185: Stones went to the Northern Territory with the Civil Construction Corp. from mid-1942 to early 1944. Latreille, *The Natural Garden – Ellis Stones: His Life and Work*, pp. 65–6.

PAGE 185: The *Home Beautiful* magazine print run was reduced to 9000 per month during the war, then was allowed to reach 40,000 in 1946; it rose to over 100,000 by the late 1950s. The print run had reached almost 19,000 in 1928 but fell during the years of the Great Depression.

PAGE 185: The informal 'Dear Gardeners' tone allowed her to add (seemingly spontaneous) postscripts and 'asides'. She sometimes created imagined dialogues with Mr Editor – who sometimes entered into the game with his own replies.

PAGE 187: The Australian Women's Land Army as a national organisation was established on 27 July 1942; see Adam-Smith, *Australian Women At War.*

PAGE 187: Olive Mellor became an instructor with the AWLA at Mont Park, Victoria. It's possible that Edna took on some Garden Army recruits, for she made The Barn more habitable with a couple of showers and chimneys at this time, and one of her c. 1940s notes refers to converting a garage into a dining room for her students.

PAGE 188: Walling, State Library of Victoria.

PAGE 188: Neil Robertson suggests that Frank Eyre of OUP Australia was the person who recognised the value of Edna's proposal; it was a sharp departure from OUP's usual publications.

PAGE 188: The quotations came on pp. 17, 34 and 9 respectively. Edna was especially fond of Reginald Farrer's robust writing on rock gardens and quoted him quite often.

PAGE 189: See Trisha Dixon's comments on gardening books of the era in 'Notes on the Second Edition' in Walling, *Gardens in Australia* – Facsimile Edition of the Author's Copy, Bloomings Books, 1999, pp. xiii–xv.

PAGE 190: ibid., p. 1.

PAGE 191: Walling, *Cottage and Garden*, p. 118.

PAGE 191: Edna included Kenneth Grahame's description of Badger's kitchen as a style guide for cottage china i.e. white plates ringed with blue lines; *Cottage and Garden*, p. 120.

PAGE 192: There is a good example of a 'hidden' person in Walling, *A Gardener's Log*, p. 52 of the 1969 edition (p. 56 of the 2003 edition). In the top right-hand corner stands a young woman in a white shirt midst the foliage.

PAGE 192: The other photographers listed were: E.L. (Ted) Cranstone, Rose Wood, Duncan Wade and Melton Greene; Vera Hodgson, later to be Ted Cranstone's wife, was also thanked for her work on Edna's films.

PAGE 193: Poem quoted in Walling, *Cottage and Garden*, p. 97.

PAGE 193: Fielden, *The Gardener's Warning*, c. 1947, printed by The Specialty Press, Little Collins St., the same press that printed Edna's three books.

PAGE 193: It's all a matter of taste of course, so here is a sample of 'L.F.' from Walling, *Cottage and Garden*, p. 133: 'Once more the earth has felt a stir /The signs of Spring are everywhere, /Again the almond tree holds high /Her rosy buds to opal sky.'

PAGE 194: Walling, State Library of Victoria; these figures appeared in what remained of an old accounts book, most of the pages had been torn out and the book 'recycled' as a folder for photo prints.

PAGE 194: Itemised costs included: car £56, wages £51, income tax £28, travel £20, p. hone £15, commercial literature £14, commercial photography £14, rates £11, cartage £10, postage £7, chemist £6, insurance £6, stationery £5, etc. (shillings and pence excluded).

PAGE 194: See Watts, *Edna Walling and her gardens* pp. 36–8.

PAGE 195: *Who's Who* was a triennial publication at this point, produced by *The Herald & Weekly Times Ltd.*, Melbourne, 13th edition, 1947. Edna's final appearance was in the 1962 edition.

PAGE 195: Broken Hill Associated Smelters P/L asked her to advise on the building of two villages, one in South Australia (not built) and the other for coalmine workers at Mount Kembla, NSW (built 1948). Edna completely rearranged the siting of these houses and brought in Alison Norris, a young Melbourne architect, to redesign the dwellings. Together they ensured that the whole was in tune with the landscape. Details regarding non-Bickleigh Vale cottage designs are limited though the Walling State Library of Victoria plan collection holds a design for R. D. Mullen of Croyden, Victoria, c. 1940. She describes herself as a 'Cottage and Garden Designer' on this plan.

CHAPTER 10: THE OPEN ROAD

PAGE 200: The lookout became known as Cinema Point; it is the highest point of the Great Ocean Road between Torquay and Apollo Bay (94 metres). The Ocean Road was started in 1919, reached Lorne in 1922 and Apollo Bay in 1932.

PAGE 200: Walling, 'Happiest Days', p. 3, Barbara Barnes private collection.

PAGE 204: ibid., p. 22.

PAGE 205: Walling, 'Happiest Days', State Library of Victoria. See www.slv.vic.gov.au/collections/treasures/walling1.html for one of the most complete transcripts, plus photographs.

PAGE 205: ibid. Another of Edna's neighbours was her friend Wing Officer Doris Carter, the hurdler who had represented Australia at the 1936 Olympics.

PAGE 206: Walling, State Library of Victoria, typescript posted to the *Herald*, 15 February 1945. Refer to Edna's 1922 statement regarding the use of Australian plants in relation to 'non-Australian' architecture on page 74 of this book.

PAGE 208: Walling, *Letters to Garden Lovers*, pp. 307–9. The Grampians is a range of westward-tilting sandstone mountains in western Victoria. The vegetation is diverse, some 800 species, and rare fauna includes the blunt-faced rat and the bush-tailed phascogale. Edna's use of the word 'garden' is significant. She applied it to the natural environment in the hope that people would value it in the same way they valued a private garden. She often talked about the importance of 'the front garden of the nation'.

PAGE 208: ibid.

PAGE 208: Harris, *Australian Plants for the Garden*, 1953. See Watts, *Edna Walling and her Gardens*, p. 48, also Webb, *Thistle Harris, a biography.* Thistle Stead née Harris 1902–90.

PAGE 209: Percival St. John's career is outlined in Aitken and Looker, *Oxford Companion*, p. 533.

PAGE 209: See *Home Beautiful*, article June 1944, Walling, *Letters to Garden Lovers*, p. 239.

PAGE 210: Walling, Barbara Barnes private collection. Edna kept this letter in her pocket index-book; it is the only letter from St. John to have survived so perhaps she kept it as a memento as much as a point of reference.

PAGE 211: Foreword, Dixon and Churchill, *Gardens in Time*, p. ix, see also pp. 84–7. The Carnegie property was Kildrummie, Holbrook, NSW; Edna had designed their Melbourne garden in 1937. Margaret Carnegie (1910–2002) established a remarkable collection of Australian art.

PAGE 213: The garden with the lake was Markdale, at Binda, NSW, created for the Ashton family in 1949.

PAGE 215: Walling, State Library of Victoria, incomplete letter cum memoir. Hephzibah Menuhin married Lindsay Nicholas in 1938 and left him for Richard Hauser soon after the war. Yehudi Menuhin married Lindsay's sister, Nola.

PAGE 216: Lorna Fielden asked the new owners of Lynton Lee to rename the house and it became Crail Cottage in 1954 – though the old name tends to persist.

PAGE 216: Edna did some radio talks for Stephanie Bini of 3UZ; recordings have not come to light.

PAGE 217: Letter from 'Twid', Joan Niewand, dated 28 December 1949; Barbara Barnes private collection.

PAGE 217: The new access road was called Devon Lane, changed to Edna Walling Lane in 1988.

PAGE 218: Walling, *Cottage and Garden*, p. 117. Very pale pink was the colour that Devonian cottages were usually painted when Edna was in Devon. My thanks to Patricia Hardy for this and many other 'Devon details'.

PAGE 218: Necessity ruled; even Edna's sister, Doris Oak-Rhind, built a house over half her Edna-designed garden in Toorak.

PAGE 220: Walling, *Country Roads – The Australian Roadside* (reprint edition), p. 18.

PAGE 221: ibid., pp. 40–6.

PAGE 221: See Bull, *New Conversations with an Old Landscape: Landscape Architecture in Contemporary Australia.*

PAGE 221: ibid., Preface.

PAGE 222: *Flowers by the Wayside* was eventually published as *On the Trail of Australian Wildflowers* by Mulini Press in 1984, having been unearthed by Jean Galbraith, edited by Victor Crittenden and assisted by Moira Pye.

PAGE 222: Walling, 'The Trees of Maroochydore – On the Coast Sixty Miles North of Brisbane', *Walkabout*, August 1953, pp. 34–5.

PAGE 223: Letter from D. A. Herbert, Brisbane, 9 April 1954; Barbara Barnes private collection.

Interlude: a dog's tale

PAGE 226: Walling, 'Tony' p. 2, State Library of Victoria. This story is adapted from Edna's four-page memoir about how she came to find Tony. Her unnamed assistant was probably Joan Niewand.

Chapter 11: Shifting ground

PAGE 229: Letter to Miss Mervyn Davis, 6 March 1962; Davis was the major force behind the formation of the AILA. Correspondence between Edna and Mervyn Davis, 1962–70, MS 10408, State Library of Victoria.

PAGE 229: This unpublished book probably had various titles and drafts. Edna also declined to become a member of the newly formed Australian Society of Authors in 1964; she didn't feel she was qualified.

PAGE 230: Beryl Mann worked for Edna for a short period during the mid-1940s; she became a highly respected landscape architect, lecturer, and committed member of the AILA; see Aitken and Looker, *Oxford Companion*, p. 398. It's worth noting that Gwynnyth Taylor became the first woman President of the Victorian National Parks Association and a founding member of the Australian Conservation Foundation; also that her daughter, Sue Forrester, has assisted her husband, Bill Molyneux, to develop Austraflora Nursery, cultivating Australian plants including the Edna Walling Plant Collection. Sue Forrester spent her childhood at Bickleigh Vale.

PAGE 230: David Higgins was taught by Edna during the war and became a landscape designer in Britain: Johnston, 'The Girl Who Loved Donkeys', p. 64. Glen Wilson received weekly tuition from Edna during 1956, she insisted he oversee the planting of the native garden she designed for the Freiberg family in Kew rather than trusting Hammond with the task. Wilson became a lecturer in landscape design, and writer on native plants and landscape issues. Edna bluntly told Rodger Elliot to pursue his dream; he worked for Edna in the early 1960s and became a native plant expert and writer. Edna recommended

Gordon Ford's work to various clients; he became a distinguished landscape designer; see Ford and Ford, *Gordon Ford: The Natural Australian Garden*, p. 18. And see references for all but Higgins in Aitken and Looker, *Oxford Companion.*

PAGE 231: Johnston, 'The Girl Who Loved Donkeys', pp. 28–30.

PAGE 231: ibid.

PAGE 232: Letter regarding the Vietnam war to Edith Cameron, 6 December 1966; Shobha Cameron family archive.

PAGE 232: Edna flirted with colour photography but didn't take to it; the quality of the colour wasn't good enough.

PAGE 232: Correspondence with *Woman's World*, April 1952; Walling, State Library of Victoria.

PAGE 233: The portrait was used to great effect on the front cover of Hall and Mather's *Australian Women Photographers 1840–1960.*

PAGE 234: Edna had at least two commissions in the Buderim area: for A. Roberts in c. 1962 and Aubrey Bowen in 1965.

PAGE 234: Edna altered her printed letterhead to 'Edna Walling Landscape Consultant' (as opposed to landscape or garden designer) during the 1960s.

PAGE 235: Walling letter to Eric Hammond, 17 February 1959, unsigned carbon copy; Barbara Barnes private collection.

PAGE 235: ibid.

PAGE 236: Interview Brian McKeever, 22 August 2002. Ruth Walker sold Downderry to the McKeevers for £2,200.

PAGE 237: Edna had a collision near Buderim on 30 July 1965 and was fined £16.

PAGE 237: Edna made at least one journey to Queensland by train.

PAGE 237: Letter to Barbara Barnes, late 1964; Barbara Barnes private collection.

PAGE 238: Mervyn Davis (1917–85) studied horticulture at Burnley (dux 1946) after serving in the WAAAF during the war; she undertook a number of landscape designs following her return to Australia in 1959 including large-scale projects for airports and depots. Daphne Pearson was her lifetime partner.

PAGE 238: General correspondence between Edna and the Misses Davis and Pearson, c. 1962–72, MS 10408, State Library of Victoria.

PAGE 239: ibid, letter from Edna to Mervyn Davis, 5 June 1966.

PAGE 239: Edna designed Mawarra in 1932, but was so incensed by a dispute over her travel expenses that she walked off the job and left it to Hammond to complete. She renewed her acquaintance with the garden when the property changed hands. See Dixon and Churchill, *The Vision of Edna Walling*, pp. 52–5. Mawarra was included in Australia's Open Garden Scheme in 2004 for the first time – as was Sonning.

PAGE 239: Edna had already given some of her garden plans to Glen Wilson to study; they too eventually found their way to the State Library of Victoria.

PAGE 240: Brian McKeever believes that Edna's spiritual beliefs are best described as Buddhist.

PAGE 240: These barely used appointment diaries were for 1959, 1960 and 1964; Barbara Barnes private collection, now with State Library of Victoria.

PAGE 240: The fire raged between Lorne and Aireys Inlet on 8 March 1965.

PAGE 240: Edna's arrangement with the Bird Observers Club was never formally legalised. The land was eventually sold in the 1990s; the club included an Edna Walling Room in its new education centre.

PAGE 241: Edna's 1964 spiritual notebook cum recycled diary. Barbara Barnes, now with the State Library of Victoria.

PAGE 241: Letter from Ted Cranstone to Barbara Barnes, March 1981, Barbara Barnes private collection.

PAGE 241: Edna designed at least two gardens for the Bowen family: in Merricks, Victoria, c. 1958 and Alexandra Headlands, Queensland, 1965.

PAGE 243: Letter to Barbara Barnes, c. March 1967; Barbara Barnes private collection.

PAGE 243: C.E. Barnes became Minister for Territories under the Menzies Government in 1963, and remained a Minister until 1972.

PAGE 244: The 'Book of Famous People' is now held by the National Gallery of Victoria. Most portraits were identified and briefly described by Edna. She lists: Algeranoff – ballet dancer, [Sir] Doug Nicholls – Aboriginal pastor, Perry Hart – violinist, William Ricketts – potter [artist], Jean Galbraith – botanist, Pierre French – journalist, Graham Smith – ballet dancer [Alistair Smith's brother], Phil Dunn & Reg Preston – potters, Esmé Johnston – journalist, Daphne Pearson – George Cross, Lorna Fielden – Australian poet, Doris Oak-Rhind – 'Dorcas', Rev. Trevor Byard, Joan Niewand, Tony [Edna's dog] – and many others.

PAGE 244: A cleaner was instructed to remove and burn all the 'rubbish' left in The Barn and this was done; interview Brian McKeever, 22 August 2002.

CHAPTER 12: 'ON THIS MOUNTAIN IT IS ALWAYS GREEN'

PAGE 248: Belated Christmas card to Edith Cameron, 29 December 1968. Shobha Cameron family archive.

PAGE 251: Walling, 'Introduction', *A Gardener's Log*, 1969 re-issue, Macmillan, p. x.

PAGE 251: See Tony Hitchin's somewhat biased 'Introduction' to Stones, *The Ellis Stones Garden Book*.

PAGE 251: Edna offered her copy of Stones's book to Kath Carr, a friend who'd become a successful garden designer in New South Wales; carbon copy of letter to Mrs Kath Carr, 10 September 1971, Barbara Barnes private collection.

PAGE 252: Letter to Daphne Pearson dated 4 August 1969; MS 10408, State Library of Victoria.

PAGE 252: Johnston, 'The Girl Who Loved Donkeys' pp. 51, 52, 56, 58; written between 1969 and c. 1971.

PAGE 253: Letter from Edna to Brian McKeever, 22 November 1972; Walling, State Library of Victoria.

PAGE 255: Letter to 'Dear Rosy pots' (identity uncertain), 20 July 1972; carbon copy, Walling, State Library of Victoria.

PAGE 256: My thanks to Trisha Dixon for the Pejar Park detail – and many others.

PAGE 256: Bligh, *Cherish the Earth: the story of gardening in Australia*, pp. 98–9. Bligh requested research details from Edna in 1969; she passed the request on to Mervyn Davis and Daphne Pearson who dealt with it for her; letters from Edna 4 August 1969, 24 July 1969 to Davis and Pearson MS 10408, State Library of Victoria.

PAGE 257: Letter to Connie Thekla, long-time friend in Victoria, 15 January 1973; carbon copy, Walling, State Library of Victoria.

CHAPTER 13: STAR BURNING BRIGHT

PAGE 262: For a list of classifications of Edna's gardens see page 268.

PAGE 263: Letter from Blanche Marshall to Peter Watts, 28 May 1977; Peter Watts. Blanche had, however, kept at least a couple of Edna's letters, significantly the one dated 22 April 1928 quoted in Chapter 6.

PAGE 263: The Marshall Garden is now protected by Heritage Victoria.

PAGE 263: Peter Watts book was published by the Women's Committee of the National Trust of Australia (Victoria) 1981; a second edition was published by Florilegium in 1991 as *Edna Walling and her gardens*, reprinted 1997.

PAGE 265: My thanks to 'The Nieces' including: Judy Hodge née Fielden, Barbara Barnes née Oak-Rhind, Val Burston née Oak-Rhind, and her daughter Susan Burston; interviews c. 2001.

PAGE 265: Especial thanks to Alistair Smith, interviews 29 December 2000 and 7 March 2001; and to Jack Manuel for making the connection.

Bibliography

Chronology of Books by Edna Walling

1943 *Gardens in Australia – Their Design and Care*, Oxford University Press
1944 *Gardens in Australia* second impression
1946 *Gardens in Australia* third impression
1947 Cottage *and Garden in Australia*, Oxford University Press
1948 *A Gardener's Log*, Oxford University Press
1948 *Gardens in Australia* fourth impression
1952 *The Australian Roadside*, Oxford University Press
1969 *A Gardener's Log*, reissued by Macmillan

Posthumous publications

1980 *The Edna Walling Book of Australian Garden Design*, a compilation edited by Margaret Barrett, Anne O'Donovan
1984 *On the Trail of Australian Wildflowers*, Mulini Press
1985 *A Gardener's Log*, revised edition edited by Margaret Barrett, Anne O'Donovan
1985 *Country Roads –The Australian Roadside*, reissue, Pioneer Design Studio
1988 *The Garden Magic of Edna Walling*, a compilation edited by Margaret Barrett, Anne O'Donovan
1990 *Edna Walling's Year: Ideas and Images from all Seasons*, compilation edited by Margaret Barrett, Anne O'Donovan
1999 *Gardens in Australia – Their Design and Care* second (facsimile) edition, Bloomings Books
2000 *Letters to Garden Lovers* (*Home Beautiful* articles 1937–1948), New Holland
2003 *A Gardener's Log*, revised edition, Viking

Unpublished manuscripts by Edna Walling

'As Far Back As I Can Remember', autobiographical draft manuscript, eleven typed pages with Edna Walling handwritten corrections, Barbara Barnes. No date.

'Australian Gardens Jacket', autobiographical draft manuscript, four typed pages with Edna Walling handwritten corrections, Peter Watts. No date.

'Memoirs with Education', eight typed pages with Edna Walling handwritten corrections, Barbara Barnes. No date.

'Father: Education', memoir handwritten on the back of recycled paper c. May 1963, five pages, no page numbers, State Library of Victoria.

OTHER WORKS CONSULTED

Adam-Smith, Patsy, *Australian Women at War*, Nelson, 1984.
Aitken, Richard and Michael Looker (eds.), *The Oxford Companion to Australian Gardens*, Oxford University Press, 2002.
Australia's Open Garden Scheme, annual listings include an increasing number of Edna Walling Gardens, ABC Books 2004–5 (on-going).
Baertz, C.N., *Guide To New Zealand – The Scenic Paradise Of The World*, Dunedin, 1906.
Bligh, Beatrice, *Cherish the Earth: The story of gardening in Australia*, Ure Smith in association with The National Trust of Australia (NSW), 1973.
Bomford, Janette, *That Dangerous and Persuasive Woman: Vida Goldstein*, Melbourne University Press, 1993.
Brown, Jane, *The Pursuit of Paradise: A Social History of Gardens and Gardening*, Harper Collins, 1999.
Bull, Catherin, *New Conversations with an Old Landscape: Landscape Architecture in Contemporary Australia*, The Images Publishing Group, 2002.
Butler, W., 'Garden Design in Relation to Architecture', *Journal of the Royal Victorian Institute of Architects*, September 1903.
Calder, Winty, *A Far-Famed Name: Braithwaite of Preston*, Jimaringle Publications, 1990.
Calhoun, Ann, *The Arts and Crafts Movement in New Zealand 1870–1940*, Auckland University Press, 2000.
Crossing, William, *Crossing's Guide to Dartmoor*, reprinted from the 1912 edition, Peninsular Press, 1993.
Dane, Clemence, *Regiment of Women*, Macmillan, 1917.
Denham, Elma, *Australasian Catechism of Carnation Culture*, (publisher unknown) 1917.
Dixon, Trisha and Jennie Churchill, *Gardens in Time: In the footsteps of Edna Walling*, Angus & Robertson, 1988
Dixon, Trisha and Jennie Churchill, *The Vision of Edna Walling: Garden Plans 1920–1951*, Bloomings Books, 1998.
Douglas, Lord Alfred, 'Two Loves', the poem was originally published in the Oxford undergraduate magazine *The Chameleon*, 1894 (and subsequent anthologies).
Fielden, Lorna, *The Gardener's Warning*, The Specialty Press, Melbourne, 1947.
Fink, Elly, *The Art of Blamire Young*, Sydney Golden Press, 1983.
Ford, Gordon, with Gwen Ford, *Gordon Ford: The Natural Australian Garden*, Bloomings Books, 1999.
Ford, Ruth, 'Speculating on Scrapbooks, Sex and Desire: Issues in Lesbian History', *Australian Historical Studies*, vol. 27, no. 106, 1996.
Foster, Jeannette H., *Sex Variant Women in Literature*, Naiad Press, 1985.
Glendinning, Victoria, *Vita: The Life of Vita Sackville-West*, Penguin, 1984.
Grahame, Kenneth, *The Wind in the Willows*, Methuen, 1973 (originally published 1908).
Hall, Barbara, and Jenni Mather, *Australian Women Photographers 1840–1960*, Greenhouse, 1986.

Hammond, Joan, A *Voice, A Life*, Gollancz, 1970.
Harris, Thistle, *Australian Plants for the Garden*, Angus and Robertson, 1953.
James, G.F., *Border Country: Episodes and Recollections of Mooroolbark and Wonga Park*, Shire of Lillydale, Victoria, 1984.
Jekyll, Gertrude, *A Gardener's Testament*: a selection of articles and notes by Gertrude Jekyll edited by Francis Jekyll and G. C. Taylor, Country Life, 1937.
Jekyll, Gertrude, *Children and Gardens*, Country Life, 1908.
Jekyll, Gertrude, *Gardens for Small Country Houses*, Country Life, 1912.
Jekyll, Gertrude, *Garden Ornament*, Country Life, 1918.
Jekyll, Gertrude, *Wall and Water Gardens*, Country Life, 1901.
Johnston, Esmé, 'The Girl Who Loved Donkeys', unpublished biography, c. 1975.
Lake, Marilyn, and Farley Kelly (eds), *Double Time: Women in Victoria – 150 years*, Penguin, 1985.
Latreille, Anne, *The Natural Garden – Ellis Stones: His Life and Work*, Viking O'Neil 1990.
Lawrence, D.H., *The Fox and other stories*, Penguin, 2001 (first published 1923).
Martin, Sylvia, *Passionate Friends: Mary Fullerton, Mabel Singleton & Miles Franklin*, Onlywomen Press, 2001.
Middlemis, Carolyn, 'Garden Design in the West – Edith Cole', *Australian Garden History*, Vol. 8 No. 2, September/October 1996.
Miley, Caroline, 'The Decorative Art of Rodney Alsop', *Australian Antique Collector*, July–Dec. 1986, pp. 78–80.
Monks, John, *Elisabeth Murdoch: Two Lives*, Macmillan 1994.
Nicolson, Nigel, *Portrait of a Marriage*, Atheneum, 1973.
Patrick, John and Janet Scott, 'Emily Gibson', *Australian Garden History*, vol. 8 no. 1, July/August 1996.
Pullman, Sandi, 'Olive Mellor', *Australian Garden History*, vol. 12 no. 1, July/August 2000.
Reeves, Simon, 'Millie Gibson Blooms Again', *La Trobe Journal*, no. 65, Autumn 2000.
Sands and McDougall's telephone and address directories, Victoria.
Shakespeare, William, *A Midsummer Nights Dream*, Signet Classics, 1963.
Shepherd, Jane, 'Six Melbourne Landscape Designers – All Women', unpublished dissertation, Faculty of Environmental Design and Construction, Royal Melbourne Institute of Technology, 1988.
Stones, Ellis, *The Ellis Stones Garden Book*, Nelson, 1976 (Introduction by Tony Hitchin).
Tanner, Howard, and Jane Begg, *The Great Gardens of Australia*, Macmillan, 1983.
Tipping, H. Avray (ed.) *Gardens Old and New – the country house and its garden environment*, Country Life, c. 1908.
Vernon, Christopher, 'Griffin and Australian Flora', *Australian Garden History*, vol. 8 no. 5, March/April 1997.
Watts, Peter, *The Gardens of Edna Walling*, Women's Committee of the National Trust of Australia (Victoria), 1981, and second edition *Edna Walling and her Gardens*, Florilegium, 1991.

Webb, Joan, *Thistle Harris, a Biography*, Surrey Beatty & Sons, 1998.
Whitehead, Georgina (ed.), *Planting the Nation*, Australian Garden History Society, 2001.
Willis, Julie and Bronwyn Hanna, *Women Architects in Australia 1900–1950*, RAIA, 2002.
Winzenried, A. P., *Green Grows Our Garden: A centenary of horticultural education at Burnley*, Hyland House, 1991.

Audiovisual, electronic and theatrical sources

New Eden, a six-part series presented by Richard Heathcote. Part 4 'Optimism' features key Australian garden designers of the first half of the 20th century: William Hardy Wilson, Edna Walling, Marion Mahony and Walter Burley Griffin, and Paul Sorensen. Gardening Australia, ABC TV, 2001.
Smith, Bryan, *Edna Walling Lives*, video documentary, A Big Country, ABC TV 1984.
Spunner, Suzanne, *Edna for the Garden*, a play for the garden, produced by Home Cooking Theatre Company, performed in the Fitzroy Gardens, 1989.
The Edna Walling Website www.abc.net.au/walling. Extensive representation of work held by the State Library of Victoria – photographs, plans, multimedia and excerpts of writing, 2001.

Picture credits

Illustrated sections

PAGE 1 William H. Walling 1916 and Harriett Walling c. 1870, studio portraits, Plymouth. Courtesy of Shobha Cameron family archive.

William Walling junior c. 1930, studio portrait by Ruth Hollick, Melbourne. This photo was reproduced in *The Home* in January 1930. Courtesy of Barbara Barnes family archive.

PAGE 2 Doris Oak-Rhind with David c. 1931 and with Barbara c. 1927. Courtesy of Barbara Barnes family archive.

Barbara Barnes and the twins outside the 1840 kitchen at Canning Downs, photographed by Edna c. 1952. Courtesy of Barbara Barnes family archive.

PAGE 3 A photo journalist caught this particularly direct look from Edna; the cutting was pasted into a scrapbook without further identification. Originally held by Barbara Barnes, now with the State Library of Victoria.

Edna at Burnley. Courtesy Noelle Kendall, Burnley College archive.

PAGE 4 Studio portrait by unknown photographer used to accompany Edna's article 'Garden Designing by Women' published in *The Australian Women's Mirror*, July 1925. Courtesy of Helen Marshall family archive.

PAGE 5 Edna's cartoon was used as the header for her *Home Beautiful* article of March 1926, p. 22. Courtesy of the State Library of Victoria.

The photograph of Edna laying Sonning's foundations was used in the same 1926 article though it would have been taken about three years earlier, possibly by Eileen Bamford née Wood. Courtesy of Claire and Bob Bamford family archive.

The building of The Cabin was celebrated in *Home Beautiful* May 1928, p. 27. Courtesy of the State Library of Victoria.

PAGE 6 The original Sonning appeared in various magazine articles between the early 1920s and 1935. This photograph appeared in *Home Beautiful* November 1933, p. 33 in an article by Mary Byles called 'Hillside and Sea-side' which featured interesting 'getaway' cottages and their owners. Courtesy of Shobha Cameron family archive.

New Sonning was featured in numerous publications; this photograph appeared in Edna's article 'The Building of Sonning 2', Home *Beautiful* January 1936, p.32, photograph by Duncan Wade. Courtesy of Shobha Cameron family archive.

PAGE 7 The very early days of The Cabin and The Barn were featured in 'Hillside and Sea-side', *Home Beautiful* November 1933, pp. 31–35. The photos almost certainly pre-date the article. It's interesting to note that Edna's cousin, Edith Cameron née Cole, indicates the presence of the Sonning garage to the right of the picture – clearly it was well camouflaged. The Sonning driveway is the road that used to be called 'Trousers Lane'. Courtesy of Shobha Cameron family archive.

PAGE 8 Miss Naismith's ballet dancers at a Red Cross fundraiser, Sonning c. 1943; photograph almost certainly taken by Edna. Private collection.

PAGE 9 Edna with Gwynnyth Taylor née Crouch; photograph by E.L. (Ted) Cranstone. Courtesy of Barbara Barnes family archive.

Edna's cousin, Edith Cameron née Cole; photograph almost certainly taken by Edna. Courtesy of Shobha Cameron family archive.

Eileen Bamford née Wood. Courtesy of Claire and Bob Bamford family archive.

PAGE 10 Road-to-Sydney holiday snap taken by Edna. Courtesy of Helen Marshall family archive.

Studio portrait of Blanche Marshall née Scharp by Jack Cato. Courtesy of Helen Marshall family archive.

The snap of Edna and Brian was taken on a beach. Edna preferred this cropped version; the uncropped one showed another dog and Edna's bare feet. Courtesy of Susan Halley family archive.

PAGE 11 Edna's photograph of Lorna Fielden appeared in *Cottage and Garden* with the caption 'The Mistress of "Lynton Lee" – and Teddy', p. 32. Edna Walling, *Cottage and Garden*, OUP, 1947.

Edna took many photographs of her offsider 'Twid' aka Joan Selnes née Niewand. This one was probably taken at Sonning c. 1948. Courtesy of Barbara Barnes family archive.

Edna and her 'secretary' Gwynnyth were featured in three of the five photographs devoted to 'The Woman Who Built Her Own Village' – i.e. Bickleigh Vale. *The Australian Women's Weekly Pictorial*, February 1939, p. 7. Originally sighted in Barbara Barnes family archive, copy from The National Library of Australia.

PAGE 12 A page from the scrapbook of Esmé Wilson née Johnston. Courtesy of Susan Halley family archive.

PAGE 13 Edna's St. Kilda letter to Esmé. Courtesy of Susan Halley family archive.

PAGE 14 Photograph of Edna taken by Barbara Barnes. Courtesy of Barbara Barnes family archive.

Edna sent this photo-greetings card of The Barn to her goddaughter, Jane Marshall. Courtesy of Helen Marshall family archive.

PAGE 15 The photograph of Edna in tweed jacket and hat was taken by Barbara Barnes when she was tucking into an al fresco lunch at the Barnes property, Canning Downs, c. 1947. Courtesy of Barbara Barnes family archive.

The photograph of Edna in shirt and tweed waistcoat was almost certainly taken by E.L. (Ted) Cranstone in the 1940s. Courtesy of Barbara Barnes family archive.

This rare photograph of Edna with secateurs (she advised restraint when it came to pruning) may have been taken by Daphne Pearson. Edna sent it to her friend Eileen Bamford in Tasmania. Courtesy of Claire and Bob Bamford family archive.

PAGE 16 Edna took hundreds of beautiful photographs of the Australian landscape during her travels, she sent this one to the Marshalls, c. 1960. Courtesy of Helen Marshall family archive.

Pictures used throughout text

PAGE (ii): Studio portrait of Edna by Francie Young of Collins Street. Courtesy of Susan Halley family archive.

PAGE (x): Edna with Brian and the Black Cat. Courtesy of Susan Halley family archive.

PAGE (xvi): Old Sonning by Cliff Bottomley. Courtesy of Helen Marshall family archive. Also used inside back cover.

PAGE 10: Young Edna – cut to fit into a locket. Courtesy of Barbara Barnes family archive.

PAGE 30: Margaret and William Walling. Courtesy of Barbara Barnes family archive.

PAGE 36: Edna boiling the billy, probably taken by Eileen Bamford. Courtesy of Claire and Bob Bamford family archive.

PAGE 58: The Walling women. Courtesy of Barbara Barnes family archive. Also used inside front cover.

PAGE 80: Edna with Brian on the 'sun porch' at Sonning. *Home Beautiful*, March 1926 p. 23. Courtesy of the State Library of Victoria.

PAGE 108: Edna with Psyche the Fiat. Courtesy of Helen Marshall family archive.

PAGE 130: Lorna Fielden's woodshed at Lynton Lee, almost certainly taken by Edna. Courtesy of Susan Halley family archive.

PAGE 168: Margaret Walling at Sonning. Edna wrote on another photo from the same photo-session 'On this seat sits my Mother – an ever willing "model" – pouring coffee.' Courtesy of Barbara Barnes family archive.

PAGE 198: Another of Edna's photo-postcards – The Great Ocean Road. Courtesy of Barbara Barnes family archive.

PAGE 228: Edna's celebrated self portrait. Courtesy of Helen Marshall family archive.

PAGE 246: Perhaps Edna's last self-portrait. She must have dragged her long mirror into the garden of Bendles to catch the best light. Courtesy of Barbara Barnes family archive.

PAGE 260: 'Essence of Edna' – part of a contemporary Edna Walling garden. Photograph by, and courtesy of, Trisha Dixon.

PAGE 299: Sara Hardy in her role as Edna Walling. Photograph by, and courtesy of Ponch Hawkes, Home Cooking Theatre Company. 1989

All the line drawings are by Edna Walling.

Acknowledgements

I am especially grateful to Barbara Barnes, Peter Watts, Trisha Dixon and Richard Aitken for their generosity and encouragement.

My sincere thanks to all those who helped with Walling-related information. The list includes: Jane Alexander, David H. Alsop, the Bamford family, Meredith Peto Beal, Sue Burston, Winty Calder, Shobha Cameron, Neil Clerehan, Richard Clough, Bruce Echberg, Freda Freiberg, Neil Greenaway, Susan Halley, Peggy Hicks, Jocelyn Jackson, Judy Hodge, Patricia Kennedy, Holly Kerr Forsyth, Jack Manuel, Helen Marshall, Nan McBean, Brian McKeever, Robyn McMahon, Dame Elisabeth Murdoch, staff at the Museum of Lillydale, Norma Pollard, Neil Robertson, Robin Scott the archivist at Methodist Ladies' College, Joan Selnes, Alistair Smith, Jane Smith, Suzanne Spunner, Joss Tonkin the archivist at Burnley College, Jo Wellington, Glen Wilson, Zoë Wilson of the Bird Observers Club of Australia, Wendy Woodford; and a very special thank you to Olga Tsara of the State Library of Victoria.

It took about five years to bring this book into being and may well have taken longer without various forms of assistance. My thanks to Julian Burnside for supporting me in the very early stages. Thanks also to the people of CERES community park for taking me on as a volunteer gardener during a period of unemployment. It was in that supportive environment that the seed of my 'Edna idea' started to grow. I am also indebted to Kate my 'Job Network Assistant' for recognising the value of that idea. And a big thank you to the Barnes family for the hospitality extended during my stay at Canning Downs.

It was a wonderful psychological as well as practical boost when I was awarded the inaugural Peter Blazey Fellowship in 2004. Sincere thanks to all those connected with the creation of 'the Blazey', and to the Australian Centre at the University of Melbourne for such a fruitful residency.

Especial acknowledgement to my friend Sylvia Martin for giving excellent editorial guidance when I was trying to find my way with the initial chapters. Resounding thanks to my partner Lois Ellis for reading every word, and for suggesting the sharp incisions that made all the difference to the structure of this book. And particular thanks to my mother Patricia Hardy for assistance, feedback, and sustained optimistic belief.

Chance brought me to Allen and Unwin's door, and it's been a dream run from the start. My thanks to Sue Hines and the Allen & Unwin team, with special thanks to the multi-talented Andrea McNamara and designer Ruth Grüner.

Fond thanks to friends – seriously neglected yet so important during this long process. Special thanks to Bettina Guthridge, Trina Parker and Michael Pearce; also to Elspeth Ballantyne; Lorraine Milne; Liz Pain and Penny McDonald; and my Feldenkrais pals Robin Laurie, Gemarja Lomas and Joan Pollock. A big cheer to the serendipitous Susan Stevenson, and to Martin, Mim and little Odette; also to Neil, Elena, Jack and John, Fritz and Jennifer, Ross, Lorna, Pen, Peta, et al.

Huge thanks to my sister Helen Ingram and nieces Beth and Samantha – so 'conveniently' living in Devon and so well placed to help with Walling research! And special thanks to the 'other part' of my family – Marcus Ellis, and Matthew, Marisa and little Kobi Noah Mowszowski. And last but never least, I acknowledge the unfailing support of a wonderful dog called Amy.

Sara Hardy playing Edna Walling, photograph by Ponch Hawkes, 1989

Index

Index

Index